Education for National Efficiency:
The Contribution of Sidney and Beatrice Webb

Education for National Efficiency: the Contribution of Sidney and Beatrice Webb

edited by
E. J. T. BRENNAN

THE ATHLONE PRESS *of the University of London*
1975

Published by
THE ATHLONE PRESS
UNIVERSITY OF LONDON
at 4 Gower Street, London WC1

Distributed by
Tiptree Book Services Ltd
Tiptree, Essex

USA and Canada
Humanities Press Inc
New Jersey

© *University of London* 1975

ISBN 0 485 11151 9

Printed in Great Britain by
W & J MACKAY LIMITED, CHATHAM

To W. H. G. Armytage

Acknowledgements

Most of the manuscript sources for this work are to be found in the British Library of Political and Economic Science. The Passfield Trustees, the Fabian Society and the British and Foreign School Society have all been most kind in allowing me to use copyright material and I am extremely grateful to them for their co-operation. Every effort has been made to clear all questions of copyright but I must take this opportunity of apologising in advance for any unwitting infringement that may have occurred.

January 1974   E.J.T.B.

Contents

INTRODUCTION

1 A Functional Theory of Education

The impact of Sidney and Beatrice Webb on educational developments in the closing years of Queen Victoria's reign has gained increasing recognition in recent years.[1] The foundation of the country's most active and influential technical education board, the revitalising of London's moribund endowed schools, the burgeoning of the polytechnics and the erection of an interlocking scholarship ladder—all have received attention. So too have the Webbs' behind-the-scenes activities at the time of the passing through Parliament of the 1902 Education Bill, followed in the next year by the extension of the legislation to London itself. Recent troubles in the London School of Economics have highlighted the extraordinary circumstances which surrounded the start of the School in 1895. But although it is true that the L.S.E. was always the 'favourite child' of the Webb partnership, it should not be forgotten that their involvement in higher education generally was considerable. The creation in 1900[2] of a teaching university for London, in itself the outcome of a long campaign in association with R. B. Haldane,[3] the start of Imperial College and the London Day Training College—the progeny was varied in its composition but united to a common purpose whose implications provide the theme of this small volume. If we consider the Webbs' educational achievements alone, Beatrice's wish at the time of her marriage that 'a considerable work' might be an outcome of the union seems amply fulfilled.

It has to be admitted from the start that it is impossible to unravel with any degree of certainty the individual contributions made by each member of 'the partnership' in any of their joint enterprises. This is a difficulty which all who have written on these two extraordinary people have had to acknowledge. Even in those areas where each seemed to be carrying out a clearly differentiated role, as for instance Sidney's chairmanship of the London Technical Education Board, or Beatrice's work as a member of the Royal Commission on the Poor Law, the impact of each upon the thinking and decisions of the other was considerable. Their natures were complementary and in all their undertakings there was inevitably a process of mutual permeation.

In some ways, it is true, their outlooks and temperaments were decidedly different. Beatrice, for example, was predisposed to see mankind framed in a metaphysical context; Sidney for his part was much more pragmatic in his approach. But few people have ever shared their lives more completely and it is doubtful whether after their marriage either ever acted independently of the other. If this is so, then the naïveté of attempting to identify their individual contributions in the realm of educational theory is at once apparent. It is for this reason that I have chosen to write of the Webbs in the plural, even when in terms of decision-taking and extent of literary output Sidney's contribution may appear to be the weightier.

It has been said that when Sidney entered public life in 1892 he was guided in his activities by 'a grand design' for educational improvement and that with this considerable advantage he was able to direct his political flair and remarkable industry to the promotion of the ends he had formulated.[4] This may be regarded as an assertion of dubious validity. As the leading member of the Fabian Society he had, it is true, written a good deal on the subject of economic and social amelioration. At a time when social injustice was being challenged by the emergence of numerous left-wing groups, the central Fabian belief was that what was really needed was the achievement of 'the national minimum' in all fields. This desirable end could best be achieved by recognizing 'the inevitability of gradualness', a process which stood in marked contrast to the revolutionary methods advocated by H. M. Hyndman's[5] Social Democratic Federation on the one hand, and on the other the escapist Utopianism of organisations like

Stewart Headlam's[6] Guild of St Matthew. But, although the belief in 'a national minimum' went right across the board of Fabian planning, with an immediate relevance to such areas of concern as factory legislation, local government, sanitation, housing and the Poor Law, it has to be said that the attention given to education at this time was little more than perfunctory.

The absence of 'a grand design' does not, however, imply that the subject was ignored for in these early years Sidney was convinced that public education, even in the limited form in which it had appeared in late Victorian England, was in its way a manifestation of socialism. This was evident enough in his contribution to *Fabian Essays*[7] and in a significant little book entitled *Socialism in England*, published in 1890. 'This branch of education', he wrote, 'has been virtually nationalised or municipalised, without loss of stimulus or failure of enthusiasm'.[8] He went on to advocate the abolition of school fees, the appointment of a Minister of Education with overall control of the system, the creation of public technical, secondary and evening schools, and the registration and inspection of private establishments—perceptive forecasting, no doubt, but hardly meriting the term 'grand design', let alone revealing any clue that Webb at this time had thought out the instrumental aspects of the subject, or given any indication that he had systematically considered what education is in itself.[9]

Scrutiny of the early Fabian Tracts reveals a similar lacuna. That he regarded education as being a necessary item in any programme of social reform, however, comes out periodically in Tracts such as *Facts for Londoners* (1889), *The Workers' Political Programme* (1890), *Questions for Parliamentary Candidates* (1891), and *Questions for School Board Candidates* (1891). It would appear that Webb, along with most socialists of the day, regarded the school boards, the agencies brought into existence as a result of the 1870 Act, as the instruments in whose hands educational advance could continue to be entrusted. There is nothing to suggest, however, that Sidney had ambitions to stand as a candidate at any school board election. For the prospect of marriage to Beatrice implied a measure of financial independence and his eyes as a consequence were directed towards a stage upon which full-blooded programmes of social reform could be enacted. In short, membership of the London County Council held out the more enticing prospect of the introduction of 'municipal socialism' on a large scale. This growing preference for the unitary, civic authority—the state in miniature, as it were—was to be of crucial importance during the course of the next ten years. Other leading Fabians might be tempted into standing for school board elections; not so Sidney, whose chief educational interests were always centred on higher education, an area which, in theory at any rate, was beyond the scope of the school boards' parliamentary mandate. What is also significant is that on the eve of his intervention in London politics, there is no mention of the subject of education in either *Questions for London County Councillors* or the important *London Programme*, both written by Sidney with the 1892 local elections in mind. If 'a grand design' was taking shape, and if he had earmarked the London County Council as the chosen instrument, he was, it must be admitted, singularly cautious in making his views known either to his fellow Fabians or to Beatrice Potter.

Unlike Sidney, whose schooling had taken place in private establishments at home and abroad, to be followed by part-time study at university level, Beatrice had been subject to all the educational vagaries that bore upon the daughters of upper-class Victorian households. The presence of a charming and devoted father, the company of numerous sisters, the periodic stays in their various properties up and down the country, the comings and goings of leading figures from the political, scientific and business communities of Victorian England—none of this could compensate the intelligent and introspective girl for the apparent hostility of a mother who was to become increasingly withdrawn as time went by. Emotional security was sought, therefore, in below-stairs relationships and intellectual development in the company of Herbert Spencer, the constant companion of her formative years.

It is difficult to conceive of Beatrice's rejection of *a priori* reasoning, in favour of a commitment to the observation of facts

and the teasing out of the principles underlying those facts, as an
outcome of the circumscribed schooling then available to the well-
to-do young ladies of mid-Victorian England. Luckily for Beatrice,
the Potter household was exceptional in that its intellectual cli-
mate was like that of a continuous university seminar with science
and religion figuring as the central issues of discussion. She was
particularly fortunate in that the leading English philosopher of
the day took it upon himself to teach her how to think and work
inductively. There was an emotional bond too, for she tells how
in her childhood he had been the only person who had consistently
cared for her.[10]

Not that she was an uncritical pupil of Spencer. Her eye was
quick to notice those occasions when the master did not follow the
precepts of empirical enquiry he was always recommending. She
also became increasingly mistrustful of his too facile application of
biological laws to the subject matter of the social sciences, and his
setting up of a whole apparatus of first principles to replace those
he had earlier rejected. As for political beliefs, she was later to
cause 'the man against the state' considerable distress when she
embraced the collectivist creed. Nevertheless, the influence of
Spencer upon her mental development is difficult to over-esti-
mate. Her wish in 1894 that the Hutchinson bequest should be
devoted to the start of a new institution in London, modelled
upon the Ecole Libre des Sciences Politiques in Paris, and to be
called the London School of Economics and Political Science, says
a good deal for the potency of that influence.

But this lay in the future. The question is whether there was in
existence an educational 'grand design' before 1892. In the case of
so assiduous a diarist as Beatrice, it might be expected that any
such aspirations on her part would have been faithfully recorded.
The answer is simple to determine: neither in *My Apprenticeship*,
nor in the manuscript diaries, is there any evidence to support the
assumption that such a design was beginning to emerge before the
time of her marriage. In fact when in 1884 the subject of education
is mentioned, there is a vehement rejection of state intervention—
'the most dangerous of all social poisons'. But this, it should

be remembered, was written some years before her political apostasy.

Not that her membership of a leisured and privileged class had prevented her from becoming acquainted with the realities of educational provision, both at home and abroad. As early as 1872, when accompanying her father on an American tour, she had visited a school in Chicago where she had marvelled at the spectacle of 'a common little negro girl sitting between two well-dressed banker's daughters, and learning the same thing.'[11] In a romantically conceived visit to working-class cousins in Bacup she had learned something about the schools of that town.[12] More significantly, working as a social investigator with Charles Booth in his *Enquiry into the Life and Labour of the People of London*, she had participated in the technique of 'wholesale interviewing', a situation in which the sixty-six school attendance officers of the East End were the key figures. And not only the attendance officers but the board school teachers themselves had been called upon to give evidence.

What she learned about the schools as a result of all this activity did not disturb her unduly. Her energies were directed elsewhere: towards establishing the facts about the scale and intensity of poverty in the world's wealthiest city, to the horrors of the sweating trades in particular, and to the considerable promise for the future held out by the growth of the co-operative movement. Like her attitude towards the emancipation of her own sex, it seems fairly obvious that the case for more educational provision did not readily engage her sympathies until after her marriage when Sidney began his work with the Technical Education Board. In *My Apprenticeship* she defends her indifference to the issue of female suffrage on the grounds that she herself had never felt the handicap of being a women. Similarly, it seems highly probable that she did not regard the absence of formal schooling in her own career as in any way a handicap. Personal experience, in other words, had told her nothing about the inadequacies of Victorian schooling. If she felt any educational deprivation at all, it was at the level of university studies, and it is significant that it was to the area of higher education that she was to direct a large proportion of her remarkable energies in the years to come.

Can the Webbs then in any way be regarded as serious educational theorists when setting out on their mission? What I have so far attempted to show is that at the time of Sidney's entry into public life there was no carefully worked-out scheme of operations, nothing that owed its vigour to any view of what education was capable of doing, either in terms of social engineering or of individual fulfilment. When in the course of the next few years it did arise, it sprang forth as a result of the Webbs' active engagement in the operation. Increasingly alarmed by experiences of obscurantism on the part of politicians and officers of the state, dismayed by what they considered to be the fumbling incompetence of those responsible for Empire in the very heyday of imperialism, Sidney and Beatrice more and more became the advocates of 'national' and, perhaps surprisingly, of 'imperial efficiency', and they came to see education as the key instrument to that end.

Thus it was that the early years of the century produce a minor spate of educational writings on Sidney's part. Ten years previously the imperative of 'the national minimum' had been advocated on the grounds of social justice; now, prompted by the disasters of the Boer War, it has been subsumed under more urgent and compelling principles, for 'national' and 'imperial efficiency' are the recurring themes. More specifically, a minimum of educational provision has become an indispensable part of the argument in the pursuit of this efficiency. This then becomes the mainspring of the Webbs' theory of education, a belief which has the undoubted merit of simplicity of conception, coherence, and economy of operation. It is an important part of an overall philosophy described by some historians as 'social imperialism'. Clearly it is not in essence a 'socialist' view of education as we would understand that term today.

Indeed it was by no means inconceivable in those years that a new party based upon the cult of 'national efficiency' might have come into being, and that, with the exception of Gladstonian

Liberals, revolutionary socialists and die-hard Tories, membership would have transcended traditional party alignments. As
it was, the 'efficiency school' embraced politicians like Lord
Rosebery[13] and R. B. Haldane, civil servants of the calibre of
Robert Morant,[14] the pro-consuls of Empire, especially Alfred
Milner,[15] and not least the Webbs. The members of the movement,
as might be expected, differed in the stress they placed on individual policies, but what united them for a number of years was
an ardent belief in the need for greater efficiency in every aspect
of life. With the example of Germany and later of Japan very
much to the fore in their thinking, this state of affairs was to be
brought about chiefly through a greater reliance on science, on
scientific and technical education, on the training of the expert,
and on the improvement of the nation's physique, the last to be
effected, if need be, through compulsory military service. It was in
essence the antithesis of the leisured and cultured liberalism of the
Victorian period and, in its seeming disregard for individual liberty,
the harbinger of much of what we may recognise to-day as the
spirit of the twentieth century.[16]

The period from 1905 to the outbreak of the Great War was a
time of comparative eclipse for the Webb partnership. Their
political manoeuvrings, or what Beatrice somewhat euphemis-
tically called their 'disinterested Machiavellianism', had alienated
old friends on the Left. It took the failure of the Poor Law campaign to cause the Webbs to lose faith in the permeation of the
major political parties and to decide instead to help shape the
emerging Labour Party. Their energies thereafter were harnessed
in new directions: the start of *The New Statesman*, Sidney's activities on the Labour Party National Executive, his career as M.P.
and member of two Labour governments, the vast range of published works. With the exception of the continuing association
with London University, and in particular the L.S.E., education
assumes a subordinate place in their interests.

Then in 1932 came the visit to the Soviet Union, a journey
undertaken, if we are to pay heed to writers of our own day, in
a state of mind bordering upon idolatry. *Soviet Communism: A*

New Civilisation, the collective fruits of their wanderings, is an extremely long work and only some thirty pages are devoted to education. On the surface the writing is purely descriptive, yet it would seem that the Webbs are identifying their own values with what they saw happening in the USSR. The school as such is regarded as but one of several educational agencies within society, and its purpose, quite unequivocally, is to turn out good citizens and productive members of the state. Under such a system there can be no 'opting out' of one's social responsibilities, as was the case with the leisured classes of the western world. As for the context in which the term is used in our own day—the self-imposed withdrawal of many of the young people of Britain and America from their parent societies—it is doubtful whether the Webbs would have had the slightest sympathy for such a phenomenon.

The fact that the theory of education that is implicit in their work was slow to emerge does not diminish its ultimate vigour, which is revealed in the selected writings that form the bulk of the present volume. The Webbs were always mistrustful of the claim that first principles should determine action.[17] They saw, for example, nothing reprehensible in the belief that conscience could be the offspring of involvement; on the contrary, the fact that it could usually be triggered off by participation or activity conveyed the seal of respectability to the process. They took no pleasure in the kind of long drawn-out discussions of terms and principles favoured in the universities of their day. *A priori* thinking of any kind was automatically suspect.[18] Essentially they were inductive thinkers, rejoicing in the accumulation of facts out of which theories could be coaxed. This was no less true in the shaping of their educational policies than it was in their thoughts on Poor Law reform or the future of industrial democracy. It is for this reason that this section has been entitled 'A Functional Theory of Education'.

Some account of the Webbs' educational accomplishments is therefore logically called for. Before going on to describe these achievements, however, it is necessary for further light to be thrown upon the source of this activity, in other words, to examine more fully the nature of Fabian socialism and Sidney's contribution thereto. It is consequently in this direction that we must now turn.

2 Sidney Webb, the Fabian Society and Municipal Socialism

Though simply expressed, the aim of the Fabian Society, an 1884 offshoot of an earlier Utopian grouping, was ambitious in the extreme. It was nothing less than 'the reconstruction of society . . . in such a manner as to secure the general welfare and happiness'. This process, it was felt, could be brought about only by the complete abandonment of the *laissez-faire* principles which had dominated the middle decades of Queen Victoria's reign. However, because Britain already possessed healthy democratic institutions, especially after the franchise reforms of 1884–85, the promotion of the goal of collectivisation demanded, not the aggressive revolutionary methods so frequently advocated by the Social Democratic Federation[19] and the Socialist League,[20] but peaceful change brought about by men and women who themselves had been thoroughly steeped in socialist doctrine.

The early members of the Society had been in the main Radicals, that is to say members of the extreme democratic wing of the Liberal Party. Not surprisingly, they liked to maintain that Marxist theory was of less consequence in the emergence of Fabianism as a political creed than the evolving English Liberal tradition, interpreted through the writings of John Stuart Mill and influenced by the continental Positivists. This however is to do less than justice to the contribution of Marx for it is unlikely that the Fabians would have taken up a socialist, rather than a radical position, had that influence not been considerable. Where they parted company with Marx was in their denial that the class struggle was the means of bringing socialism into existence. Unlike some countries abroad where democratic institutions were conspicuously absent, Britain was in a position to reach the socialist millennium through peaceful change. This belief was the source of what came to be known as 'the inevitability of gradualness'. Such an evolutionary approach to social and economic change did not imply, so most Fabians maintained, the starting of a new political party but the 'permeation', for the time being at any rate, of the existing parties.

Although not a founder member of the Society, Sidney Webb had quickly established himself as its intellectual mainstay,[21] a process facilitated not only by the scale and thoroughness of his writings but also by his apparent personification of the Fabian *zeitgeist*. Certainly it would be a mistake to regard Webb himself as educationally under-nourished. Although forced by family circumstances to leave school at fifteen, his education both at home and abroad had been in its way sound, thanks to the concern shown by enlightened parents. As an external student of London University he had read Law and in 1885 had been called to the Bar. By this time, having climbed the necessary preliminary rungs, he had entered the upper division of the Colonial Office, an early product, as Asa Briggs has reminded us, of the system of open competition and promotion by merit.

The path had not been easy, yet, save in his limited response to the arts,[22] the result was vastly impressive, a judgment enthusiastically held by men as varied as E. R. Pease[23] and George Bernard Shaw. A steadfastness of purpose, a formidable intellect, and powers of memory which the years could not wither, had produced not only a scholarship which was overwhelming, but an extraordinary ability to marshal evidence and support hypotheses. All this evoked an admiration so total on the part of his friends that his reputation frequently crossed the barrier between myth and reality.

In short, Webb, having himself been exposed for so many years to the excitement of intellectual growth, was aware of what the emancipatory power of education could be. The comparative lack of attention given to educational advance in the early Fabian reform platform is therefore puzzling, particularly to the late twentieth century radical spirit which regards it as indispensable in the journey towards the new Jerusalem.

Two questions must now be put and answers attempted. First, just how crucial was Webb's role in the Fabian Society during these early years? Secondly, if educational advance did not figure strongly in the early Fabian reform programme, what issues were considered to be important? Fortunately, the tremendous volume of propaganda that poured forth from the Society during these years provides ample documentation for charting its priorities in the field of social and economic reform with some degree of confidence.

In the light of its subsequent record the Utopian ancestry of the Fabian Society may cause some surprise. According to E. R. Pease, the Fabian secretary for many years, its members were at first 'ethical, sentimental and vague, thinking of reconstructing society in accordance with the highest moral possibilities'. Somewhat falteringly, the right road was indicated by Bernard Shaw and Frank Podmore,[24] but it was Webb, newly recruited by Shaw, whose passion for precise facts led the Society along the path which it has followed ever since.[25] What Webb succeeded in doing was turning the Society from a not very notable group of earnest seekers after truth into a powerful intellectual force armed with a new and practical social gospel, a gospel which demanded state intervention in place of an uncaring individualistic ethic. This was to be effected, not by revolutionary means, but by 'the application of scientific thinking to politics'.

Pease may have been somewhat intemperate in his admiration for Webb, but his claim that Sidney was without question the main inspirational force of the Society throughout its first thirty years, and further that, quite apart from the many Fabian publications bearing his name, any seemingly anonymous works were almost certainly the results of his labours,[26] receives frequent confirmation, even from such a notable egotist as Bernard Shaw. For his part Webb was self-effacing to a fault. Indeed, so unwilling was he to take the personal credit, even when this was deserved, that the myth of 'the new Machiavelli' was born. Beatrice evinced much pleasure at the time when Sidney's reputation for behind-the-scenes manipulation was at its height. Still, there were to be unfortunate consequences, not least in the growing disinclination of the London Progressives to accept a merely subordinate role in the decision-taking.

However perplexing Webb's apparent anonymity within the Society might be, it is thus by no means too facile an assumption to identify the policies of the Society during these years with those which Sidney had first conceived. In its seemingly impossible task of transforming Britain into the Welfare State, the spotlight was brought to bear upon those critical areas where reform was most urgent and where at the same time it stood a reasonable chance of being carried out. The early Tracts, therefore, eschew abstract concepts such as the theory of the state or definitions of social justice. As has been stated earlier, abstract theorising at this level was to the Fabians neither relevant nor interesting. Instead, the Tracts are concerned with practical issues such as the feasibility of the eight-hour day, the nationalisation of land, leasehold enfranchisement, the demands of the farm labourer, and so on. The documentation was impressive: data and statistics tumbled forth in profusion, providing the intellectual leavening so badly needed by the radical left.

Without question the most influential of all Fabian writings was *Fabian Essays*, first published in 1889 and regarded as a seminal work, particularly on account of its economic analysis, by a whole generation of radicals and socialists both at home and abroad. There is a marked similarity between Webb's contribution to the *Essays* and to *Socialism in England*, published in the following year, to which reference has already been made.[27] In both works the basic Fabian belief in the importance of 'the national minimum' predominates. Without it the people of Britain will be denied the safety net so essential to a civilised society, a net which should be placed under all the more critical areas of existence. But factory legislation, sanitation, housing, local government, the Poor Law—the creation of a 'national minimum' in each of these areas was not only to be justified in terms of individual happiness; it was essential for the welfare of the State, as the evidence from Germany so abundantly made clear.

Not only that: it was all evidence of the growing swing towards collectivist solutions of pressing social and economic problems. It was only to be expected that Webb would be criticised by Radicals for his apparently over-ready identification of state intervention with socialism. The Radical reluctance to acknowledge fully the real destination indicated by this growing collectivisation comes out time and again. By 1890, however, Webb had worked out his political theory much more thoroughly and he was certain that the increase of state intervention in areas which had hitherto been the exclusive preserve of free enterprise was leading the country inexorably in this direction.[28]

In *Socialism in England* public education is given its place in this on-going development. Curiously enough, this open recognition of the place of education in the collectivist scheme of things is in marked contrast to *Facts for Socialists* which makes no reference whatsoever to the subject, but which was regarded by some as providing the truest insight into Webb's political credo. It must also be remembered that *Questions for London County Councillors* and the important *London Programme*, both written by Sidney with the 1892 local elections in mind, are also devoid of any mention of education, an omission all the more startling when one bears in mind that, quite apart from his own candidature, Sidney claims that one most important consequence of the municipalising of London will be a development of the *character* of its citizens. Astonishingly, he forbears at this stage to mention that the schools may have a contribution to make in this direction.

Of equal significance is the lack of interest in the subject at the level of national politics. It certainly does not feature in the famous Newcastle Programme of 1891, on the basis of which Gladstone was returned as Prime Minister for the fourth and last time. The true extent of Fabian influence in the formulation of the Programme is difficult to establish with any degree of certitude. In all probability it was rather small but Fabians like Pease and Shaw thought otherwise. It was in their eyes a supreme example of the effectiveness of permeation as the major weapon in their armoury. One must conclude therefore that, despite Beatrice's subsequent recollections, the Webbs, like all good socialists and radicals, considered the school boards, which had been brought into existence by the 1870 Act 'to fill the gaps' left by voluntary agencies, to be perfectly adequate for the task in hand. Certainly there is nothing in the Fabian writings to imply any loss of faith in the boards. In both *Questions for Parliamentary Candidates* (1891) and *Facts for Londoners* (1889)—the Tract which supplied a complete programme of municipal socialism—Webb expresses satisfaction with the work of the boards, asks for an increase in the number of their higher grade schools, schools which were in fact providing a new sort of secondary education for the people, and demands an extension of the free meals service, a measure which at the time was an article of faith with socialists of all complexions. These demands appear, along with many others, in *Questions for School Board Candidates* (1891). Although Sidney may have had misgivings about the restriction of school board control to the area of elementary education, there is every indication of satisfaction with these exercises in 'primary democracy'.

As yet, however, unlike Annie Besant[29] and Stewart Headlam,[30] he had gained no practical experience in the field of educational administration. This was to come in 1892 when he was elected to the London County Council as one of the members for Deptford and, almost immediately, found himself chairman of its Technical Education Committee. At this stage of his career, Sidney had high hopes that the public services that would result from the collectivisation of English society would hinge more upon the recently established county councils than upon Whitehall. The permeation of those councils was therefore a fundamental part of Fabian strategy. As this process was to have such important repercussions on the future shape of the English educational system, not least in our own day, some consideration of the claim that the Fabians, and more particularly Webb, were the founders of 'municipal socialism' is called for.

The claim springs from the scale of Fabian propaganda during the three years which followed the first county council elections in 1889. Webb's contribution was to open the eyes of fellow members of the Society to what was for them a whole new field of operations. As a consequence the Fabians tended to overrate the originality of his proposals. More objective accounts of the period scotch the notion that the Fabians were pioneers in the field. G. D. H. Cole, for instance, maintained that, 'save in the field of education, the Fabians on the L.C.C. appear to have made, and to have attempted, little that had not been attempted by the London Radicals, under the leadership of J. F. B. Firth' and that in general they behaved more like Radicals than Socialists.[31] R. C. K. Ensor, another prominent Fabian, took care to stress that municipalisation had always been an empirical growth in England and only in later years 'did the young intellectuals of the Fabian Society seize on the process, christen it "municipal socialism" and base on it a philosophy of politico–economic evolution.'[32] The identification of the Fabians with London—a bye-product perhaps of Webb's undoubted passion for that worst-governed of cities—and their rather condescending attitude towards provincial Fabianism come out very strongly in Pease's *History of the Fabian Society*. But what Pease himself always took care to stress was that much of what they were proposing to do had in fact long since been put into practice by the great cities of the provinces, especially in the Birmingham of Joseph Chamberlain.

What was proposed for London was in fact past history for the Midlands. Contemporary Liberal opinion saw little novelty in what the Fabians had to say about municipal reform. W. T. Stead's opinion was that 'Mr. Sidney Webb . . . aspires to be Mr. Chamberlain of London'. *The Speaker*, a Liberal journal, in reviewing *The London Programme*, declared: 'On this occasion Mr. Webb writes more as a Radical than as a Fabian, and, except on one subject . . . every reform he advocates is certainly in- cluded in the programme of every Liberal and Radical in Lon- don.'[33] A few years later Lord Rosebery spoke for the majority of Liberals when he claimed that 'these things are not Socialism at all. They are a vital necessity for a great city.'[34]

But even though Webb's ideas were not so uniquely original as some Fabians believed, his impact, disregarding for the moment his major contribution in the field of technical education, was considerable. In the first place he became as a theorist the successor to Firth, who was killed in an accident in 1889, and whose organisation, the Municipal Reform League, faded out of existence shortly afterwards. In only one important respect was there a major point of difference for, whereas Firth was a centraliser by conviction, Webb adopted a more flexible approach, and in the early years at any rate took up a middle position between this policy and the sort of decentralisation through the metropolitan boroughs that Chamberlain was advocating for London. In short, Webb was prepared to act quite pragmatically in so far as centralisation was concerned. What was important was efficient government. If a decentralised system could bring this about he was content. If not, as in the case of the school boards some years later, then centralisation was the answer. Even then, if only to protect the liberties of the citizen or consumer, a system of checks and balances would have to be created.[35]

Secondly, the flood of Fabian publications over the next few years, although perhaps stating little that was fundamentally new, produced the desired effect. At the time of the next round of local elections in 1892, the Progressive Party, a heterogeneous grouping of all those elements seeking an active administration,[36] had definitely recognised *The London Programme* as the most up-to-date statement of its objectives. Mention must also be made of the London Reform Union, the propaganda body of the Progressives, which was always well staffed with Fabians. It was therefore not surprising that the character and format of the pamphlets issued by the London Reform Union bore a marked resemblance to the Fabian Tracts.

Perhaps, as Alan McBriar has pointed out, the really important difference between Fabians and Radicals was a psychological one. In the Fabian propaganda there is a more evident note of self-assurance. Every reform that is advocated seems to be part of a comprehensive scheme. It was this which was so important in the maintenance of Fabian morale. Unlike the Radicals they had a feeling of leadership and a sense of knowing which way the world was going. It was all part of the emerging Fabian myth.[37]

Even so, the Society had been singularly uninterested in the first London County Council elections. In 1892 however, persuaded by Webb that the promotion of socialism should not be restricted to the parliamentary arena, they secured six out of a total of 118 seats on the County Council. The claim that thenceforth their influence was totally disproportionate to their numbers needs of course to be substantiated and unfortunately all the *Minutes* of the L.C.C. and of its committees tend to eschew personalities. In general, the personal element reveals itself only in opposition and the fact that Webb was such a superb committee man makes the unravelling of his influence baffling on occasion. His generally acknowledged self-effacement and the logical implications of the process of permeation make matters even more difficult.

The real fruits of Fabian intervention in local government were in the area of educational advance—a fact which, when one considers just how little attention had been previously given to the subject, is mildly ironic. Some account of how the county councils came to be involved in public education—more specifically in technical education—is therefore called for.

During the early decades of the nineteenth century Britain's industrial supremacy had been very much taken for granted. Lulled into a complacency that was the result of the country's early industrialisation and the favourable position in which the Napoleonic Wars had placed her, there seemed little reason to believe that Britain would ever cease to be 'the workshop of the world'. Suffice it to say that by the middle of the century, Britain was producing about two-thirds of the world's coal, 'perhaps half its iron, five-sevenths of its small supply of steel, about half of such cotton cloth as was produced on a commercial scale, and forty per cent (in value) of its hardware'.[38]

The challenge to the country's industrial supremacy arose from the development of the new science-based industries, which, with a few notable exceptions, came to be dominated first by Germany and later by the United States. Even at the time of the spectacularly successful Great Exhibition of 1851, the very heyday of Britain's pre-eminence, there had been signs that trouble lay ahead. Thoughtful observers were prepared to attribute at least a part of Britain's comparatively poor showing in the new industries to an inadequate system of technical education and scientific research. Prince Albert was one of those observers and his comments to the Commissioners of the Great Exhibition singularly perceptive:

The improvement in locomotion, the increased means offered by science for the extraction, preparation, or culture of the raw material, have lessened the peculiar local advantages of certain nations, and have thus depressed the relative value of the raw material as an element in manufacture; while they have immensely increased the value of skill and intelligence as the other great element of production.[39]

The answer could lie only in the provision of more technical education.

The immediate result was the setting up of the Department of Science and the Department of Practical Art, both of which were to amalgamate a few years later. This new body—the Department of Science and Art—was to perform sterling work. In the main, however, the tempo of change remained leisurely until the Paris International Fair of 1867, an occasion in which Britain won a mere ten out of ninety sections and British exhibits were described by one caustic observer as 'slovenly intruded heaps of raw material mingled with pieces of rusty iron'. The significance of the setting up in the next year of a Select Committee to inquire into the whole subject was heightened by the onset in 1873 of the 'Great Depression' which signalled the end of the truly buoyant years of Victorian capitalism. The years 1870–71 also saw the rise to full nationhood of Imperial Germany. Matthew Arnold's recently published report on *Higher Schools and Universities in Germany* went at least some way towards accounting for the phenomenal rise of German power and influence.[40]

The year that saw the birth of the Fabian Society was also the year in which the *Report* of the Royal Commission on Technical Instruction was published. The Commission, under the chairmanship of Bernhard Samuelson, recommended an extension of technical education at home, with help from the rates for this purpose. The Liberal government of the day was however distracted by the Irish question and remained inactive, thus causing the emergence in 1887 of an influential group of scientists and politicians who were committed to reform in this critical area. This body, the National Association for the Promotion of Technical Education, kept up a steady pressure on all fronts and the result two years later was the passing of the Technical Instruction Act. The Act empowered the new county and county borough councils, brought into existence in the previous year, to assume responsibility for this branch of education. In the following year A. H. D. Acland,[41] chairman of the National Association, succeeded in diverting the revenues of a tax on beer and spirits—the so-called 'whisky money'—to the councils for the greater provision of technical education. This revenue, together with the product of the penny rate that the Act empowered the county councils to raise, provided the lubricant that was necessary in order for the machinery to operate.

Even so the London County Council was extremely dilatory in taking any step in this direction, preferring instead to divert its whisky money for the purposes of rate relief whilst it indulged in a somewhat futile attempt to wrest more money from the City Corporation for educational purposes. This inaction provoked the wrath of the National Association, which showed itself highly critical of the delay. The first real evidence of Sidney Webb's concern was seen just before the 1892 local elections, when there was a flurry of activity involving himself and leading members of the technical education lobby. The result of all this was his appointment as chairman of the Council's first Technical Education Committee. Coming as it did within days of his initiation into local government, this was, to say the least, surprising. The closeness of the link with the National Association is revealed in Webb's choice of Hubert Llewellyn Smith,[42] secretary of the Association, to survey London's needs and to report in due course to the Technical Education Committee, known from 1893 onwards under the more familiar 'Technical Education Board'.

Thus it was that Sidney's entry into the educational world was not dictated by any particular interest in elementary education, nor for that matter in the endowed grammar schools. Parliament had given educational responsibilities to the new authorities. As far as the L.C.C. was concerned, those powers had been allowed to go by default. The situation called out to be exploited. It was the subsequent experience of being responsible for the conceiving and execution of policies in the field of technical education that provided the practical frame of reference for the Webbs' instrumental theory of education to germinate and grow. It is true that it was the area of higher education that attracted them the most, Beatrice especially. But, underpinning the efficiency of colleges and universities, as the German experience so forcefully demonstrated, was the quality of schooling at the elementary and secondary levels. There was therefore a need to bring about a 'national minimum' in all the schools and higher educational establishments of London, a city which, as Sidney constantly took pains to point out, was, in terms of wealth and population, as well favoured as many a nation state.

The concept of 'national efficiency' became superimposed upon this as a result of a growing impatience with what they considered to be the amateurism and frequent incompetence of Britain's political, social and military institutions. The training of the expert in all fields was thus of supreme importance in the struggle for national survival. The start of the London School of Economics in 1894 must be viewed in this perspective. By 1902–3, with the disasters of the early months of the South African War so painfully confirming 'England's shame', the Webbs' faith in increased educational provision as the means of bringing about the desired change reached its zenith.

At the local level too the problem of inefficiency was becoming obvious. Despite their earlier satisfaction with the work of the school boards, the Webbs had come to believe that *ad hoc* bodies as such were unsatisfactory instruments for educational advance. If the goal of 'national efficiency' was to be pursued in all seriousness, it was important that these embodiments of primary democracy should go. Some short account of the work of the L.C.C.'s Technical Education Board and its relationship with the London School Board must now be given.

3 The London Technical Education Board, 1892-1904

Sidney Webb's feeling for London remained strong throughout his life, a state of mind all the more remarkable when one considers his normal placidity of temperament. To his dying day he loved his birthplace with a passion of surprising intensity.[43] In 1892 the prospect of rectifying the deficiencies in technical education in the nation's capital must have been an exciting one.[44] Not only that, it offered a splendid opportunity for a further application of collectivist policies in an area where 'self-help' had proved woefully deficient. But before the inadequacies of technical education could be put right, they had to be surveyed by the sort of expert indispensable to Fabian policy-making. The appointment of Llewellyn Smith to do this was to be of the greatest importance. Not only was he secretary to the National Association for the Promotion of Technical and Secondary Education,[45] he was also a fellow worker with Charles Booth in his classic *Inquiry into the Life and Labour of the People of London*. Not surprisingly, the *Report* that emerged a few months later was so thorough in its scope that it was to serve as a blueprint for the next decade.

Confirming the gloomy picture that had been described in an earlier work, the shortcomings of London's provision of technical education were starkly contrasted, not only with the facilities available in France and Germany—these countries were generally acknowledged to be well ahead—but with other parts of Great Britain. The indictment was considerable but so was the opportunity for reform and in the compass of two hundred pages Llewellyn Smith outlined what was needed.

His proposals were accepted almost immediately by the Technical Education Committee and early in the following year the Committee's recommendations were in turn approved by the County Council. Webb's proposal to replace the Committee by a Technical Education Board, twenty of whose members were to be Council nominees and the other fifteen to represent outside interests—a formula much favoured by local government con- stitution-makers from that time to the present day—also won the approval of the Council. The device had the merit of allowing far- reaching plans to be fathered of a kind which, if they had been advanced in the Council itself, would have antagonised those self-same interests. For, with his usual prescience, Webb realised that if the Council simply created another committee, without any outside representation, there would be jealousy and hostility from all quarters—from the London School Board, the City Livery Companies, teachers and trade unionists. In order to conciliate potential opposition, therefore, the proper course was to invite outside representation from the beginning, but at the same time leaving a working majority of elected members. It is significant that the device of the mixed delegated committee was later written into the Education Act of 1902 as the pattern for the pro- posed Education Committees of the new L.E.A.s.

As a result of his labours, it might have been expected that Llewellyn Smith would have been the natural choice for the post of Secretary to the Board. This was not to be for Dr William Garnett, a rising expert in scientific education, was appointed in- stead. Both Chairman and Secretary co-operated closely during the Board's lifetime, although it should be said that in their reminiscences many years later there was a singular reticence on each side in acknowledging fully the achievements of the other.

There is a well-known account by Beatrice of how Sidney told Acland and Sir John Donnelly,[46] the permanent head of the Science and Art Department, that in a city like London every conceivable subject specialism had to be learned by someone if the place was to function at all. It should be remembered that in the 1890s there was a growing tendency to regard much of secondary education as 'technical' in the sense that it promoted 'fitness for life'. Certainly there were encouraging precedents, for, owing to a very generous interpretation of 'technical instruction', a whole range of subjects was already being encouraged by technical education committees up and down the country. The outcome of the meeting was a very broad concession on the part of Acland that Science and Art grants-in-aid could cover all the sciences and all the arts. 'We can now lawfully teach anything under the sun except ancient Greek and Theology', Sidney is reported to have remarked following this visit. Hyperbole on his part perhaps, but his jubilation, as he looked at the prospect that lay ahead, was understandable, for now the T.E.B. could count on government support in expanding the scope and provision of secondary education in the metropolis.

With the problem identified and its powers made clear, the Board could now go ahead. It was probably the result of Sidney's own educational experiences which made him wish to erect 'two educational ladders for every Londoner', one for climbing by day, the other available in the evening. By doing this it would be possible for poor children to rise from the elementary schools, through the secondary schools and, if they had a true head for heights, as far as university studies. The creation of several hundred 'junior county' and 'intermediate' scholarships, as well as numerous scholarships of a more specialised nature, provided the means to bring this about.

No effort was spared by Webb to make the 'ladders' reach levels hitherto regarded as inaccessible. At the end of his tenure of office he liked to claim that there was a more serviceable ladder for the London child than was available to its counterpart in any American, French or German city. To our contemporary radical spirit scholarships for secondary schooling may smack of élitism and notions of scarcity. Even in the 1890s such critical attitudes were not unknown. It is interesting to note for example that Keir Hardie[47] and Will Crooks[48] were bitterly opposed to the competitive philosophy inherent in all this. But the truth was that by no stretch of the imagination could the Webbs be regarded as egalitarian in the sense in which that word is so often used to-day. Their growing belief that the schools should act as agencies for the sifting of the talent necessary for the efficient running of the meritocratic state comes out very strongly in a speech made by Sidney in 1897 in the presence of the future Edward VII:

We have endeavoured to build up here the greatest capacity-catching-machine that the world has ever yet seen. Time has yet to show to what extent we shall be successful in discovering hidden treasures of genius and ability and practical wisdom which, as we believe, exist in almost as large a proportion among the children of the poorer sections of the community, as among those more favoured in pecuniary fortune. We have hitherto been compelled to recruit our able men, our captains of industry, our leaders of science, mainly, though not entirely, from those who have had the advantage of good education and further culture than falls in the ordinary course to the lot of most of us; but perhaps in the future we may look also for a considerable portion of the intelligence and wisdom of the nation to those lowlier sections of society who are represented here tonight . . . What we have done and what is being done for these scholars is not done for themselves alone. It is not even done to give pleasure and pride and honour to the parents who are here tonight. We hope and trust that the public money which we are now expending this way will come back to the community in the future multiplied a hundredfold.[49]

In such pronouncements Platonic assumptions are immediately evident and there was more than a whiff of Platonism in the air many years later when Beatrice recorded in her diary her reactions to a review of one of their larger literary works by their old friend, R. B. Haldane:

Haldane believed more than we did in the existing governing class: in the great personages of Court, Cabinet and City. We staked our hopes on the organised working class, served and guided, it is true, by an élite of unassuming experts who would make no claim to superior social status, but would content themselves with exercising the power inherent in superior knowledge and longer administrative experience.[50]

The decade of the 1890s was a crucial one in the emergence of the Webbs' functional philosophy. Increasingly it seemed to Beatrice and Sidney that political morality lay in changing the composition of the social hierarchy so that merit would more and more become the criterion of social mobility. An élite hitherto based upon the accident of birth or wealth was to be replaced in the fullness of time by what would be recognised to-day, unfortunately often in a pejorative manner, as a meritocracy whose goal would be quite simply the pursuit of 'national' and 'imperial efficiency'. Given limited resources at the secondary-school level, it was important that these new guardians should be selected by tests, and rise by means of 'the scholarship ladders'. This then was the vision which increasingly gave purpose and direction to the Webbs' educational schemes.

When confronted by the starker implications of this social philosophy Sidney inevitably recoiled, as is evident in what he had to say in addressing the Association of Technical Institutes in 1909:

I want no hewers of wood and drawers of water; no class destined to remain there and prevented from rising because we do not provide for it . . . Our convenience! Our comfort! Our comfort is to stand in the way of enabling these people, our fellow-citizens, to attain anything better than being mere hewers of wood and drawers of water! I must apologise for having been betrayed into a little heat, but I do object to the notion that for our convenience we are to keep hewers of wood and drawers of water.

On occasion a certain ambivalence of attitude undeniably peeps through, as for instance when he seems to imply that a scholarship system will not in itself be sufficient to produce trained people in sufficient numbers to take their place in the new 'organic state' he increasingly favours. In the following passage he hints at the substitution of 'the ladder' by some new principle of selection. Its nature is, unfortunately perhaps, not specified and there is an undoubted sting in the tail:

But the really democratic purpose of public education was not to dole out elementary education to all and sundry, nor yet to develop a race of scholarship winners, but to train up the most efficient and most civilized body of citizens, making the most of the brains of all, and, in the interests of the community as a whole, developing each to the 'margin of cultivation'. We must discard the old notion of education free of cost as a grant of charity to the poor; we no longer think that a free opening of all avenues to individual ability is the true ideal. What Collectivists demand is the equipment of the whole body of citizens, each in accordance with his particular aptitudes and capacities, for the service of the community, *as far and as freely in each case as the interests of the community require.*[51]

The truth was however that, despite these early hints of comprehensivisation, a belief in a limited pool of ability was implicit in all the decisions taken by the Webbs during this very busy period in their lives, just as it was in most of their public and private utterances. Consider, for example, the description of London's secondary schools in Sidney's contribution to H. Bryan Binns' *A Century of Education*, published in 1908. There is nothing here which in any way anticipates the growing egalitarian spirit within the Labour Party in the post-1945 period. Sidney's justification for his rather complacent view of London's secondary school provision is in fact the *Report* of the Taunton Commissioners back in 1868. The writing is structured around notions of the different grades of secondary schools, each grade reflecting the needs of the different social classes. Fabian radicalism comes through in his enthusiasm for the scholarship system which will make it possible for ability, no matter from what quarter it has emerged, to be recognised and nurtured. 'This, however, and not "common schools", has already become, in education, the Democratic ideal.' Only in the 1930s in the course of the Webbs' visit to the Soviet Union do we see an unqualified enthusiasm for the virtues of the common school. This however is to jump ahead to a period in which the world had become a vastly different place and their thinking had as a consequence undergone considerable change.

Nevertheless, measured in practical terms, the effects of the development of London's scholarship system were considerable. In the first place, the Technical Education Board w s brought directly into contact with the elementary and secondary schools, and the friendly relationship that ensued had an important influence on the future development of secondary education.[52] What the scholarships also succeeded in doing was to bring 'a steady stream of clever boys and girls to the languishing endowed secondary schools, to the expanding technical institutes and to the unfilled classes of the university colleges'.[53] Safeguarded by the usual conditions of inspection and carefully devised codes of regulations, the Board started to make annual grants to the host of independent institutions to which its scholars were sent. Schools, colleges, and institutions, hitherto unaware of, or unconcerned with, the existence of similar bodies to themselves, became gradually welded into a co-ordinated whole and began to assume a corporate consciousness in place of anarchic independence.

Had the Board decided to build its own schools and colleges under the powers given to the County Councils by the Act of 1889, it is conceivable that a lot of this might not have taken place. For Webb there was a threefold advantage in his decision to subsidise existing institutions. He was able to avoid delay in the building of new schools; he escaped the friction that would have resulted from further competition in London's educational system; and he was able to begin to establish 'a unity in diversity' by introducing some central supervision over a whole host of semi-independent bodies. The fact that the Technical Education Board of the London County Council came in large measure to act as a highly successful local education authority did not escape the attention of the Royal Commission on Secondary Education, reporting in 1895. For the policy makers of 1902 it provided an argument of considerable magnitude in the reshaping of the local control of England's educational system.

The most influential educational agency in the capital was of course the London School Board which lost little time in applying for grants from the County Council for its higher grade and organised science schools. These were readily forthcoming, as was help for its evening classes. Having educated himself largely in his spare time, Webb always had a soft spot for those who had to study under this handicap. In *London Education*, published in 1904, Webb affirmed his belief that all young people under the age of twenty-one should be enrolled at some sort of evening class. And at all costs such evening schools were not to be considered in isolation. They were an important element in London's educational system so that, if the need arose, a student would be able to progress from an evening class right up to the level of university studies.

Quite separate from the institutions of the School Board were London's ninety endowed schools, fifty of which applied to the T.E.B. for financial help. Before the Board's intervention many of these had been in a state of acute financial depression which had taken its toll of staffing, amenities and morale. Scholarship fees and grants of all sorts now began to revive these tired and drooping institutions, so creating what Beatrice was pleased to call 'an unexpected *renaissance* in desirable variety'. Critics of the endowed secondary schools and the partisans of the School Board's higher grade schools were angry that the T.E.B. had intervened to preserve institutions which had seemed likely to fulfil a collective death wish. Their supporters, predictably, felt emotions of a different order. Webb himself was quite sure that what was beginning to emerge in London in the 'nineties was a system of public secondary education, and he took care at subsequent L.C.C. elections to see that the Progressive Party was given the credit.[54]

Rather more spectacular was the increase in the numbers of polytechnics, art schools and technical institutes during his tenure of office. Some of these already existed on the ground as a result of private effort and the backing of the City Livery Companies. A most welcome reinforcement had been provided by the City Parochial Charities Act, an 'elegant piece of modernization' which had pooled all the bits of accumulated capital stored in the obsolete charitable endowments of the City of London.[55] Because he felt these establishments were catering for a *'nouvelle couche sociale'* Webb had a particular affection for them and lost no opportunity of stressing their need for support from a radically-minded representative body such as the L.C.C.

Not only was there an increase in the number of monotechnic establishments providing for such specialisms as building, printing and navigation. The number of polytechnics was also to more than double during the decade. This rate of growth was gratifying, but more distant goals were being formulated, goals which envisaged the inclusion of polytechnic courses as accredited areas of university teaching and the recognition of polytechnic teachers as teachers of London University. The lever that Webb intended to use to prise open the door was a financial one, namely the promise of T.E.B. subsidies. As yet, however, the University was simply an examining body. Not until it was reformed along the lines being drafted by Webb and R. B. Haldane would subventions begin to fall from the L.C.C. cornucopia. It was for this very reason that Webb had opposed an early suggestion that there should be a university representative on the T.E.B. And although at Webb's prompting L.C.C. grants were already being given to King's College, University College, and Bedford College, it was made quite clear that no money would be forthcoming, even to a reformed teaching university, unless there was an inclusion of certain polytechnic courses within the University itself.

Another institution whose inclusion in the University was essential to the Webbs was the London School of Economics and Political Science, without question 'the favourite child' of the partnership. The unique and 'picturesque'[56] circumstances which surrounded the birth of the L.S.E. are by now well known: the extraordinary windfall of £10,000 entrusted to Webb under the will of Henry Hunt Hutchinson, the obscure Derby Fabian, to promote 'the propaganda and other purposes of the Fabian Society and its Socialism, and towards advancing its objects in any way that may seem advisable'; the fund-raising opportunism of Beatrice in snaring Charlotte Payne-Townshend, who neglected to marry Graham Wallas, preferring Bernard Shaw instead; the prescience of the Webbs in sensing the quality of W. A. S. Hewins,[57] the School's first Director; the calibre of the early teachers working in conditions which would have daunted lesser spirits.

Beatrice's reactions to the news of Hutchinson's suicide, confided to the intimacy of her diary a few weeks after the event, are extremely revealing, as they indicate that the Webbs had been

thinking for some time about starting a higher educational establishment directed to research and teaching in the field of economics.[58] As early as 1888 Sidney had enthused over the quality of
economics teaching in the Massachusetts Institute of Technology,
but the spur to action, in other words involvement in the practical
business of educational administration, still lay in the future.
When, early in 1894, the 'Gresham University' Commission
stressed the need for studies of the sort pursued in Paris in the
Ecole Libre des Sciences Politiques, Webb, as Chairman of the
T.E.B., was very much concerned with putting right deficiencies
in higher education, and the news of the Hutchinson bequest
came as manna from the heavens. More specifically, it presented
an opportunity to teach the sort of down-to-earth economics that
would be very different from the theoretical and philosophical
subject taught at the older universities.

Beatrice was jubilant that the training of the expert so badly
needed in the pursuit of 'national efficiency' could now begin in all
seriousness:

It looks as if the great bulk of the working men will be collectivists
before the end of the century. But Reform will not be brought about by
shouting. What is needed is *hard thinking*. And the same objection
applies to sending nondescript socialists into Parliament. The radical
members are quite sufficiently compliant in their views: what is lacking
in them is the leaven of knowledge. So Sidney has been planning to
persuade the other trustees to devote the greater part of the money to
encouraging *Research* and Economic study. His vision is to found,
slowly and quietly, a 'London School of Economics and Political
Science' a centre not only of lectures on special subjects but an association of students who would be directed and supported in doing original
work. Last evening we sat by the fire and jotted down a whole list of
subjects which want elucidating—issues of fact which need clearing up.
Above all, we want the ordinary citizen to feel that reforming society
is no light matter and must be undertaken by experts specially trained
for the purpose.[59]

The most pressing question that the Webbs had to face was

whether the spending of the modest sum in question could legiti-
mately be diverted towards the start of an educational institution
whose *raison d'être* was dispassionate study and research as
opposed to the dissemination of left-wing propaganda. In the
extract just quoted Beatrice quite obviously assumes that the two
aims will bring about the same result. Sidney however was
obviously uneasy, and it is interesting to trace his tactics during
the twelve months that elapsed between the news of Hutchinson's
death and the start of the L.S.E. in the autumn of 1895.

Even Bernard Shaw was aghast at the manoeuvrings of his
friend, all the more so when he learned the names of the other
bodies that Webb had approached for funds. Voicing the dismay
of leading members of the Society at what appeared to be a
diverting of Fabian resources from their legitimate purpose, he
indulged in a splendid display of Shavian fireworks:

What I wanted to say myself was about the Hutchinson business. At
the last executive discussion of it Webb quite terrified me by showing
an appalling want of sense of the situation; and my most violent efforts
failed to wake him up: he kept on making exactly the speeches he
makes to the Chamber of Commerce and the County Council (T.E.B.)
about it. When Bond Holding and Martin[60] began to stare with all
their eyes, he first attempted to prove that Acworth[61] was the greatest
living authority on railways; then that his object was 'abstract research' (meaning a kind of research in which Bosanquet[62] and Miss
Dendy would arrive at exactly the same conclusions and produce the
same information as Wallas and Miss Stacy);[63] then, feeling rather
hurt at the evidence of scepticism of Martin as to the feasibility of this
academic ideal, he hinted that the bequest had been left to him to dis-
pose of as he thought fit, and that the executive had nothing to do with
it. The general impression left was that the Hutchinson trustees are
prepared to bribe the Fabian by subsidies for country lectures and the
like to allow them to commit an atrocious malversation of the rest of
the bequest; and that as the executive is powerless, the best thing to
do is to take the bribe, and warn future Hutchinsons to be careful how
they leave any money they may have to place at the disposal of
Socialism. This won't do. First, Hewins must be told flatly that he must,
in talking to the Guild of St. Matthew and the other Oxford Socialists,

speak as a Collectivist, and make it clear that the School of Economics will have a Collectivist bias. Any pretence about having no bias at all, about 'pure' or 'abstract' research, or the like evasions and unrealities must be kept for the enemy. Second, Hewins must be told that he MUST get somebody else than Acworth and Foxwell[64] to put in the bill. It is easy to say where are the men: the answer is that that is precisely what Hewins is being paid out of Hutchinson's money to find out. Third, the Collectivist flag must be waved, and the Marseillaise played if necessary in order to attract fresh bequests. If the enemy complains, it must be told that the School has important endowments the conditions of which are specifically Socialist; and that if the enemy wants specifically individualistic lectures, he must endow too. Meanwhile the Fabian must be kept in mind of the fact that Acworth was chosen by the L.C.C.; and Webb positively must not declare that he is an authority on the subject, or indeed that he is anything but hopelessly wrong and invincibly stupid on it, which is the solemn truth.

You see we must be in a position at any moment to show that faith has been kept with Hutchinson. If Webb is ever publicly convicted of having served up the County Council and the Chamber of Commerce on toast to the ghost of Hutchinson, everyone will laugh and think it an uncommonly smart thing. But if he is even suspected of having tampered with a trust of ten thousand pounds from a private benefactor, then we shall lose our character for being straight in money matters; and none of us can afford to do that. And it is so very simple to avoid anything of the sort. All that is necessary is to avoid shocking the common sense of the public and the I.L.P. or Fabian critic by talking about academic abstraction and impartiality. Even if such a thing were possible, its foundation out of Hutchinson's money would be as flagrant a breach of trust as handing it over to the Liberty and Property Defence League, since it was expressly left to endow Socialism. Further, the Fabian Executive must not be told that it has nothing to do with it. It was by an act of special providence that Bland[65] was absent on that disastrous occasion. He would certainly have moved then and there that the subject be dropped and that the Fabian executive, having no control of the Hutchinson bequest, declines to make itself responsible for its administration by discussing it in any way. To me the attitude of Martin, who is quite friendly to us, is very alarming. He is willing to admit good-naturedly that nothing else could be done; but it is quite evident that he also feels that if the money had been left to him, he would have managed very differently. Much more terrifying is the temporary (let us hope) suspension of Webb's wits. The moment I read that prospectus in the Chronicle, I saw that it would have to be carefully explained to the Fabians. My dismay when Webb did not even understand why the subject had been put on the agenda paper was acute. Please show him this letter and allow it to rankle.[66]

Webb however had already sought the advice of counsel in the person of R. B. Haldane, 'that steadfast fellow conspirator for the public good', as Beatrice later described him. Haldane had confirmed the right of the Hutchinson Trustees to act without consulting the Fabian Society and had advised that the provision of public instruction in economic and political science could be regarded as a proper use of trust funds. Sidney was now secure in an apparently impregnable legal fortress; but that he still had some doubts is apparent from the care he took to avoid the will being challenged in the courts.[67]

His immediate objective was to start the School of Economics in the shortest possible time; the long-term aim was to weave it into the fabric of the University. Amazingly enough, when one considers the difficulties, he had by 1900 managed to achieve precisely this. The Hutchinson money had been the spur to action, but if the L.S.E. was to become a constituent part of the University he could not afford to have it associated with any one political grouping. Hence his wish to keep the spending of the money in the hands of the Trustees and not with the Fabian Executive who might in any case have been tempted to use too large a proportion of the bequest for the purposes of political propaganda.

One notable Fabian who had criticised Webb for appropriating socialist funds for his own educational ends was the future Labour Prime Minister, James Ramsay MacDonald. When in 1902, in a correspondence which was perverse but entirely logical, MacDonald wrote to the Principal of London University, alleging that the University had embraced a politically motivated establishment to its bosom, the dismay of Sir Arthur Rücker was at once apparent. So too was that of Sidney, as is evident from the anxious note that runs through a whole series of letters to Beatrice who at the time had taken Bertrand Russell's first wife, Alys, away to Switzerland in order to provide some distractions from her growing marital concerns.[68]

Despite his anxiety, however, Sidney was quite secure. The ground had been well prepared. He could now show that the Hutchinson bequest had never formed part of the L.S.E.'s actual endowment, for in the strictly legal sense the School had never enjoyed any endowment 'other than the subscriptions and donations given to it'. The Hutchinson money was, he maintained somewhat disingenuously, only one of many donations. There were certainly no ideological strings attached and the School's financial backers and its teachers represented all shades of political opinion.[69] MacDonald was doubtless puzzled by Sidney's lack of consistency, but Shaw's admiration for the political acumen of his friend presumably increased as he saw the real motive for the inclusion of academics like Acworth and Foxwell on the staff of the School.

The prospect of a permanent grant from the coffers of the T.E.B. provided the means whereby the London School was successfully engineered into the University and it was to this end that Webb and Haldane were most closely associated in the 1890s. As a rising star in the sector of the Liberal firmanent which at the time of the Boer War was to be labelled 'Limp'—an acronym for Liberal Imperialist—and the personal friend of A. J. Balfour who was shortly to become Prime Minister in place of his uncle, Lord Salisbury, Haldane's role was to be crucial. But so too were Sidney's backstage activities, more especially the conciliation of sectional interests such as those represented by Convocation and the various London colleges, and his part in the actual drafting of successive Bills.[70]

Yet no two men could have been physically and temperamentally so unlike, as Beatrice herself repeatedly pointed out in her vivid pen-portraits. In one respect, however, there was an important similarity. This was in their personal experiences of higher education. Haldane had studied at Edinburgh and later at Göttingen. The nature of Sidney's experience of higher education has already been touched upon. What was to be of considerable significance in the restructuring of London University was that neither man had been educated at Oxford or Cambridge, an omission which in their view did not appear to be unduly debilitating.

The *Report* in 1894 of the Commission on the proposed Gresham University recommended a single university for London, one which would combine the existing system of examinations for 'external' degrees with the examination of internal students who had taken an approved course at a college recognised by the university. Unfortunately it proposed a form of government which found favour with none of the interested parties. Together Webb and Haldane drew up a compromise constitution which seemed to have more chance of acceptance and embodied their scheme in a Private Member's Bill introduced in the House of Lords. The Bill was, however, killed by opposition from the bishops. In 1897 it failed again with the result that Haldane then persuaded Balfour to bring the Bill forward as a Government measure the next year. It still met with much opposition, but was finally carried, thanks to a very telling speech by Haldane himself. By drawing attention to the possibility of financial support from the L.C.C. and by lauding the work of the polytechnics and of the London School of Economics, institutions which deserved a rightful place in a reform University of London, Haldane exploited the arguments that Webb had so carefully marshalled.

The Commission under Lord Davey[71] that was set up as a result of the University of London Act itself underwent a share of Fabian permeation and in the early months of 1900 Webb was able to announce that many of the polytechnic courses had been accepted by the new University, that their teachers had been duly accredited, and, not least, that the London School of Economics had been included in a form which made it almost identical with the new Faculty of Economics.

When we bear in mind the inauspicious beginnings of the L.S.E., the jubilation of the Webbs is understandable. Although Beatrice's optimism about the linking of economics with the natural sciences was, as it turned out, wildly premature, a diary extract of the time is worth quoting as it gives an insight into their curriculum priorities for the education of the experts needed to run the twentieth-century nation state:

We have got the School recognised as a Faculty of Economics, we have secured a site and a building, free of cost, and an income of £2,500 devoted to economics and commercial science. Sidney will be a member of the Faculty and will probably represent the County Council on the Senate. Best of all he has persuaded the Royal Commission to recognise economics as a science and not merely as a subject in the Arts Faculty. The preliminary studies for the economics degree will, therefore, be mathematics and biology. This divorce of economics from metaphysics and shoddy history is a great gain. We have always claimed that the study of the structure and function of society was as much a science as the study of any other form of life, and ought to be pursued by the scientific methods used in other organic sciences. Hypotheses ought to be used, not as the unquestioned premiss from which to deduce an unquestioned conclusion, but as an order of thought to be verified by observation and experiment. Such history as will be taught at the School will be the history of social institutions discovered from documents, statistics and the observation of the actual structure and working of living organisations.[72]

Thus it was that the training of the expert geared to 'national' and 'imperial efficiency' became the L.S.E.'s *raison d'être*, and not the production of socialists which but a few years previously had been the argument used to silence Fabian critics. It may well have been the case that Webb believed that, in the end, the dispassionate study of society would inevitably turn people into socialists. Certainly this was his answer to Haldane at the time he had consulted counsel, but the stress placed upon this objective diminishes with the passage of time and the growth of the cult of efficiency. Beatrice's diaries show how little faith they chose to put in the knowledge and competence of the socialists of the 1890s. They were clearly convinced that socialists themselves would continue to be ineffective unless they really understood the complexities of the society they were setting out to reform. The strength of

Sidney's feeling about socio-economic research is shown in a letter he wrote to Mrs Bernard Shaw:

. . . only in this path of scientific study lies any hope of remedying social evils, or relieving individual misery. I am furious when I read of bequests to the Poor Box, or the Lifeboat Society, or the Hospital—it is worth more to discover one tiny improvement that will permanently change conditions ever so little for the better than to assuage momentarily the woes of thousands.[73]

There is here perhaps some implication of a socialist commitment but what is more important is the leavening of knowledge. Whether the shade of Hutchinson approved of the change of emphasis must remain a matter of fireside speculation.

In the long run there can be little doubt that the London School of Economics has contributed to the thinking and activity of the Fabian Society, and more widely perhaps to socialist thinking at large. It has not, however, in the judgment of a recent Director of the London School, contributed exclusively to socialist thinking, and may even on balance have been an influence against rather than for socialist policies.[74] But such a sequel would not have unduly dismayed the Webbs whose educational priorities must always be seen in the promotion of social efficiency through the training of the expert.

With the birth of the new London University there came for Sidney a seat on the Senate. Although he could never be as dominant on this body as he had once been on the Technical Education Board, he nevertheless enjoyed a unique position. This was determined by the size of the L.C.C. grant, by 1902 one quarter of the total University income, and also because he had over the years acquired a reputation for success in extracting funds for what seemed forlorn causes. Consequently his presence was an invaluable asset to any growing institution. This dual role on both T.E.B. and Senate was also to reap direct results in the shape of two brand-new institutions. These were the Imperial College of Science and Technology and the London Day Training College. Each was born out of the prevailing ardour for 'national efficiency'; in its maturity each has achieved a notable pre-eminence.

The Llewellyn Smith *Report* of 1892 had stressed 'the enormous and unquestioned importance of the thorough training of teachers'. London's position was a difficult one. The only training colleges that existed were sectarian in character and had proved to be quite incapable of providing trained men and women in sufficient numbers to cope with the rapid expansion of the 1890s. The result was that many potential teachers had of necessity to go far afield in order to receive their professional training.

All manner of public-spirited individuals and professional bodies had drawn attention to the disastrous consequences of this deficiency. Convocation, for example, had asked for the establishment of a Faculty and Degree in 'Formal Pedagogy'. The Education Department in Whitehall had let it be known that it would welcome any move in the right direction but seemed singularly reluctant to take the initiative itself. In the long run it was the London School Board which, judging the period when the Davey Commission was sitting to be propitious, suggested to the T.E.B. that a day training college should be included in the reorganised University.

Webb was a prime mover in the meetings which followed, particularly those between the T.E.B. and the Senate. All his political and managerial skills were deployed to the best possible effect, not least in the face of criticisms from John Burns[75] and other School Board champions, who were seemingly unaware of the fact that the original overtures to the T.E.B. had come from the School Board itself. Predictably too there was opposition from the increasingly vociferous 'anti-higher education' body on the L.C.C., an opposition which found its chief exponents in Ramsay MacDonald and J. E. Gregory. But the 'sweet reasonableness' of the Fabian prevailed, a handsome new annual grant was extracted from the L.C.C., and in October 1902 the London Day Training College, now the London University Institute of Education, began its existence with the future Sir John Adams as the first Principal.

The story of the beginnings of the Day Training College once again provides a revealing insight into the methods used by Webb in 'making ideas viable'. He always avoided following the advice of the many people who would have waited until conditions were completely favourable before the launching of any new undertaking. His belief was that any start was better than none and this was as true of the Day Training College as it was of the London School of Economics and the University itself. Modifications and improvements could always come later.

At this time the Webbs' attitude to the elementary schoolteacher was curiously ambivalent. It will already be apparent that, despite the broad sweep of the T.E.B.'s responsibilities, their chief educational pre-occupations concerned higher education. They were fully alive to the importance of teachers as civilising agents in the late-Victorian industrial wens, but, as political tensions grew, misgivings about the teachers' religious and political loyalties came to the fore. In 1903, a year which was critical for the future of London education, one of their most telling arguments in persuading the Conservative administration not to divide the metropolis up into ten boroughs was their avowal that education in London would be unduly dominated by the elementary schoolteachers, thanks to their disproportionate representation on the borough councils. The radical leanings of the teachers were already sufficient to frighten an administration which was in danger of losing its grip and Sidney's stratagem was successful. Only in later years did the Webbs set out to woo the teachers. In 1918, for instance, there appeared Tract No 187, *The Teacher in Politics*, a publication which makes it quite clear that the growing professional identity of the teachers was recognised as a major force in the future development of the Labour Party.

But as far as scientists and technologists were concerned Sidney's attitude was one of unqualified approval. Clearly, they were in his view the agents of Britain's regeneration. He was after all the Chairman of London's Technical Education Board, brought into existence to help remedy the growing imbalance in the provision of technical education between Britain and her continental rivals. It was not surprising, therefore, in view of Haldane's intimate knowledge of Germany, that there should once again be concerted action between the two men. The fruit of their labours this time was the start of yet another higher educational establishment—the Imperial College of Science and Technology.

The contrast Llewellyn Smith had drawn between the training given to British engineers and chemists and to their counterparts abroad, particularly in Switerland and Germany, had made sad reading for those who felt that in this international race, it was the very existence of Britain that was at stake. It was not in numbers that the country was deficient, according to Llewellyn Smith; the crucial issue was one of quality. Indeed the fear was expressed that Britain was 'overstocking the market with "half-baked" engineers, instead of training the same or even a smaller number to the highest possible pitch'.[76] But the *Report* did not recommend the foundation of any new institution; what it wanted was the proper co-ordination of the existing colleges, the raising of the standards of student entrants and the creation of a teaching university. Four years later this was followed up by the *Report of the Special Sub-committee on the Teaching of Chemistry*. Webb was a member of this committee and of a similar body which presented its *Report on the Application of Science to Industry* in July 1902. The latter document, particularly, was full of gloomy forebodings and partially re-iterated the dismal sentiments of Webb's two articles in *The Times* the previous summer in which he had drawn attention to the dangers of foreign competition. Cassandra-like, he had pointed a warning finger at the coal-tar industry which had recently been lost to Germany, largely because Britain simply did not know what to do with the tar she produced. Unless something were done at home he feared that electro-chemistry might become the prerogative of the Germans in the same way. There were deficiences, too, in other fields. In tanning, for example, we were falling hopelessly behind: hides were being sent to the United States to be tanned and then brought back to England. The list of deficiencies was comprehensive and included such diverse items as brewing and sewage disposal. The same criticism, Webb claimed, held true of most branches of engineering. Though much ground had been lost, however, there was still hope; lessons could be drawn and the remedy applied.[77] The solution he outlined in further contributions to *The Nineteenth Century*[78] and the *Cornhill Magazine*.[79] In contrast to the Llewellyn Smith *Report* ten years previously, he now felt that a completely new type of institution was needed—a British 'Charlottenburg', comprising an extensive and fully equipped institute of technology with special departments for mining, metallurgy, naval architecture and marine engineering, railway engineering, electro-chemistry, optics and various branches of chemical technology.

In calling for a British 'Charlottenburg' Webb was obviously influenced by Haldane who had been greatly impressed by the rising tide of German industrialisation which had followed closely on the victory over France in 1870–71. A key factor, in Haldane's opinion, was the close link between the universities and German industry, a situation which had no parallel at home. He was less favourably impressed with the divorce between the German universities and the great technical colleges, but at Charlottenburg he saw his ideal. This great technical *Hochschule*, working alongside the University of Berlin, had cost £500,000 to build, and £55,000 a year to maintain, but every year there emerged from its doors 1,200 fully trained technologists. In 1890 the vision that Haldane brought back with him to England was the foundation of a similar college in the capital city of the Empire, one which would become the centre of Imperial scientific technology. The real stumbling block was, as might have been expected, the question of finance; but the raising of a £500,000 endowment was a task to which Haldane applied himself with characteristic energy and determination. Lord Rothschild[80] and the two South African magnates, Sir Julius Wernher[81] and Alfred Beit,[82] all gave handsomely, although it should perhaps be said that University College became in the process the poorer by £100,000, for this was the sum that the South African millionaires had originally earmarked for it.

The major role of Haldane in all this cannot be denied. Yet Sidney was always there in the wings and even on occasion making an entry on to the lavish stage of the Edwardian country house. When Haldane visited Rothschild he went in the company of Cecil Rhodes; when he visited Wernher and Beit he took Sidney along with him. The meeting between socialist and pluto-crats was by all accounts congenial, Sidney finding Wernher to be 'the best of fellows according to his own lights'.

Once again, the Webb–Haldane combination proved irresis-tible. The problem of the site was resolved. The Treasury was persuaded to transfer control of the Royal College of Science and the Royal School of Mines to the new institution. The City and Guilds of London College was brought in. By July 1903 the future of the Imperial College of Science and Technology seemed secure.

The period was of course the heyday of Britain's imperial dream, a dream that socialists like John Burns and Ramsay Mac-Donald found hard to accept. It was the Fabians' stand on the issues raised by the South African War which had precipitated MacDonald's departure from the Society. The Webbs and the Fabians generally felt little sympathy with the cause of the Dutch farmers and in fact took a wry pleasure in pointing out that neither of the white races seemed to be unduly concerned with the rights of the vast majority of the population. This lack of sympathy with the Boers resulted in a close association with the Liberal Im-perialists, whose enthusiasm for Empire they hoped to supplement with a full-blooded programme of social reform. To the 'Limps', in whose circle Haldane was a leading figure, acting as the link between the Webbs on the one hand and Asquith and Sir Edward Grey on the other, 'national' and 'imperial efficiency' were articles of faith. The credo of 'social imperialism' held little appeal for more tender-hearted beings like Ramsay MacDonald who found them-selves as a consequence siding with the Pro-Boer element within the Liberal Party.

The mutual antipathy of the Webbs and MacDonald was played out in the debating chamber of the London County Council and in the committee rooms of the Technical Education Board. Quite apart from the question of the War, it proved increasingly difficult to persuade MacDonald and the working men on the

Council that money devoted to ventures in higher education represented a true educational priority. The fact that these developments occurred at a time when the Webbs were taking up a position which was essentially hostile to the school boards[83] and were supporting the policy of giving extra help to denominational schools served only to add fuel to the blaze. More and more were Sidney and Beatrice forced to expend time and energy persuading the London Progressives that 'national efficiency' was in itself a worthwhile pursuit. The drain on their mental and physical resources must have been considerable and Beatrice particularly was apt to feel the strain:

Fagged with combination of work and entertaining. Before the Charlottenburg scheme was launched we spent ourselves, money and energy, in tuning the Press . . . and trying to keep the Progressives straight. But of course they unconsciously resent having situations 'prepared' out of which there is only one way, i.e. ours.[84]

At moments of real frustration she hit back, albeit in the restricted compass of her diary:

. . . they are not much to be proud of—a good deal of rotten stuff;[85] the rest upright and reasonable but coarse-grained in intellect and character . . . the ordinary Progressive member is either a bounder, a narrow-minded fanatic, or a mere piece of putty upon which any strong mind can make an impression, to be effaced by the next influence—or rather the texture is more like gutta percha, because it bounces back to the old shapeless mass of prejudice directly you take your will away.[86]

What seems to have taken the Webbs by surprise was the strength of the working men's attachment to the school boards, which a Liberal government had brought into existence a generation before 'to fill the gaps' in elementary education that voluntary effort had not been sufficient to remedy. They seem to have constantly underrated the intensity of this feeling which was partly the result of the board schools' divorce from Anglican dogma and partly because it was based on a belief that *ad hoc* administration was in a sense 'purer' as it seemed to be a manifestation of 'primary democracy'. By way of contrast, the county councils, the all-purpose, unitary, civic authorities which experience had taught the Webbs to favour, were forced to execute policy through mixed delegated sub-committees. They were therefore subject to charges of remoteness and insensitivity—complaints that have certainly not diminished over the years.

In retrospect Beatrice claimed that Sidney's policy had from the beginning been one of centralisation. This seems far from certain. As has already been stated,[87] in the early years Sidney almost invariably took up a mid-way position between the centralising position favoured by J. F. B. Firth on the one hand, and on the other the federal approach that Joseph Chamberlain found so congenial. In his early works, for example, Sidney opposes the abolition of the school boards that Firth was advocating and even recommends the introduction of new *ad hoc* authorities for other functions of local government. It is therefore not possible to label Sidney a centraliser or decentraliser without qualification. In a very penetrating contribution to *The Webbs and Their Work*, Alan McBriar suggests that what caused Sidney, of necessity, to become a centraliser was a growing awareness of the unnecessary expense, the unhealthy cleavage between elementary and higher education, and the inevitable confusion which arises when authorities overlap in their functions.[88]

The 1902–3 break with the Progressives was, on the face of it, rather surprising as so many of them had been nurtured on Firth's centralising doctrines. It is therefore highly probable that they would not have been antagonistic to the abolition of the school boards had it not been for the plan to give rate assistance to the voluntary schools. The working men on the L.C.C. were poised therefore to find new virtues in the institutions of primary democracy.

Beatrice's claim that the centralisation of London's educational service loomed large from the beginning is certainly not borne out if examination is made of Sidney's earlier writings. In *Facts for Londoners*, written in 1889, it is quite apparent that he regarded control of elementary schooling by the London School Board as axiomatic. Tracts such as *Questions for Parliamentary Candidates* and *Questions for School Board Candidates*, both written in 1891 with important elections in the offing, assume that any school receiving public money will automatically come under school board control. If Sidney did believe in these early years in county council dominance in education, he did not chose to reveal his intentions to his fellow Fabians, nor, one suspects, to Beatrice herself. It was only in the fullness of time that Sidney felt it necessary to cut back the school boards and once again one is struck by the realisation that Fabian intervention was dictated not so much by *a priori* belief but by a realisation that the boards' administrative efficiency left much to be desired.

In 1895 the Liberals went out of office and a Unionist government was returned with Sir John Gorst as Vice-President of the Education Department. The policy thenceforth was the harassing of the school boards by administrative means. Yet in spite of the Webbs' obvious pleasure that they had succeeded in persuading the members of the Royal Commission on Secondary Education to regard the county councils in a favourable light, there is not the slightest shred of evidence that Sidney was ever identified with Gorst's policy. That having been said, it must be admitted that relationships between Gorst and the Webbs were at this time close, although the Minister's ineptitude over the ill-fated Education Bill of 1896 caused Beatrice to rail against yet another manifestation of national inefficiency:

The discreditable failure of this complicated measure is only another instance of how impossible it is nowadays to succeed in politics without technical knowledge of the great democratic machine. The last Liberal Government went out discredited because their members were mere prigs thrust into office—the present Government are going the same way. 'In these matters I am a child', says Balfour! We do not want clever school boys at the head of our great departments . . . Who would trust the building of a bridge to a man who started with such an infinitesimal knowledge of engineering as Balfour and Gorst have of national education and its machinery ?[89]

It is possible of course that Beatrice's disappointment was in part a consequence of a realisation that a splendid opportunity for turning the county councils into educational overlords had been thrown away. One thing is certain: either Sidney was not yet convinced that the boards stood in the way of administrative efficiency or he was too politic to say so openly.

In the following year the Education Code was amended so that in future the grants of the Science and Art Department could be paid to one educational authority only in each area. As Chairman of the T.E.B., Sidney made no move to apply for such recognition for this would naturally have been interpreted as hostility to the London School Board. In fact, for most of 1898 Sidney and Beatrice were away from England on a world tour and when the application was made by the new Moderate chairman they were many thousands of miles away. In later years William Garnett claimed that he had been responsible for the initiative being seized, in the same way that his hand was behind the challenging of the school board expenditure by the two London ratepayers which led eventually to the Cockerton Judgment and the administrative gap which made the passing of a new education act a matter of urgent political necessity. Webb, we are led to believe, played no part in these initiatives. Of course, what cannot be ruled out is that Webb may have briefed Garnett to make the move when the time was ripe. The difficulty lies in discovering whether the omission of Webb's name from Garnett's recollections was made out of a regard for historical accuracy or whether it was occasioned by a reticence to acknowledge fully the achievements of his chairman. On the face of it, however, it would appear that Sidney played no part in these manoeuvrings. There can be little doubt that from 1899 to 1902 he appears as the advocate of conciliation, seeing his role as that of comforter of outraged school board sensibilities.

Beatrice's second assertion about Sidney's policy towards the school boards is more readily substantiated than her first. By the time of their return to England in January 1899, he had determined, she relates, to bring about county council control of public education. The immediate result was the most potent of all Fabian Tracts, *The Education Muddle and the Way Out*. There is a striking

similarity between its contents and the provisions of the great
Education Act that appeared on the statute book three years later.
Graham Wallas and Stewart Headlam were powerless to stem the
centralising tide that increasingly dominated Fabian thinking at
this time and the Webb formula for administrative sanity was
adopted as providing the only sensible 'way out'.

But although Tract No. 106 recommended the giving of extra
money to the Church schools and the dissolution of the great
majority of the school boards, Sidney made it quite clear that the
largest boards were to be spared.[90] Their very size made it
possible for them to operate efficiently; and efficiency rather than
centralisation was held to be the cardinal principle. In the Education Act of 1902 all the boards except one were swept away, but
this innovation of Robert Morant, who had drafted the Bill, came
as a complete surprise to Webb who up to this point had not
visualised dispensing completely with the services of so many
well-tried public bodies.

As far as the issue of rate aid to the voluntary schools was concerned, the Webbs' stand both puzzled and dismayed their non-
confirmist and secular friends, who simply could not understand
how two avowed socialists could in all conscience hold such a
position. For that matter, the Webbs, Sidney especially, were
unable to appreciate the feelings of outrage displayed by non-
conformists and secularists. So intent was Sidney to pursue the
goal of 'national efficiency' that the giving of rate-assistance to the
church schools seemed to him to be of minor import. Rationalist
and sceptic he might be, but if millions of people wanted this sort
of education, there seemed to him to be no reason at all why they
should not be given it. It was this sense of tolerance, seen at its
best in two rather rueful sounding Fabian Tracts,[91] which his
left-wing critics simply could not understand, nor indeed forgive.

Beatrice was even more tolerant about the granting of public
money to the voluntary schools. An unwillingness to accept the
starker implications of materialism is ever-present in her diaries.
Not only is there a personal longing for a greater transcendental
reality but there is evidence of a frequent, if at times self-conscious,

attendance at church. Beatrice's justification for their stand on the church schools is succinct and not without relevance to our own day:

I could only shelter myself by the argument that the reform of the Church was not the work I had undertaken to do, or which I was trained to consider. The practical alternatives before us constituted a very simple issue; whether we were to throw our weight against the continuance of the present form of religious teaching and help to establish pure materialism as the national metaphysic; or whether we would accept, provisionally, as part of the teaching in the schools, the dogmas and ritual of the Christian Church of today. For my own children, and for those of other people, I deliberately believed the lie of materialism to be far more pernicious and more utterly false than the untruths which seem to me to constitute the Christian formula of religion. Moreover, we are face to face with the fact that the vast majority of the English people, are as far as they think at all, convinced Christians. By insisting on secular education, I should not only be helping to spread what seems to me a bad kind of falsehood, but I should be denying to others the right to have their children taught the creed they hold to be positively true. I see no way out of the dilemma, but the largest variety possible of denominational schools, so that there may be the utmost possible choice for parents and children, and, let me add, the widest range of experiment as to the results of particular kinds of teaching on the character of the child and its conduct of life.[92]

The solitary *ad hoc* body that was excluded from the scope of the 1902 Act was, ironically enough, the London School Board. London was altogether too sharp a thorn to be handled with comfort, as Sir John Gorst took care to point out. The main difficulty was that many Conservatives had an intense dislike of the L.C.C. as a result of its policy of municipal socialism and were now thinking in terms of control by the metropolitan boroughs which had arrived on the scene as a result of the London Government Act of 1899.

Webb fought tooth and nail, using all the acknowledged techniques of permeation, in an attempt to have the one clause in the Bill which excluded London struck out, but without success. Thus it was that in the first half of 1903 he was faced with a renewal of the wire-pulling and lobbying that had been such a feature of educational politics in the previous year. And this time he had to do without the help of Morant who, pleading the excuse of 'a rotten staff'[93] and overwork, declined to co-operate.[94] There were two broad strategies that had to be pursued. The first was to persuade the Anglican bishops that the L.C.C. was much more likely to be generous to the voluntary schools than would the boroughs, which would be unduly dominated by the elementary school teachers. Strictly speaking, however, borough control was not the only alternative to L.C.C. overlordship, for so disturbed had the government become by the growing non-conformist discontent in the country—a discontent being reflected in disastrous bye-election results—that there was even talk of retaining the London School Board. With this as a possible outcome, the Webbs' second objective was to persuade the by now thoroughly suspicious L.C.C. Progressives that a logical extension of county council powers was the only policy which could make sense. In view of the non-conformists' intensity of feeling over the church schools' issue, this was to prove a difficult, not to say frustrating task.

It was, however, to be successful. The manoeuvrings with Unionist M.P.s, wining and dining the Prime Minister, the nightly conversations with Anglican bishops and Roman Catholic dignitaries, the canvassing of the professional associations, the creation of a favourable public opinion through the leader columns of the press—the years 1902–3 represent the high point of Fabian permeation.

The increasing potency of the campaign can be seen in the successive stages of the London Education Bill. Sidney had been extremely worried over the sequence of government proposals, which seemed to reflect the responses of an administration that was in danger of losing its nerve. There was at one time for example the plan for a vast *ad hoc* authority on the lines of the Water Board. This was followed by a plan for a smaller board with L.C.C. representatives in a majority, but still essentially an *ad hoc* body. In the long run, however, the government gave way, with the result that the London Education Act laid down that London was to be treated in exactly the same fashion as the rest of the country. The Webbs were jubilant at the outcome but such massive campaigning resulted in their being placed in a singularly exposed position in their relationships with many of their left-wing friends.

As a result of the defeat of Graham Wallas and Stewart Headlam in the Fabian councils, the educational policies of Sidney Webb had become the official policy of the Society. Left-wing opinion has been highly critical of the Society's attitude during this important period of English social history. Some historians have seen its members adopting an unhelpful, not to say perverse, role. The development of the higher grade schools and the emergence of more 'realistic' curricula within their walls have been interpreted as adumbrations of post-1945 educational reform. Now, with the demise of the school boards and new policies at the Board of Education, the clock had been put back for a generation. The voice of the people had been suppressed. Alone in all the more significant groupings of the Left, the Fabians had allied themselves with the forces of clericalism and reaction.

That the Fabian Society appears in a maverick role during these critical years cannot be denied. Neither can the feeling of outrage on the part of non-conformists, secularists and the advocates of primary democracy who saw the abolition of the school boards as a completely reprehensible step. Although the Fabians had played no part in the events leading up to the suppression of the higher grade schools and therefore to the need for major educational legislation, their very active part in the shaping of the Acts of 1902–3 is indisputable. So also is the knowledge that they were supported by no other left-wing organisation.

The prevailing fear of the Left was that the new L.E.A.s were likely to be dominated by propertied and moneyed interests. In the mood of anguish created by the threat to the school boards they were seemingly oblivious to the fact that most boards were too small to be efficient, that many others were dominated by those self-same interests they feared so much, and that the depressing state of mind known as 'Diggleism'[95] had held sway for astonishingly long periods even in such reputedly progressive bodies as the London School Board.

It should be said that there had been some justification for their fear in the original Bill, which proposed that the co-opted members of the new education committees should be in a majority of one. But when that Bill was withdrawn, the L.C.C. formula for having county council representatives always in the majority was written into the new legislation. There was certainly no more likelihood of clerical dominance on the county and borough councils, even with a large co-opted element, than had been the case with the boards. As far as Sidney Webb was concerned, it was quite unthinkable that the placing of public services like education under the control of the councils would lead in any other direction than towards the realisation of the collectivist utopia. Compared with 2,500 miscellaneous *ad hoc* bodies, they were much more strongly placed to achieve this goal. But, in any case, there can be little doubt that, as far as Sidney was concerned, 'national efficiency' was a much more relevant and interesting question.

THE TEXTS

I Lord Rosebery's Escape from Houndsditch

Despite the unfavourable impressions that were the result of their first encounter with Lord Rosebery in March 1900,[96] the Webbs, through the good offices of Haldane, continued to cultivate him.[97] Beatrice reveals their motives with all her usual candour. At the time the Webbs were convinced that, however vague Rosebery's references to social problems might be, they were entirely consistent with their own belief in the need to promote 'the national minimum' in every way possible. With Haldane in his habitual role of honest broker, they were sustained in the belief that they would be able to persuade the wealthy Whig aristocrat to adopt a social policy of an unmistakably progressive stamp. This then was a positive reason for the growing intimacy between the Webbs and the man who but five years previously had been Prime Minister. But in their desire to permeate the Liberal leadership there was a negative motive as well, for not only did the Webbs share the general antipathy of 'the efficiency group' for the sadly underrated Campbell-Bannerman but they were increasingly exasperated by the stand of the pro-Boer faction. Rosebery, despite all his limitations, struck the Webbs as being the likeliest party leader to espouse the sort of social programme which they believed in so profoundly.

The part played by Rosebery between 1900 and 1902 was an extraordinary one. The Unionist government of the day, despite the parliamentary mandate given to it in 'the khaki election' of 1900, was already showing signs of fatigue and a falling-off in public confidence was inevitable. But the Liberals themselves were in considerable disarray as a result of the strains that the South African War had precipitated. Only an abnormal situation like this can explain why so many hopes were pinned on Rosebery during these years. But not only did his name arouse the hopes of demoralised Liberals; the part he played as the acknowledged high priest of the cult of efficiency drew him much support from the Conservative ranks and also from the leaders of the Fabian Society.

Another shared enthusiasm that brought the Webbs and Rosebery together was their wish to expand the provision of higher education. In 1901 Rosebery was persuaded to become the President of the London School of Economics and in his turn he saw to it that Lord Rothschild, a cousin by marriage, became Treasurer. Help was also given by Rosebery in getting 'the Charlottenburg scheme' off the ground in 1903.

Curiously enough, Beatrice seems to have been of the opinion that it was they who had been manipulated by Haldane into becoming followers of Rosebery.[98] On the other hand, Shaw, whose manifesto, *Fabianism and the Empire*,[99] had turned out to be very much to Rosebery's liking, saw an opportunity for the Webbs to exercise their skill as 'tool wielders', with Rosebery as the 'political tool . . . screaming for somebody to come and handle him'.[100]

This then was the origin of the article which appeared in *The Nineteenth Century* in September 1901, under the title, 'Lord Rosebery's Escape from Houndsditch'.[101] In this article, Webb appeals to the Liberal Imperialists to discard the last vestiges of Gladstonian policies and create a live opposition based upon a political programme which would promote 'the national minimum' in all fields, not least in education. It is the clearest exposition possible of the harnessing of large parts of the original Fabian reform programme to policies which could now be held to be above party lines of cleavage: the well-being of the nation and the efficiency of Empire might be said to depend directly upon the implementation of these policies. It is for this reason and because in it Sidney Webb places education in its full social context that the article is quoted in its entirety.

Predictably, it excited much attention on publication. Campbell-Bannerman[102] was far from pleased and wrote without enthusiasm of 'admirable sentiments which I have heard enunciated by other and greater men: which may be master and which scholar I do not know'.[103] Rosebery, equally predictably, was vastly impressed. 'I hope you will keep Webb out of London, or have him protected by the police,' he wrote to Beatrice, 'for his life can hardly be safe since the publication of his article in the *Nineteenth Century*—the most brilliant article that I have read for many a day'.[104] A few weeks later he was using the ammunition that Webb had provided in his famous Chesterfield speech, the main feature of which was that if the Liberal Party were to be returned to power it would first have to abandon all the old programmes and adopt a bold policy of educational, administrative and social efficiency.

That Rosebery was becoming embarrassed by this liaison with the Webbs is plain, however. To Campbell-Bannerman there was an unconvincing denial that he had in any way been 'permeated'.[105] Campbell-Bannerman was not so sure: 'All that [Rosebery] said [at Chesterfield] about the clean slate and efficiency was an affront to Liberalism and was pure claptrap,' he complained. 'Efficiency as a watchword! Who is against it? This is all a mere rechauffé of Mr. Sidney Webb, who is evidently the chief instructor of the faction.'[106]

By the beginning of 1902, Rosebery seems to have largely abandoned his desire either to create a new 'national' party or to re-invigorate the parliamentary opposition. His true position remains ambiguous to this day. There is some truth in Beatrice's description of him as a man who lacked strong convictions, caring only for appearances and the striking of popular poses. The renewed polarisation of the political parties that was an immediate outcome of the 1902 Education Bill seems to have cut the ground from under his feet. From now until the time of Lloyd George's emergence as a 'national' statesman, there was a period of renewed confidence in traditional Liberal values and methods. As for the Webbs, though they continued to pay court to the Liberal Imperialists they became increasingly exasperated with the growing ambivalence of Rosebery's position.

Mr. Gladstone, as we now learn upon the unexpected testimony of Lord Tweedmouth, regarded the last twenty years of his life as having been spent in 'patching up old clothes'. His achievements as a sartorial artist in politics approached, it must be admitted, the miraculous. But the patched-up suits of 1880, 1885 and 1892, though they served their immediate purpose, have, on the expanding conditions of contemporary politics, proved wretched wearing material. Not even Mr. Gladstone could have patched them up again. With amused dismay the new generation of Progressives have lately witnessed Sir Henry Campbell-Bannerman piecing together the Gladstonian rags and remnants, with Sir William Harcourt[107] holding the scissors, and Mr. John Morley[108] unctuously waxing the thread. Mr. Asquith and Sir Edward Grey are sufficiently up to date resolutely to refuse even to try on the repatched garment, but they are not in a position to decline to associate with those who still believe the Gladstonian cut to be fashionable. Lord Rosebery is the only person who has turned his back on Houndsditch and called for a complete new outfit. This is the first step towards the regeneration of the Opposition. I say the Opposition advisedly, for the political opportunity of the moment is not for a regeneration of Gladstonianism or of 'the Liberal Party', or of anything else that had its day in the last century, but solely for a live Opposition. That Opposition, when it comes, may call itself the Liberal Party or any other name that may be convenient. But it is certain that it will not be the old Gladstonian Party—quite the contrary, in fact—and that it will not become a political force until, meeting the new needs and expressing the new aspirations of the twentieth century—dealing, as Lord Rosebery rightly says, 'in a new spirit with the new problems of the age'—it thereby makes itself into a practicable alternative to the Conservative Government.

What then is the matter with the Liberals? For fifty years, in the middle of the last century, we may recognise their party as 'a great instrument of progress', wrenching away the shackles—political, fiscal, legal, theological and social—that hindered individual advancement. The shackles are by no means wholly got rid of, but the political force of this old Liberalism is spent. During the last twenty years its aspirations and its watchwords, its ideas of daily life and its conceptions of the universe, have become increasingly distasteful to the ordinary citizen as he renews his youth from generation to generation. Its worship of individual liberty evokes no enthusiasm. Its reliance on 'freedom of contract' and 'supply and demand', with its corresponding 'voluntaryism' in religion and philanthropy, now seems to work out disastrously for the masses, who are too poor to have what the economists call an 'effective demand' for even the minimum conditions of physical and mental health necessary to national well-being. Its very admiration for that favourite Fenian abstraction, the 'principle of nationality', now appears to us as but Individualism writ large, being, in truth, the assertion that each distinct race, merely because it thinks itself a distinct race (which it never is, by the way), has an inherent right to have its own government, and work out its own policy, unfettered by any consideration of the effect of this independence on other races, or on the world at large.

Of all this the rising generations of voters are deadly tired. When they hear the leading Liberal debater shouting the Liberal war cry of fifty years ago, 'Peace, Retrenchment and Reform', and explaining it as a claim for absolute quiescence in Downing Street, with the Treasury cutting down all expenditure, and the Cabinet doing nothing but tinker with the electoral machinery, what can they say but 'You are old, Father William'? And when they turn from Whig aspirations to Whig proposals, they see the official Liberal leaders, for lack of any live principle, committing themselves to a medley of projects which the man in the street, no less than the experienced administrator, regards as impracticable.

Unable to conceive their own obsolescence, the Liberals of the old rock account for the collapse of their party by the personal quarrels of their leaders. They have haled those leaders to the Reform Club, and insisted on a public outpouring of affection and esteem to reassure the nation as to their solidarity. The leaders have outpoured accordingly in moving copiousness, and we have now no excuse for doubting the warm friendship for Sir Henry Campbell-Bannerman that underlies the resolution of so many of his colleagues to allow no public utterance of himself or his admirers to pass without prompt and explicit repudiation. But though this Reform Club farce has imposed on nobody—not even on the actors themselves—it has reduced the illusion of Liberal solidarity to confirm another and more dangerous illusion, namely, that it is the South African War that has wrecked the Liberal Party. On the contrary, the war has raised the old Liberal guard from insignificance to unpopularity, for the party had fallen so low that even unpopularity was a promotion. Lord Rosebery is only emphasising the obvious when he insists that the impotency of the Liberal Party, as an instrument either of opposition or of government, dates from much further back than the Boer ultimatum. Have we so soon forgotten the contemptuous disgust with which, in 1895, the great mass of Englishmen turned away from the Liberal Party? The collapse does not date even from Mr. Gladstone's proposal in 1886 to set up Ireland as a self-governing state. The smashing defeat of 1895 was only the culmination of a steady alienation from Liberalism of the great centres of population, which began to be visible even in 1874. London and Lancashire have ever since persisted in this adverse verdict. The most startling feature of the election of 1885—still prior to the Home Rule Bill—was the extent to which Liberalism was rejected by the boroughs. All that has happened since that date has but confirmed the great centres of population in their positive aversion to Gladstonianism. This, and not the ephemeral dispute about the war, is the bottom fact of the political situation. Thirty years ago the great boroughs were enthusiastic for Liberalism. By an uninterrupted process of conversion they have now become flatly opposed to it. The fact that to-day the Conservative Party finds its chief strongholds not in the lethargic and stationary rural counties, drained of their young men, but in the intellectually active and rapidly growing life of the towns (containing two-thirds of the nation), proves that the Liberalism of Sir William Harcourt and Mr. Morley is not the Progressive instinct of the twentieth century. The Progressive instinct always exists, and will always, in time, raise up an opposition to the party which strives to maintain the vested interests of the existing order. The Liberal Party can be strong only in so far as it is the political organ of that Progressive instinct. It held that position for so large a part of the last century that it came to believe that it held it by natural right. How is it that it has now lost it?

The answer is that, during the last twenty or thiry years, we have become a new people. 'Early Victorian' England now lies, in effect, centuries behind us. Such things do happen. The processes which make one generation differ from another operate sometimes slowly and imperceptibly, sometimes quickly and even suddenly. At one period centuries may pass without any discoverable difference in the mind or character of a nation. At another new ideas are precipitated and new parties crystallised almost before the old parliamentary hands have time to prove their visionariness. Such an epoch of transformation we now recognise, to cite only one instance, in the reign of Elizabeth. We note, within a single generation, a distinct change in the content of men's minds. Their standpoints are shifted. Their horizons are suddenly enlarged. Their whole way of considering things is altered, and lo! a new England. In the same sense, the historian of the future will recognise, in the last quarter of the nineteenth century, the birth of another new England. Elizabethan England changed because Englishmen became aware of new relationships. They saw themselves linked on, almost suddenly, with the past in classic antiquity, and with the future in America. The England of this generation is changing because Englishmen have had revealed to them another new world of relationships, of which they were before unconscious. This time is not a new continent that the ordinary man has discovered, but a new category. We have become aware, almost in a flash, that we are not merely individuals, but members of a community, nay, citizens of the world. This new self-consciousness is no mere intellectual fancy, but a hard fact that comes home to us in our daily life. The labourer in the slum tenement, competing for employment at the factory gate, has become conscious that his comfort and his progress depend, not wholly or mainly on himself, or on any other individual, but upon the proper organisation of his Trade Union and the activity of the factory inspector. The shopkeeper or the manufacturer sees his prosperity wax or wane, his own industry and sagacity remaining the same, according to the good government of his city, the efficiency with which his nation is organised, and the influence which his Empire is able to exercise in the councils, and consequently in the commerce, of the world. Hence the ordinary elector, be he workman or manufacturer, shopkeeper or merchant, has lost his interest in individual 'rights', or abstract 'equality', political or religious. The freedom that he now wants is not individual but corporate freedom—freedom for his Trade Union to bargain collectively, freedom for his co-operative society to buy and sell and manufacture, freedom for his municipality to supply all the common needs of the town, freedom, above all, from the narrow insularity which keeps his nation backing, 'on principle', out of its proper place in the comity of the world. In short, the opening of the twentieth century finds us all, to the dismay of the old-fashioned Individualist, 'thinking in communities'.

Now the trouble with Gladstonian Liberalism is that, by instinct, by tradition, and by the positive precepts of its past exponents, it 'thinks in individuals'. It visualises the world as a world of independent Roundheads, with separate ends, and abstract rights to pursue those ends. We see old-fashioned Liberals, for instance, still hankering after the disestablishment and disendowment of all State Churches, on the plea of religious equality; meaning that it is unfair to give any public money or public advantage to any denomination from which any individual taxpayer dissents. But if it be so, all corporate action is unfair. We are all dissenters from some part or another of the action of the communities of which we are members. How far the maintenance of a State Church really makes for national well-being—how otherwise than by national establishment and public endowment we can secure, in every parish, whether it cares and can afford to pay for it or not, the presence of a teacher of morality and an exponent of higher intellectual and social life—is a matter for careful investigation. But the notion that there is anything inherently wrong in compelling all citizens to help to maintain religious observances or religious instruction of which some of them individually disapprove, is part of the characteristically Whig conception of the citizen's contribution to the expenses of the social organisation, as a bill paid by a private man for certain specific commodities which he has ordered and purchased for his own use. On this conception the Quaker is robbed when his taxes are spent on the Army and Navy; the Protestant is outraged by seeing his contributions help to support a Roman Catholic school or university; the teetotaller is wronged at having to provide the naval ration of rum. What nonsense it all sounds in the twentieth century! The Gladstonian section of the Liberal Party remains, in fact, axiomatically hostile to the State. It is not 'little Englandism' that is the matter with them; it is, as Huxley and Matthew Arnold correctly diagnosed, administrative Nihilism. Hence in politics they are inveterately negative, instinctively iconoclastic. They have hung up temperance reform and educational reform for a quarter of a century, because, instead of seeking to enable the citizen to refresh himself without being poisoned or inebriated, and to get the children thoroughly taught, they have wanted primarily to revenge their outraged temperance principles on the publican and their outraged Nonconformist principles on the Church. Of such Liberals it may be said that the destructive revolutionary tradition is in their bones; they will reform nothing unless it can be done at the expense of their enemies. Moral superiority, virtuous indignation, are necessaries of political life to them; a Liberal reform is never simply a social means to a social end, but a campaign of Good against Evil. Their conception of freedom means only breaking somebody's bonds asunder. When the 'higher freedom' of corporate life is in question, they become angrily reactionary, and denounce and obstruct every new development of common action. If we seek for the greatest enemy of municipal enterprise, we find him in Sir Henry Fowler.[109] If we ask who is the most successful opponent of any extension of 'the Common Rule' of factory legislation to wider fields of usefulness, the answer is Mr. John Morley. And when a leader is needed by those whose unalterable instinct it is to resist to the uttermost every painful effort towards the higher organisation of that greatest of co-operative societies, the State itself, who than Sir William Harcourt, at his most eloquent, can be more surely depended upon? Not that I have any right to reproach these eminent ones for standing by their principles. The principles were fresh once—in the last quarter of the eighteenth century. Their exponents' minds were fresh, too—about the middle of the nineteenth. But Adam Smith is dead, and Queen Anne, and even Sir Robert Peel; while as to Gladstone, he is by far the deadest of them all. It is kinder to say so bluntly than to encourage his survivors to attempt to conjure themselves into office by a name which, in its owner's lifetime, ended by being hardly able to command even a Scotch constituency; for we cannot believe that Midlothian would have proved safer than Newcastle or Derby had its greatest Liberal representative contested it in 1895. And I confess that I feel the hopelessness, even the comic absurdity, of seeming to invite his more elderly lieutenants, at their ages, to change their spots—to turn over a new leaf and devote themselves to obtaining the greatest possible development of municipal activity, the most comprehensive extension of the Factory Acts, or the fullest utilisation of the Government departments in the service of the public. I know too well that they quite honestly consider such aims to be mischievous. They are aiming at something else, namely, at the abstract right of the individual to lead exactly the kind of life that he likes (and can pay for), unpenalised by any taxation for purposes of which he individually disapproves. They are, in fact, still 'thinking in individuals'.

This same atomic conception of society, transferred from the State at home to the British Empire as a whole, colours the Liberal propaganda of Home Rule for Ireland, and its latest metamorphosis, the demand for the independence of the Transvaal. There is good argument for the devolution, within the United Kingdom, of local business to provincial assemblies, in the interest of the efficiency of the House of Commons itself. There is every reason to prefer, for the rebuilding of the civilisation of British South Africa, the model of the Australian Commonwealth rather than that of Malta or Mauritius. But Irish Home Rule and Boer independence are passionately advocated on the plea of the abstract right of these 'nationalities' to separate existence. For the very reason that these races are assumed to have ends which differ from, and perhaps conflict with, those of the British Empire as a whole, it is asserted that they must, in justice, be allowed to pursue these ends at whatever cost to themselves and to their neighbours. What *vieux jeu* all this 'Early Victorian' nationalism now seems! What have we, the citizens of a commonwealth of four distinct races in these little islands alone (five if we include our Jews); of fellow citizens in our states over sea sprung from all European nations, conspicuously French, Italian, and Dutch; of countless tribes and castes of all human colours and nearly all human languages; what, in the name of common sense have we to do with obsolete hypocrisies about peoples' 'rightly struggling to be free'? Our obvious duty with the British Empire is deliberately so to organise it as to promote the maximum development of each individual state within its bounds. As with the factory or the slum at home, this maximum of individual development will not be secured by allowing each unit to pursue its own ends without reference to the welfare of the whole. The central idea of the old Liberalism, hostile as it was to the development of the State within these isles, was naturally unsympathetic to the deliberate organisation of the Empire over sea.

Has then the nation become Conservative? Not in the least. The pleasant-mannered young gentlemen of no occupation, the portly manufacturers and the estimable country squires who sit on the Conservative benches, as every one who knows them personally will admit, no more share the feelings of the new England of the town electorate than does Sir William Harcourt. Far from having learnt to 'think in communities', there is no satisfactory evidence of their having, in politics, learnt to think at all. Their very triumph is not their own. They are elected, not in order to put Conservatism into power, but in order to keep Gladstonianism out. Two advantages, indeed, they have, which make their election possible. The modern Conservative candidate is politically a man without prejudices. No abstract principle forbids him to listen sympathetically to any proposal for reform. Hence he seems on the platform less belated than the official Liberal, with his stock of shop-soiled principles at full price. And, most useful of all at the present juncture, the modern Conservative, unlike the Gladstonian Liberal, is quite happy and ungrudging in paying out the Imperialist commonplaces which convey to a constitutency a stimulatingly bluster-ous impression that he is conscious of the British Empire as a whole. Into this blusterous impression the enthusiastic voter is allowed to read as much consciousness as he himself has attained to of Imperial rights, duties and interests in the sphere of world politics. This, how-ever, is mere hustings manner. Conservative cabinets at work, like Conservative members in the House of Commons, show themselves no more in accord with the new England of the twentieth century than do the Liberals. When the question is one of making any more effective use of the State departments, Sir Michael Hicks-Beach[110] is as old-fashioned as Sir William Harcourt. As to our Presidents of the Local Government Board, they are about as much at home in twentieth-century municipal affairs as King James the First would be in a modern trade arbitration. Whether they are called Fowler, Chaplin,[111] or Long,[112] makes no difference that is discoverable by the provincial town-clerks or the chairmen of the committees of the London County Council; all alike are impenitent decriers of the magnificent social structure that is rising all over the country, ignorant of their duties, missing their great opportunities, and naturally hostile to any extension of the local government activity which has already far outgrown their knowledge and capacity. In the efficiency of the War Office and Admiralty, the elector has, to put it as moderately as possible, no more confidence to-day than he had seven years ago. It may be an injustice to meritorious Ministers in humbler station, but there is every reason to believe that the British public takes Lord Salisbury as the type of his own Government. Now Lord Salisbury simply does not believe in the possibility of improvement in human affairs—a view which is rather the philosophy of an independent income and a peerage than of the mass of electors existing in obviously improvable circumstances.

But to expatiate on the disappointment of the country with the present Government would be to hit a Ministry when it is down. Lord Salisbury's Ministry has disgusted not only the educationists and the temperance reformers but also the Churchmen, the philanthropists, the municipal councillors, the business men, the Services and the Naval Leaguers. And yet this much-slighted Government is as strong, elector-ally, as ever it was. We keep it in office lest a worse thing befall us—to wit, a Government of Gladstonian ghosts. And until an alternative

Government that has thoroughly purged itself of Gladstonian Liberalism comes in sight, the 'Cecil dynasty', as the Radical papers love to call it, will reign *faute de mieux*.

Where, then, is this alternative Government likely to be discovered? Ten years ago, had I been then writing such an article, I might have persuaded myself that only in the rise of an independent Socialist party could the alternative be found. For Democratic Socialism, as a theory of economic and political State organisation, has at least the double merit of being based on the latest political science, and in accord with the aspirations of the new England of to-day. Indeed, we can now see that the rise of the organised Socialist movement in England after 1880 was only one symptom of the political change of heart which the nation was experiencing. Just for this reason the propaganda of practical Socialism has, during the last twenty years, had a great effect on English thought. In my judgment it has powerfully contributed, and will certainly continue to contribute, to the decay of the old political creeds. But, looking back on the last two decades, we see that this effect has come, not so much in causing people to abandon their political parties, or to abstain from using the party watchwords, as in forcing upon their attention an altogether novel criticism, and in changing their whole way of looking at things. What hinders the formation of a separate Socialist party in England is always that the increase of Socialism is so much faster than that of professed and organised Socialists. The effect of the Socialist propaganda on our matter of fact nation is like the overflow of a flooded river. It extends horizontally with a certain rapidity, but vertically only with extreme slowness, perhaps never reaching any high point. It first wets everyone's boots, and then steals unobtrusively over the ankles and knees, producing an amphibious condition in which the elector or statesman, whilst strongly objecting to being called a Socialist, or to join any avowedly Socialist organisation, nevertheless becomes convinced that an enlightened and progressive interpretation of his traditional political creed, Conservative or Liberal, demands the addition of collectivist items to the party programme. But by the time the professed Socialists were weaned from their primitive policy of the 'conversion of England' and the formation of an all-powerful Socialist party, to a policy of permeating the existing parties, the political horizon was widened by the rise of Imperial questions, and the advent of modern world-politics. The Socialists, having no definite views of their own on foreign policy, immediately found their boom of 1885–1892 collapsing;

and for a time they could only account for this by 'the apathy of the working classes'. When the war came the secret was out. Outside the two spheres of labour and local government the majority of the Socialist leaders proved to be, notably with regard to the British Empire, mere administrative Nihilists—that is to say, ultra-nationalist, ultra-Gladstonian, old-Liberal to the finger-tips. They out-morleyed Mr. Morley in their utterances on the burning topic of the day; and now the Independent Labour Party is as hopelessly out of the running as the Gladstonian Party. On the issues of 'nationalism' and the Empire, Mr. Hyndman and Mr. Keir Hardie find themselves, in fact, by honest conviction, on the same platform as Sir Wilfrid Lawson and Mr. Labouchere.[113]

It appears, then, that without some new grouping of the electorate, without the inspiration of some new thought, no virile and fecund Opposition, let alone an alternative Government, is conceivable. No front Opposition Bench can be really effective—still less can it cross the floor of the House of Commons—unless it expresses, not alone the views of its own political partisans, but also the inarticulate criticism of the mass of the community. Outside the narrow ranks of the 'political workers' of either party, the millions of citizens are quietly pursuing their ordinary business—weavers at the loom, mechanics at the lathe, teachers in the schools, ministers of religion toiling in the slums of our cities, doctors going their rounds, manufacturers at their mills, merchants and bankers journeying daily to their offices, patient investigators working out scientific problems, public-spirited men and women struggling 'gegen die Dummheit' on Town Councils and School Boards. It is these men's judgments on public affairs, these men's impressions and aspirations, which, in the England of to-day, give force and backing to the words of statesmen. And if now we inquire what it is that comes into these men's minds when they read their newspapers, when they, in their particular calling, impinge on some corner of public administration, or when, in their own lives, some public disaster comes home to them, there is but one answer. They are not thinking of Liberalism or Conservatism or Socialism. What is in their minds is a burning feeling of shame at the 'failure' of England—shame for the lack of capacity of its governors, shame for the inability of Parliament to get through even its routine business, shame for the absence of grip and resourcefulness of our statesmen, shame for the pompous inefficiency of every branch of our public administration, shame for the slackness of our merchants and traders that transfers our commercial supremacy to the United States, shame for the supineness which looks on unmoved at the continued degradation of our race by drunkenness and gambling, slum life, and all the horrors of the sweated trades, as rampant to-day in all our great centres of population as they were when officially revealed fifteen years ago. This sense of shame has yet to be transmitted into political action. Lord Rosebery's quick political wit seizes this fact, and rightly pronounces that 'the country is ripe for a domestic programme', which shall breathe 'new life into the administrative dry bones of our public offices'. The party and the statesmen whom these men will support, the leaders for whom they are hungering, are those who shall convince them that above all other considerations they stand for a policy of National Efficiency.

But let no politician delude himself that the utterance of this or any other shibboleth, however eloquently worded, will open for him the gates of power. The Tapers and Tadpoles of to-day, like those of sixty years ago, still put their faith in a 'good cry'. Above all, they say, avoid a programme. Do not commit yourself to any particular reforms. Deal only in phrases, and say that you cannot prescribe until you are called in. This, however, is merely the obsolete pedantry of the Tadpole-Taper trade. It is 'Early Victorian' politics. No leader will attract the support of the mass of unpolitical citizens—who in this juncture, at any rate, alone can give a decisive vote—without expanding his thesis of National Efficiency into a comprehensive and definite programme. Nay, he must do more. He must understand his programme, believe in his programme, be inspired by his programme. He will, in fact, lead the English people—eager just now for National Efficiency, they care not how—only by becoming a personified programme of National Efficiency in every department of life.

Here Mr. Asquith is on the right tack:

What is the use of an Empire [he asks] if it does not breed and maintain in the truest and fullest sense of the word an Imperial race? What is the use of talking about Empire if here, at its very centre, there is always to be found a mass of people, stunted in education, a prey to intemperance, huddled and congested beyond the possibility of realising in any true sense either social or domestic life?

To-day, in the United Kingdom, there are, Sir Robert Giffen tells us, not fewer than eight millions of persons, one-fifth of the whole population, existing under conditions represented by a family income of less than a pound a week, and constituting not merely a disgrace, but a positive danger to our civilisation. These are the victims of 'sweating' in one or other of its forms, condemned, as the House of Lords' Committee emphatically declared, to 'earnings barely sufficient to sustain existence; hours of labour such as to make the lives of the workers periods of almost ceaseless toil; sanitary conditions injurious to the health of the persons employed and dangerous to the public'.

The first and most indispensable step towards National Efficiency is the healing of the open sore by which this industrial parasitism is draining away the vitality of the race. There is no doubt about the remedy, no uncertainty among those who have really worked at the problem. We have passed through the experimental stage of factory legislation, and we now know that it is no mere coincidence that these eight millions of persons correspond almost precisely with the sections from whom we have hitherto withheld the effective protection of the Factory Acts. 'Every society is judged', says Mr. Asquith, 'and survives, according to the material and moral minimum which it prescribes to its members'. Note the word 'prescribes'. But when Mr. Asquith was in office he found, as Mr. Ritchie[114] has found, that the usual timid little Factory Bill was a thankless undertaking, received sulkily by the House, and either ignored by the electorate or denounced for its omissions and concessions by capital and labour alike. The statesman who is really inspired by the idea of National Efficiency will stump the country in favour of a 'National Minimum' standard of life, below which no employer in any trade in any part of the kingdom shall be allowed to descend. He will elaborate this minimum of humane order— already admitted in principle in a hundred Acts of Parliament—with all the force that eloquence can give to economic science, into a new industrial charter, imperatively required, not merely or even mainly for the comfort of the workers, but absolutely for the success of our industry in competition with the world. With the widespread support which this policy would secure, not only from the whole Trade Union world and the two millions of organised co-operators, but also from ministers of religion of all denominations, doctors and nurses, sanitary officers and teachers, Poor Law administrators and modern economists, and even the enlightened employers themselves, he would be able to expand our uneven and incomplete Factory Acts into a systematic and all-embracing code, prescribing for every manual worker employed a minimum of education, sanitation, leisure, and wages as the inviolable starting-point of industrial competition.

But factory legislation alone, however effective and complete, can secure Mr. Asquith's 'moral and material minimum' only so far as the conditions of employment are concerned. Even more than in the factory, the Empire is rooted in the home. How can we build up an effective State—how, even, can we get an efficient army—out of the stunted, anaemic, demoralised denizens of the slum tenements of our great cities? Can we, even as a mere matter of business, any longer afford to allow the eight millions of whom I have already spoken—the 'submerged fifth' of our nation—to be housed, washed, and watered worse than our horses? Is it not clear that one of the first and most indispensable steps towards National Efficiency is to make really effective that 'National Minimum' of sanitation which is already nominally compulsory by law? This means a great extension of municipal activity in town and country. It means a new point of view for the Local Government Board, which must cease to do evil and learn to do well, by dropping its lazy routine of obstruction and discouragement, and rousing itself to be prompt with its stimulus, eagerly oncoming with its help, and, when necessary, swift and ruthless with its compulsion. For the Local Government Board has, though no President seems to be aware of it, an even higher duty in sanitation than stimulus and help. It is the guardian of the National Minimum. To it is committed the great trust of seeing that no single family in the land is denied the indispensable conditions of healthy life. So far as house accommodation, ventilation, good drainage and pure water are concerned, Parliament has long ago embodied this National Minimum of sanitation in universally applicable Public Health Acts, which it is the duty of the Local Government Board to enforce upon local authorities just as drastically as these ought to do upon individuals. Can anything be more preposterous in a business nation to allow (as a succession of Presidents of the Local Government Board have long allowed) one locality after another, merely out of stupidity, or incapacity, or parsimony, demonstrably to foster malignant disease and bring up its quota of citizens in a condition of impaired vitality? Why does not the Local Government Board undertake a systematic harrying up of the backward districts, regularly insisting, for instance, that all those having death-rates above the average of the kingdom shall put themselves in order, improve their drainage, lay on new water supply, and insure, by one means or another, a supply of healthy houses sufficient to enable every family to comply with the formula of 'three rooms and a scullery', as the minimum necessary for breeding an even moderately Imperial race? Every medical officer knows that it is quite possible, within a generation after the adoption of such a genuine enforcement of the National Minimum of sanitation, to bring down the average death-rate by at least 5 per 1,000, and the sickness experience by at least a third. The equivalent money gain to the community would be many millions sterling. A single friendly society, the Manchester Unity of Oddfellows, would, it has been calculated, save a quarter of a million annually in benefits alone. I measure my words when I say that the neglect of the Local Government Board to enforce even the existing legal National Minimum of sanitation caused, last year, more deaths than the whole South African War.

A Ministry really inspired with a passion for National Efficiency would, however, know how to use other instruments besides compulsion. The Government must set itself, as Mr. Asquith aptly puts it, 'to raise the standard of life'. This is specially the sphere of local initiative and corporate enterprise, of beneficent competition rigorously stopped by law from the downward way, but freed, stimulated and encouraged in every experiment on the upward way. We have seen how the Local Government Board has necessarily to be always coercing its local authorities to secure the National Minimum; for anything beyond that minimum the wise Minister would mingle premiums with his pressure. He would, by his public speeches, by personal interviews with mayors and town clerks, and by the departmental publications, set on foot the utmost possible emulation among the various local governing bodies, as to which could make the greatest strides in municipal activity. We already have the different towns compared, quarter by quarter, in respect of their death-rates, but at present only crudely, unscientifically and perfunctorily. Why should not the Local Government Board avowedly put all the local governing bodies of each class into honorary competition with one another by an annual investigation of municipal efficiency, working out their statistical marks for excellence in drainage, water supply, paving, cleansing, watching and lighting, housing, hospital accommodation, medical service, sickness experience and mortality, and publicly classifying them all according to the result of the examination? Nay, a Ministry keenly inspired with the passion for National Efficiency would call into play every possible incentive to local improvement. The King might give a 'Shield of Honour' to the local authority which had made the greatest progress in the year, together with a Knighthood to the mayor, and a Companionship of the Bath to the clerk, the engineer, and the medical officer of health. On the other hand, the six or eight districts which stood at the bottom of the list would be held up to public opprobrium, and, in the last resort, their elected bodies summarily dissolved, in order to give the inhabitants an opportunity to choose more competent administrators.

If honour and shame fail to appeal to the ratepayers of our most backward communities, there remains the potent lever of pecuniary self-interest. For England has, almost without being aware of it, invented exactly that relationship between central and local government which enables the greatest possible progress to be made. To let each locality really manage its own affairs in its own way—the anarchic freedom of American local administration—is not only to place an intolerable burden upon the poorer districts, but also to give up the all-important principle of the enforcement of a National Minimum. On the other hand, to subject the local authorities to the orders of a central government—the autocratic Minister of the Interior of continental systems—would be to barter away our birthright of local self-government for the pottage of bureaucratic administration. The middle way has, for half a century, been found through that most advantageous of expedients, the grant in aid. We see this in its best form in the police grant. When each locality did its own 'watching' in its own way, thieves and highwaymen enjoyed as much liberty as the local governing bodies themselves. When this state of things became unendurable, eager reformers urged a national police force. But England had an anti-Napoleonic horror of a centralised gendarmerie, acting under orders from London. The solution was found in an empirical compromise. Parliament has, since 1856, required by statute that every county and every borough in Great Britain shall maintain an efficient police force. This is the policy of the National Minimum. But as the local authorities very much disliked providing anything like enough police, and as the enormous growth of an uneducated and almost desperate 'proletariat' which was produced by the industrial revolution forced successive Governments to be very much in earnest about police efficiency, they applied a potent stimulus to it. A grant in aid of the cost of the local police force was offered to the justices and town councillors—at first one-quarter, and now one-half, of their actual expenditure on this service, however large this may be. As the grant is conditional on the force being maintained in efficiency, the Home Office is able, without impairing the independence, or offending the dignity of the local authorities, to inspect all the provincial police forces. The Home Secretary has no power to order any improvement. But his annual inspection enables him to call pointed attention to any shortcomings, and to observe, with circumlocutory official politeness, that if the defect should not have got itself remedied, somehow or another, before the next inspection, he might find himself under the regrettable necessity of withholding the certificate without which the grant cannot be paid. The result of this constant expert criticism and central pressure, coupled with the unlimited grant in aid, is that the strength and efficiency of the provincial police forces has increased during the past generation by leaps and bounds, without any loss of local autonomy, and without the creation of any centralised bureaucracy. We need not consider whether this very great development of the county and borough police was or was not required for national efficiency. The point is that, as successive Ministers really wanted it, they were able, by their fortunate discovery of the instrument of the grant in aid, *varying automatically with the growth of the service, and conditional on its efficiency*, to bring about the improvement they desired. The story of the establishment and pro-gressive efficiency of the English provincial police force is destined to become a classic example of the perfect relationship between central and local self-government.

Unfortunately, Ministers have had so little desire for efficiency in any other branch of local government, and have made so little study of the subject, that grants in aid have been, in other directions, per-verted into mere doles in relief of the rates. Gladstone—to whom the very idea of promoting the utmost possible efficiency of government was alien—simply hated them all, even the police grant, with an un-discriminating hatred. The great bulk of the Liberal Party has echoed him, knowing no better. But the grants in aid are there, to the extent, all told, of some fifteen millions sterling annually; and no Ministry dependent on the ratepayers' vote will ever dream, by withdrawing this subsidy, of suddenly raising rates by two shillings in the pound. The outcry of Sir William Harcourt and the old-fashioned section of the Liberal Party is therefore mere echolalia, a much worse complaint, by the way, than megalomania. What we have to do is to give up all pretence of abolishing grants in aid, or even of objecting to their inevitable increase, in order to enlist their aid in the promotion of National Efficiency. A mere rearrangement of the existing infertile subventions would enable a separate grant to be made, on conditions similar to those of the present police grant, in aid of each branch of local administration which it is considered desirable to promote, not only for police and schools but for such humdrum but fundamentally important services as roads and bridges, paving and lighting, water-supply and housing, baths and wash-houses, parks and libraries.

Passing from the municipal services of daily life to the collective provisions for those sections of the community who are avowedly unable to provide for themselves, what a vista of urgently needed reform is opened up by the Poor Law! Three-quarters of a century ago the nation was saved from hideous disaster by the little knot of social investigators who, by inventing the workhouse test, found the means of stopping the pauperism of the able-bodied. The central department charged with Poor Law administration adopted this invention, and has lived on it ever since. Liberal and Conservative Ministers alike have since done their best, even at the cost of some public uneasiness, to maintain the 'principles of 1834'. But a Government department cannot, any more than a business undertaking, go on living for ever on a single invention. The semi-penal workhouse was excellent for its purpose of a test of able-bodied destitution. We now know that it is the worst possible place for the children, the sick and the aged, who comprise the vast majority of present-day 'paupers'. But the Local Government Board has never incorporated this new truth. It exhausts its energies in trying to prevent Boards of Guardians from giving outdoor relief, without insisting, with equal positiveness, that the children, the sick and the aged shall, at all costs, be saved from the workhouse. The policy of National Efficiency, applied to the Poor Law, would replace the present critical and repressive attitude of the Local Government Board by a positive programme of Poor Law reform. What an energetic President would take in hand would be, not only the vigorous discouragement of outdoor relief to the able-bodied (women no less than men), but an equally vigorous insistence on the humane treatment of the aged, the most scientific provision for the sick, and, above all, the best possible rearing of the 'children of the State.' In no branch of the work of the Local Government Board is there more opening for improvement than in the case of the children. Here and there, indeed, enlightened Boards of Guardians have, after many difficulties, extracted the approval of the central department for carefully considered plans of 'scattered homes' and 'cottage homes', 'boarding-out' and emigration. But in scores of unions up and down the country the Local Government Board tolerates, year after year, a treatment of pauper children quite 'Early Victorian' in its parsimonious thriftlessness. There are still thousands of children in actual workhouses, still tens of thousands in ophthalmic barrack schools; the level of their education is still such that, to give only one example, not a single pauper child in all London has ever won one of the London County Council's junior scholarships. In spite of the decay of apprenticeship, practically nothing has yet been done to give them any genuine technical instruction; and hundreds of them are still annually bundled off the hands of the Guardians into such occupations as haircutting and shaving, from which they are destined, in too many cases, to recruit the ranks of unskilled labour. Or take again the treatment of the sick poor. When a man is ill, the only profitable thing for the community is to cure him as thoroughly as possible with the least possible delay. Yet it cost years of patient struggle before Mr. William Rathbone and other far-sighted philanthropists could force the Local Government Board to require trained nurses, or even to allow Boards of Guardians to train nurses, for the sick poor. Even to this day, whilst some workhouse infirmaries are nearly as well equipped as a good hospital, they are all seriously understaffed. What is far graver, the Local Government Board allows dozens of unions to go on, year after year, with workhouse infirmaries so foul, so badly equipped, and so destitute of adequate medical and nursing staff—in short, so far behind the standard of an up-to-date general hospital—as plainly to delay recovery. Year after year its own officials report the same shortcomings—in one case going so far as to declare that the Guardians ought to be indicted for manslaughter. Yet no President has grit enough to put his foot down, and enforce, upon these backward unions, even the standard of the rest. Nevertheless, the 50,000 indoor pauper children and the 100,000 pauper sick constitute no trivial part of the human material out of which our Empire has to be built.

So far I have been dealing with the prevention of disease and premature death, and the building up of the nervous and muscular vitality of the race. This, it is clear, the twentieth century will regard as the primary duty of Government. As such, it must necessarily form the principal plank in any Imperial programme that will appeal to the Progressive instinct of the country. But it is not enough that we rear a physically healthy race. The policy of National Efficiency involves a great development of public education. Here again the law is in advance of the administration. So far as the schooling of children is concerned, Parliament has long since endorsed the policy of a National Minimum, to be compulsorily enforced on every locality and every individual. The guardian and interpreter of this National Minimum is the Board of Education. No Education Minister has ever found the House of Commons cut down his estimates, or express anything but satisfaction at the growth of the education vote. The Board of Education, moreover, has full powers to fine, dissolve, and even to supersede any local authority that fails in its duty. So far as instruction up to fourteen is concerned, it is clearly not the fault of Parliament if any child, in any part of the kingdom, is denied the most efficient education that pedagogic science can devise,

Unfortunately we have never yet had a Prime Minister or a Chancellor of the Exchequer who had any conception of the duty of the Government to insist on National Efficiency in education, or, with the one exception of Mr. Arthur Acland, an Education Minister who had any power of standing up either against his own permanent staff, or against the unwarranted but frequent interferences of the Treasury with educational policy. Unfortunately, too, both Conservatives and Liberals have, in dealing with primary education, been hampered by the particularism in schools which stands in the way of any national policy of education. One party has backed denominational schools, and has only grudgingly admitted the need for School Boards. The other party, with at least equal intolerance, has backed Board Schools and only grudgingly allowed denominational schools to exist. The result of this sectarian and unsectarian narrowness, and of the incapacity of the Education Department itself, is that, after a whole generation of nominal compulsion, we are still only at the beginning of the task. Over at least a third of England, the schools, the training of the teachers, the scope and content of the curriculum, and even the attendance of the children, are so inferior as to amount to a national scandal, whilst only in the picked samples of a few towns do we rise to the common level of Switzerland. It is in the class-rooms of these schools that the future battles of the Empire for commercial prosperity are being already lost. What the country now needs, and what it will presently clamour for—perhaps too late—is a national policy in education. It is tired of the old particularism in schools. So long as freedom of conscience is maintained, and reasonable public control secured, the younger generation cares not a jot what particular modicum of religious instruction is combined with the secular education. It has not the slightest wish to starve out the Church or the Roman Catholic schools, and really prefers them to go on supplying a useful alterntive to municipal administration. And seeing that we cannot possibly shut up the voluntary schools (which educate half the children in the land), the ordinary non-political citizen cannot see why the old feud should any longer be allowed to paralyse national education; why both sets of schools cannot once for all be frankly accepted as equally parts of the national system; why the Board of Education cannot do its statutory duty and firmly bring up all schools, whatever their management, to the same high (and annually rising) national standard of secular efficiency; and why the whole cost of these necessary improvements should not be freely granted, under reasonable conditions of audit and control, from national funds. And the tantalising thing is that all this needs no further legislation. The Duke of Devonshire could decree it all to-morrow, after one Cabinet Council, by a stroke of the pen. All that stands between us and a really effective National Minimum of education is a strong Education Minister who really knows his business, who is backed by his Cabinet against the natural resistance of the Chancellor of the Exchequer to the necessary increase of the grant, and who will stand no insubordination from either his own or the Treasury clerks.

But all this concerns only primary education, which the nation thought that it had settled so long ago as 1870. It is now prepared to see the building up of an equally national system of secondary education, and even of university education of a certain sort. In nothing, indeed, has the present Government incurred more discredit than its failure to carry through its secondary education proposals, except perhaps in the timidity of the proposals themselves. The man in the street cannot be interested by carefully minimised reforms, effecting nothing but such half-hearted changes as only experts can understand. He, no more than Mr. Balfour, can bring himself to care about a mere change in the name of the present Technical Education Committees. His imagination and patriotism must be roused by a large-hearted plan for bringing the whole of our educational machinery up to the level of that of any other country. Assure him politely that energetic local authorities here and there will presently provide technical schools and a scholarship ladder, and he will not even pretend to understand what it means; but he will wake up if he is told that the whole system is to be so reorganised that every clever child, in every part of the country, shall get the best possible training that can be devised. To get this done he quite realises that there must be a substantial grant in aid of secondary education. Moreover, the man in the street, though he knows nothing accurately, has got into his mind the uncomfortable conviction that Germany and the United States are outstripping us, not merely in general education and commercial 'cuteness,' but also in chemistry and electricity, engineering and business organisation in the largest sense. Not that I would pretend that our friend in the street knows much about these subjects. But when he sees in his local paper that tenders have been received by the local authority for the latest thing in electrical plant, and that the leading English firms not only ask about double the price quoted by the best German-Swiss companies, but naïvely fortify their absurd demands by promising, if they get the contract, to put up the necessary works to execute it (thereby confessing that it is their inexperience that they offer as an inducement), then even the suburban tradesman's mind begins to clear, and to make itself up on the subject. Nothing would be more widely popular at the present time, certainly nothing is more calculated to promote National Efficiency, than a large policy of Government aid to the highest technical colleges and the universities. The statesman who first summons up courage enough to cut himself loose from official pedantries on this point, and demand a grant of half a million a year with which to establish in the United Kingdom a dozen perfectly equipped faculties of science, engineering, economics, and modern languages would score a permanent success.

I can indulge in no further detail. The policy of National Efficiency here sketched out for the Home Office, the Local Government Board, and the Board of Education, needs, of course, to be worked out in equal detail for the other departments. The reorganisation of the War Office and the substitution of a system of scientific fighting for our present romantic and incapable 'soldiering'; the energetic rehandling of the Budget (which now yields no more per head than it did a hundred years ago), so as to assert the claims of the State as the sleeping partner in the unearned increment both of urban land values and the huge gains of monopolised industry; the reform of local taxation on the lines of an assessment according to site-value instead of the present penalising of the building and improving of houses; the rescue of our present 'tied' refreshment houses from the tyranny of the brewer, and the adjustment of their number and hours of business to the actual needs of each locality; the reform of the House of Commons by confining all ordinary speeches to a quarter of an hour, and the increased devolution of business to committees—all these are but points in the same policy of National Efficiency by which every part of the central and local machinery of the State needs to be knit together into an organically working whole.

To sum up. What the mass of non-political citizens are just now craving for is virility in government—virility in South Africa, virility in our relations with the rest of the world, and, by no means least, virility in grappling with the problems of domestic administration. It is now evident even to Conservatives that what with lack of faith and lack of knowledge, what with the dominance of vested interests and the paralysing infection of political cynicism, no such virility is to be hoped for in the present Government. The nation is looking around for an alternative, but can find none. The war has completed its disgust with old-fashioned Liberalism, with its complaisant insularity, its fanatical intolerance, and its unscientific Individualism. At the beginning of the twentieth century, Gladstonianism is as dead as the dodo, and Jingoism is going the way of all rowdy fashions when they have been slept on.

So far Lord Rosebery and Mr. Asquith, Mr. Haldane and Sir Edward Grey are right in their diagnosis. The nation sees that these men, in their different opportunities, have had the courage to cast off the old clothes. But at present we are all in the dark as to what is to be the new outfit. Before the non-political citizen will rally to a new standard, he will need to be convinced that those who raise it not only accept the principle of National Efficiency, but have a clear vision of how they intend to work this principle out in each of the departments of State activity. Lord Rosebery is struck by the repeated electoral successes of the Progressive party in the London County Council. But these successes were not gained by any enunciation of general principles, or merely by the declaration that the Progressives stood for progress, or for efficiency in the abstract. They were, as Lord Rosebery knows, won by a persistent and all pervading propaganda of a detailed programme of reform in every department; resolute, and even extreme in its character; put forward by a group of men who had definitely thought out what they intended to get done; and who, at the risk of calumny and misunderstanding at the West-End and in the City, did not shrink from painting the sky red with their projects. Thus it was that they gathered into one irresistible force, strong enough to carry their party through four successive general elections, the whole Progressive instinct of the Metropolis. Now, the up-to-date business man or Progressive-minded workman is satisfied that Lord Rosebery and Sir Edward Grey know their own minds about the Empire, and that they have both the knowledge and the conviction necessary to get done what they wish. But in this respect, to the man in the street at any rate, they offer no advantages over Lord Salisbury and Mr. Chamberlain. The question is, What steps would their alternative Government take to insure the rearing of an Imperial race? What action have they in mind for healing the open sore of the sweated trades: what do they intend to do with the Poor Law: what plan have they thought out for stimulating and directing the utmost possible municipal enterprise in sanitation and housing: what is their scheme for a comprehensive national system of education from the infant school to the university: what are their practical conclusions as to increasing the grants in aid and assessing site values: how do they intend to transform the present silly procedure of the House of Commons: do they propose to simply neglect the military situation? It is on questions of this sort that they must, during the next few years, mark themselves out from their opponents, and convince us that they have a faith and a programme rooted no less in knowledge than in conviction. To think out such a programme is, of course, irksome, and, as every political Polonius will advise, to commit yourself to it is inconvenient—if you do not believe in it. But, to create a live Opposition—still more, to construct an alternative Government—this new thought and this new propaganda must be undertaken. If even one-half of the study and conviction, money and capacity, were put into such a campaign for the next five years that Cobden and Bright put into the Anti-Corn Law League, the country could be won for a policy of National Efficiency. Without the pledge of virility which a campaign of this sort would afford, the nation will not be persuaded.

Such a campaign cannot be undertaken by any one man, however eminent. It involves the close co-operation of a group of men of diverse temperaments and varied talents, imbued with a common faith and a common purpose, and eager to work out, and severally to expound, how each department of national life can be raised to its highest possible efficiency. If he does nothing but plough his own furrow, Lord Rosebery will, I fear, have to plough it alone.

II The Education Muddle and the Way Out

The Education Muddle was first discussed by the Fabian Society on 26 May 1899, a time, it will be noted, when Webb was publicly deploring any decrease in the powers of the school boards. It was published as Tract No. 106 by the Society in January 1901. The name of the author does not appear on the frontispiece but Edward Pease is insistent that the scheme was 'entirely the work of Sidney Webb'. The passage through the Fabian debating chamber was singularly stormy and accounts for the unusually long period which elapsed between the time of the first discussion and the date of publication. Opposition to Webb came chiefly from the Society's two other education experts, Graham Wallas and Stewart Headlam, both of whom were critical of the proposals favouring sectarian education and the abolition of the vast majority of the school boards. The struggle was acute and the damage done to old friendships irreparable but Webb's point of view was to prevail.

The Tract is the most telling of documents. Within the compass of eighteen pages there is set forth a trenchant analysis of the chaos existing in English education, a list of the possible solutions, followed by the only 'way out' which will meet all the circumstances and answer all the arguments. The work is a skilfully woven fabric of facts and conclusions, leading in turn to a re-affirmation of the credo of 'the national minimum'. In addition, as with so many Fabian Tracts, it possesses a subtle emotional force. What the writer appears to be attempting is the arousal of a feeling of outraged intelligence on the part of the reader. With the facts as they were, what other conclusions can possibly be drawn but those which have just been put forward?

The Tract proved to be an immediate best-seller: twenty thousand copies were quickly circulated and a second edition was necessary before the end of the year. But even before the official date of publication, non-Fabian eyes had perused it from cover to cover for Sir John Gorst had asked for fifty galley pulls to be despatched to Whitehall.[115] Not only was it read by high departmental officials, it also went the rounds of members of the Government who evidently found it profitable reading. Well might the editor of *Fabian News* feel justified in striking a self-satisfied note when referring to *The Education Muddle* barely one month after publication: 'It is a pronouncement of no small importance, and has already attracted much curiosity in influential quarters. It is probable that a Government measure on the subject will shortly be announced.'[116]

Our educational machinery in England has got into a notable mess. Some places have two or three public authorities spending rates and taxes on different sorts of schools, whilst others have none at all. In one town the clever boy or girl finds in the infant school the lowest rung of an unbroken ladder to the university; whilst in the very next county there is no rescue for talented poverty from the shop or plough. Some school districts are too small to maintain a decent primary school; others are large enough to run a university. The central organization is as chaotic as the local. The various educational institutions in the United Kingdom—taking only those supported out of the rates and taxes—are officially under the charge of no fewer than ten separate Cabinet Ministers; and their several departments usually scorn to consult together.

The result is that, although we spend on education in the United Kingdom every year nearly twenty million pounds of public money of one sort or another, from rates, taxes or public endowments, we get a very inadequate return for it. In English education to-day, waste and want go hand in hand.

I THE LOCAL AUTHORITIES

THE PRESENT MUDDLE

There are, in England to-day, two distinct sets of local educational authorities, acting in the same areas, and sharing the provision of schools between them. These are (i) the School Boards, (ii) the County, Borough and Urban District Councils.

The School Boards, of which there are now 2,527, have unlimited powers of rating, but are, in other respects, narrowly restricted in their scope. They can maintain only 'elementary' schools, as defined by the Acts and by the Day and Evening 'Codes' annually issued by the Education Department. But they do not maintain or control even all the elementary schools. More than half the children in elementary day schools, and more than one-third of the young people in evening continuation schools, are in the so-called 'voluntary' or denominational schools. Where a School Board exists, it is responsible for enforcing attendance at school upon all the children of the district, whether they go to Board or voluntary schools. But in more than one-third of England (measured by population) no School Board exists. Over this large area, the children must attend denominational schools, and these are under no local public control. In these parishes the duty of enforcing school attendance is entrusted to the local sanitary authority—that is, in rural parts, the persons who are the Guardians of the Poor. Even in the two-thirds of England in which School Boards exist, they are not allowed to have schools of their own if there is already a sufficient supply of places in 'voluntary' schools, however unsuitable such schools may be for the special educational needs or religious opinions of the locality. The effect of this is that in over 10,000 parishes there is none but a denominational school. These 'voluntary schools' (though four-fifths of their cost is provided from taxes) are nominally governed by 'boards of managers,' who are practically self-elected; while the real work of administration is usually performed by the minister of religion (Anglican or Roman Catholic) to whom the school 'belongs'. The Government puts the School Boards, the public educational authorities within their respective districts, exactly on the same footing as these little nominal committees of managers. Moreover, by a piece of official pedantry, every alteration in the Code intended to improve a village school under this irresponsible private management, is made to apply equally and identically to the largest and most efficient borough School Board. The School Boards were, in fact, established by Mr. Forster in 1870 merely to 'fill up the gaps' in the then existing system of 'voluntary' schools, and they have been treated as stopgaps ever since. They are closely scrutinized by jealous eyes in order to prevent them from providing 'secondary' or 'technical' education, however much their constituents may need or desire this. Nevertheless, so numerous are the children of school age that the English School Boards in 1899–1900 spent about £9,500,000, an amount which had increased in each of the two preceding years by about 4 per cent. The English voluntary schools in the same year spent about £5,300,000 which had increased in each of the two preceding years by about 10 per cent. Of the totals the Government found about £3,600,000 and £4,150,000.

The County, Borough and Urban District Councils, on the other hand, whilst narrowly limited in the amount they can spend on education, enjoy a large freedom as to its kind or scope. The Technical Instruction Acts, 1889 and 1891, prohibit their teaching any child who is in the standards of an elementary school, but impose no upward limit of any kind. Hence the London County Council, like the Town Councils of Manchester, Nottingham, Bristol, Newcastle, etc., can help to maintain a university. The instruction must be confined to 'technical education,' but this has been so defined as legally to include every subject of study except 'theology, Greek and Shakespeare'.[117] The result is that Town and County Councils now maintain and aid hundreds of schools (above the elementary standards) of every kind— grammar schools, science and art schools, commercial schools, cookery schools, trade schools, and what not. In most towns, the Town and County Councils do not, in fact, confine themselves to anything that can properly be described as technical education. They have, without express statutory warrant, assumed the position of secondary education, and even university authorities; and in this they have been encouraged by the Education Department. But though they have thus stretched their powers, and enlarged their responsibilities, their funds are strictly limited.

The County Councils (51 in England) and County Boroughs (62) can spend on 'technical education' what is known as the 'whisky money' (the additional duties on beer and spirits imposed by the Local Taxation Act, 1890), and in 1899–1900 they did so spend £804,000 out of £867,000. They can spend also up to a penny in the pound from the

County or County Borough rates. In 1899–1900, twenty-two County Boroughs added in this way £44,960 to their whiskey money expenditure. No County Council has yet levied a rate on the whole county for education, but in a few cases the Council levies a rate on a part of the county at the request and for the benefit of the rural districts concerned. The Non-County Boroughs and Urban District Councils can, in addition, levy a penny rate of their own for technical education, and 262 of them now do so, to the extent of £36,894 a year.

The total expenditure on education by these municipal bodies now amounts to about a million sterling, and it is increasing at the rate of about 5 per cent a year. In addition, they exercise, by their inspection and grants, more or less control over about a million sterling a year of educational endowments devoted to secondary and higher education.

CONFLICT AND OVERLAPPING

These two distinct sets of local authorities come everywhere into more or less acute rivalry and conflict. The School Boards were the earlier in the field, and they have frequently provided 'higher grade schools' and evening continuation schools of high type, scarcely to be distinguished from those started by the Town and County Councils. But this occasional overlapping is not, of itself, a serious evil, and, moreover, it is one which mutual consultation and consideration might easily set right. Nor is the waste of public money owing to this overlapping at all large in amount. What is serious is the educational chaos caused by the arbitrary separation of one part of education from another; the total absence of any considered scheme for fulfilling the whole educational needs of any one district; the lack of any coherent system for the promotion of scholars from school to school; the stupendous inequality between one district and another; and the deadening effect upon the primary schools of their confinement within rigid limits, and the exclusion of their teachers from the opportunity of being transferred to other branches of education. What is wanted, in the interests alike of the public, the children and the teachers, is

ADMINISTRATIVE UNITY

There ought to be, in each district of convenient size, one public educational authority, and one only; responsible for providing and controlling all the education maintained in the district out of public funds, whether it be literary, scientific, commercial, artistic or technological in type—whether it be, for any of these types, primary, secondary or university in grade.

THE POLICY OF DRIFT

But there is, as yet, apparently not much chance of our getting this administrative unity. Having 'drifted' into the present muddle, the only easy course is to go on drifting; and this is what nearly everybody, statesman and schoolmaster alike, is vigorously doing. The last Liberal Government did nothing but 'drift', so far as education was concerned, the short time it was in power; and Mr. Acland, unable to gain the ear of the Cabinet for so dull a subject, was reduced to making untiring administrative attempts to patch up a crazy structure.

In 1896 the Conservative Government half-heartedly attempted to unify local educational administration by forming 'education authorities' from the Councils of Counties and County Boroughs. They did not believe it possible to abolish the School Boards, and preferred, on the line of least resistance, to subordinate them to the new authorities. The Bill passed its second reading by an immense majority, but was lost owing to the revolt of the smaller or non-county boroughs, who objected to the surrender of their independence, and joined the opponents of the clauses intended to strengthen denominational education. Since then the chiefs of the Department have announced their intention of securing the objects of the defeated Bill, by a combination of administrative action and small Bills. This means that they have given up any serious attempt to think out the problem as a whole, and that the policy of least resistance has slipped back into a policy of drift. The School Boards are weak; therefore bit by bit their power is being taken from them—but they are still retained in existence. The County Councils are strong; therefore bit by bit their powers are being increased, but there is no suggestion that they should receive that unrestricted rating power and that control of all educational grades which alone would make them efficient educational authorities. The Church is powerful and the Church schools are in want of money. Therefore a new source of confusion is introduced by the creation of 'associations of voluntary schools', which secure the control of an important section of education to the official hierarchy of the various denominations.

Year after year we are promised a Secondary Education Bill, and it is safe to assume that it too will follow the line of least resistance and least thought. The School Boards may unfortunately still further be restricted both in their day and in their evening schools, and the Councils may be given increased power, but will still be subject to a narrow rating limitation, and still confined to special educational grades. But just as easy writing makes bad reading, so easy legislation makes bad adminis-tration. The School Boards and the denominational school managers would still be in charge of the education of nearly three million children, and an expenditure of over twelve millions sterling annually, whilst every year the educational results of that expenditure would be en-dangered or even gravely impaired. Already it is difficult to create public interest in School Board elections. Already it is common to find only one-fifth of the electorate taking the trouble to vote, and as the School Boards are elbowed out by their stronger municipal rivals, this decay of public interest must increase. A body elected on a small poll is always in peril. The Board schools have bitter enemies. In all sections of the community there are to be found many who think that to provide anything beyond the 'Three R's' for the manual labourers is illegitimate and absurd, whilst they dismiss with contempt the claim of elementary teachers to be or to become an educated class. As long as the County and Town Councils are kept without responsibility for or knowledge of the primary schools, they will tend to believe that the only real educa-tion is to be found in the technical schools which they maintain, or in endowed secondary schools which they inspect and aid, and which are open to all who can afford to pay the fees, and to a selected few of those who cannot. Their natural partizanship for their own schools inevitably tends (even if unconsciously) to reinforce that powerful social prejudice which resists any development of 'primary' education beyond the preparation for a life of hewing wood and drawing water. It has been suggested that this might be prevented by giving the School Boards the statutory rights to a few representatives on the education committees of the Councils. But such representatives would be in a permanent and helpless minority, and their presence would do little except increase friction; while the division of the responsibility of the Councils might tend to produce that decreased interest which is the result of indirect election.

One method, however, of connecting the Councils with primary education is so perfectly consistent with the policy of drift that it has been already foreshadowed, and may be adopted at any moment. The Councils, while still separated from the Board schools, may be empowered or required to assist efficient 'voluntary', that is denominational, schools in their district. This would make the position of the Board schools absolutely impossible. The Councils would tend to become partizans not only of the social interests of the technical and secondary schools, but also of the religious interests of the demoninational schools, and religious tolerance for teachers would, like the teaching of French or algebra to children without fee or scholarship, seem to be one of the 'fads' of an unreasonable and discredited faction.

Thus, whilst reform is difficult, delay is dangerous. The 'policy of drift' will not save the School Boards, and will probably destroy all chance of an enlightened development of elementary education for the mass of the people.[118] Every year the Town and County Councils become stronger and more grasping; every year the importunities of the Anglicans and the Roman Catholics for increased grants of public money for their denominational schools become more pressing; every year the muddle increases.

THE CLAIM OF THE SCHOOL BOARDS TO BE THE SOLE EDUCATIONAL AUTHORITIES

If the 'policy of drift' is thus so dangerous to elementary education, and if everything points to unification as the remedy, why should we not adopt the Liberal and Nonconformist cry of 'School Boards everywhere and for everything?' This proposal—to place the whole of public education in each district under the control of the body already elected by the citizens to manage the greater part of it—seems at first sight irresistible. Closer consideration proves, however, that it is impracticable as a solution of the present difficulties, and that even if it were possible, it would not be desirable. We simply *cannot* make the School Board the universal authority for secondary and technical education, because:

(1) In one-third of England School Boards do not exist. It was exactly for this reason that the School Board was ignored in the Technical Instruction Act of 1889, and the new powers were given to the County, Borough and Urban District Councils, which together cover all England.

(2) School Boards are so fiercely hated by large sections of the people, so little desired by the ordinary man, and so energetically

opposed by positive majorities of the local electors, that their compulsory establishment in places where they are not petitioned for,
and where they are not absolutely required to provide new schools,
is politically impossible—even if it could be defended on principles
of Democracy and Local Self Government.

(3) Even where School Boards exist, their districts are, in the vast
majority of cases, absolutely unsuitable for anything beyond elementary education. Out of 2,527 existing School Boards, 2,085 govern
populations of less than 5,000. It will certainly be impossible for many
years to come in England to maintain even one good secondary
school for boys and girls in a population as small as 20,000. Only
about 300 out of the 2,527 existing School Boards deal with such a
population. Higher education, and more specialized education
would, of course, be outside the possibilities of many even of these
larger Boards. To make the School Board the sole authority for all
education within its district would necessarily involve abolishing
nine-tenths of the existing School Boards, and creating new bodies
for much larger districts than single parishes, or even than small
boroughs. There would still remain the difficulty of providing for the
purely rural areas divorced from their urban centres. But even if it
were possible to adopt the existing School Boards as the authorities
for secondary and technical education, it would not be desirable,
because School Boards have inevitably become the scene of religious
quarrels, and experience shows that their election is almost always
made the occasion for a struggle between religious denominations.
No one would wish to infect secondary and technical education—
hitherto mainly free from sectarian squabbles—with this deplorable
strife.

THE CASE FOR A NEW EDUCATIONAL AUTHORITY

Many defenders of School Boards now admit with regret that it is
politically and geographically impossible to make the existing School
Boards the sole educational authorities for their respective districts.
They urge that the best way to secure administrative unity in education
is to create a brand-new body; to divest the County, Borough and
Urban District Councils of all their present educational powers; to
abolish all School Boards; to divide England up afresh into suitable
districts; and to make each district elect an Education Council, to

which should be entrusted all the education within its area. But this too, on examination, is found to be both impracticable and undesirable, because,

1. It would involve the maximum of disturbance of local property, finances and vested interests, and would combine in one irresistible opposition (i) the 2,527 School Boards and the 1,200 County, Borough and Urban District Councils, all objecting to have their freehold schools taken away from them, (ii) all their officials whose salaries would be disturbed and their very places jeopardized, (iii) all the members of Parliament, not understanding what it was about, but desperately wirepulled by the aforesaid local bodies and their officials, and (iv) all the ratepayers who would expect their rates to be raised by the change. No House of Commons would look twice at such a Bill; and no Cabinet would propose it.

2. It would almost certainly transfer to the elections of the new bodies, and so enlarge and perpetuate, the religious animosities and sectarian strife that now dominate School Board elections and obstruct educational progress. All experience indicates that, at any rate in the England of this generation, public bodies directly elected to manage schools will be elected largely on theological grounds. The proposed new Educational Councils, though elected for wider educational functions, and often for larger areas, would tend to be merely the existing School Boards under a new name.

We come thus into direct conflict with those who, so far as matters educational are concerned, still cherish a belief in the necessity of an *ad hoc* body. This demands separate consideration.

THE STORY OF THE 'AD HOC' BODY

It is now often urged, in support of the School Boards, or of the proposal to create elected Educational Councils, that the business of providing and managing schools is of so special a nature that it is best entrusted to a separate public body elected *ad hoc* (that is to say, for this special business only). This is not the reason why School Boards were invented. Whatever good arguments there may be for an *ad hoc* body for school management, the School Board, as we know it, is merely one of the few survivors of what was once a large class. A hundred years ago most of the local government of the English towns was carried on by *ad hoc* bodies, chosen in all sorts of ways, for all sorts of different functions. During the eighteenth century, as the urban population increased, it became absolutely necessary to provide for more local government. No statesman thought out any general system. What happened was that one bit after another was stuck upon the structure of the old township government—in one place a special board of commissioners was appointed to drain the marshes; in another a separate body of governors and directors of the poor was elected to provide a workhouse; elsewhere a board of trustees was set to keep a road in repair; or a special 'lamp board' would be constituted to pave and light the streets. It was the age of *ad hoc* bodies, elected, co-opted, appointed or constituted in every conceivable way, and literally thousands of them came into existence. In 1834, when the Poor Law was reformed, there was no public body either in the rural districts, or in the unorganized urban districts, to which the new work could possibly have been given. A new *ad hoc* body had therefore to be created. The result of this historical accident is that there are people to-day who have come honestly to believe that the management of a workhouse and the administration of relief is a matter of so special a nature that it must be entrusted to an *ad hoc* body. When, in 1870, Mr. Forster carried the Education Act, efficient town councils existed in the boroughs, and it was at first proposed that the School Board should be nominated by these Town Councils, of which they would virtually have been statutory committees, with independent powers. But in the rural districts no responsible local authority could be found, and the great population of London was in the hands of the Vestries. Indirect election was objected to by the Radicals, and the various denominational bodies insisted on 'a representation of all parties and all religions'. So Mr. Forster gave way, and directly elected School Boards were created. Now many people have come to feel that there is something inherently reasonable and natural in having a separate elected body to look after schools. This is not the opinion of Germany or Austria, France or Switzerland, where they know something about education. In all these countries the public body that manages other local affairs also manages the schools. The hesitation to carry the *ad hoc* theory to its logical conclusion shows an inherent doubt in its validity. Mr. Chaplin's proposal to create a special authority for defective poor law children met with universal condemnation, and during the debates on the London Government Bill, 1899, the suggestion that Boards of Guardians should be abolished and their duties handed over to municipal authorities, met with general acceptance, especially from experts like Canon Barnett. We have, in fact, ceased to believe in the need for *ad hoc* authorities. During the last sixty years they have been as far as possible absorbed and abolished.

The success of Town and County Councils, with their varied functions, is evidence that separate bodies for separate services are superfluous. There is at least as much difference between main drains and lunatic asylums, between street sweeping and technical education, between prevention of infectious disease and providing music in the parks as there is between 'purely municipal', poor law, and educational functions—problems no less difficult, duties no less important, are involved in the actual work of a modern municipality as in any of the three separate services.

THE WAY OUT

If, then, it is impracticable and undesirable, either to make the School Boards the sole educational authorities, or to supersede them and all other existing educational bodies by brand-new Educational Councils, how are we to get administrative unity ? What we have to work towards is the concentration in a single elected body for each locality of all the public business entrusted to that locality. Leaving Poor Law aside, as outside the purpose of the present Tract, let us consider how, on this principle, we can get out of the Education muddle.

First, as to the unit of area. It is at once clear that the large towns must be kept as distinct educational units. Birmingham and Manchester, Liverpool and Leeds, can neither be broken up nor merged. Outside the large towns, seeing that we want unity of all grades of education, the unit of area must, it is clear, be much larger than the parish; and as a large part of the educational machinery is already organized by the County, it does not seem either practicable or desirable to adopt any other area.

Leaving out of account for a moment London and the County Boroughs, we propose that, in the 50 Administrative Counties which make up the rest of England, the County Council should be made responsible for the provision and maintenance of every kind and grade of education within its area. All School Boards existing within the County should be abolished, and their schools transferred to the County Council. The annual cost of maintaining these and other public schools should become an equal charge throughout the County, levied in the ordinary County rate. The first duty of the County Council should be to prepare and submit to the Board of Education for criticism (but not for control) a complete survey of the existing educational provision for the whole County, from the elementary school to the university, coupled with a plan for its completion and improvement. The Council should have full and free powers to experiment in schools and subjects, and of initiation in new forms of instruction, subject only to the consent of the Board of Education. Finally, it should control any public educational endowments belonging to the locality, administer the 'whisky money', and have unlimited powers to levy rates for the aiding and supplying of every description of education within its district.[119]

We have here the basis of a complete and systematic organization of education (outside London and the 62 County Boroughs), based on the principle of administrative unity. But there are difficulties in the way, and objections to be overcome, with which we must deal one by one.

(a) The Non-County Borough

The first difficulty that confronts us is the claim of the Non-County Borough and the large Urban District to escape from the County, and to be made, like the County Borough, a completely independent educational unit. On the one hand it is undesirable even to appear to limit the activity of an energetic and growing town. On the other, we have the practical impossibility of disturbing the 'whisky money' distribution, which now goes to the Counties and County Boroughs; and cutting off from the Counties nearly all their schools and institutes, which have naturally been placed in the urban centres. The solution must be found in a proper organization of functions and powers. The educational system of the County must be organized as a whole, the little market towns taking in it their proper place as educational centres for the adjacent districts. But, in this system, the local administration, including the whole management of the institutions in the towns, should be delegated by the County Council to a responsible local committee for each Non-County Borough or Urban District. This local committee might consist, in the main, of persons nominated by the Borough or Urban District Council, together with the County Councillors for the district, at least two women, and possibly other persons interested in education. These committees could be allowed, subject to the ultimate control of the County Council, to spend a definite sum annually allotted to them by the Council, plus any special rate in their own area that the Borough or Urban District Council could be induced to levy.

(b) The Absence of Women, and often of Persons with Educational Experience, from County and Borough Councils

It is said that County and Borough Councils, though they usually contain some experienced administrators, are unfit to manage schools, because (i) they often include no men of educational experience or interested in the subject, and (ii) women are not eligible to sit upon them.[120] To get over this real difficulty, and also to facilitate efficient administration, the County and Borough Councils should be required by statute to appoint special educational committees. Under the Technical Instruction Acts the Town and County Councils have spontaneously developed this organization for educational purposes, entrusting the execution of their powers to committees on which are co-opted persons whose presence and advice may be, for one reason or another, desired. This system has worked so well that it ought to be continued. The local authorities for education would then be the Town and County Councils acting each through a statutory committee consisting of a majority of councillors and of certain co-opted individuals. In order to preserve unity of control, no other authority or body of persons should have a statutory claim to representation thereon; but, if only (pending an alteration of the law) to ensure the presence of women, the Town or County Council should be required to submit for the approval of the Board of Education the proposed composition of its committees. These committees, like other committees, should not have the power to levy a rate, otherwise all the simplification of finance would be lost. At the beginning of the financial year the committee would present its budget, and after getting it passed would administer the allotted funds without further interference by the Council.

(c) The Need for Local Supervision

But the County is a large area, and it is rightly urged that no County Council can properly undertake the actual management of the schools in all its parishes. It is not suggested that it should do so. The work of the Education Committee of the County Council would be to frame a scheme for providing and maintaining such schools, of such grades and types, and in such localities as the circumstances of the County require. It should provide both the capital cost and the annual maintenance of these schools; frame regulations for their government; inspect them by its officials; and appoint all the head-masters. But the detailed administration of the several institutions, the selection of assistant-masters, and as much else as possible should be delegated to a local committee, appointed by the County Council for each parish or for each institution. For this local committee, two alternatives present themselves. Either the County Council might be required to appoint the local Parish Council, or the County Council might be left to appoint whom it chose among the local residents, with the addition of two or more members nominated by the Parish Council.

(d) How to Deal with the Voluntary Schools

Every County Council would find the greater part of the elementary education in its district in the hands of voluntary schools, owning no allegiance to it or to any other local authority; but often starving for lack of funds, and grossly below any reasonable standard of educational efficiency. It is politically impossible to abolish these voluntary schools; and whatever we may think of the theological reasons for their establishment, their separate and practically individual management does incidentally afford what ought to be, in any public system of education, most jealously safeguarded, namely, variety, and the opportunity of experiment. What we have to do with the voluntary schools is to put them under the control of the local educational authority; to improve and strengthen their committees of management; to raise their efficiency; and especially to provide better salaries for their teachers; to make impossible the tyrannical vagaries of foolish clergymen in the village schools; and, to bring these into co-ordination with the rest of the educational system.

We propose that the County Council should be allowed to offer a grant in aid up to, say, five or even ten shillings per head per annum to all the voluntary schools in the County, to be spent in increasing the salaries of the teaching staff, or otherwise raising the efficiency of the schools; and in all cases subject to the following conditions, viz.:

(a) The County Council to be allowed to inspect the schools, frame regulations for their administration, and audit their accounts.

(b) All future appointments and dismissals of teachers to be subject to its confirmation.

(c) The appointment, subject to its approval, of a committee of managers, which should invariably include two members to be annually nominated by the Parish (or Urban District or Borough) Council; meet at least once in every term, appoint its own chairman and clerk, and have brought before it all school business (including the appointment, suspension, or dismissal of teachers, the school log, and the school accounts); be responsible for the whole management of the school; and transmit copies of its minutes annually to the County Council.

The Education Committee of the County Council should be empowered to provide additional school places when in its opinion the existing denominational school accommodation, though sufficient, was unsuitable to the demands of the district. In this way the Church schools would remain strong where the Church was strong, but a sufficient remedy would be provided for substantial Nonconformist grievances. A right of appeal to the Board of Education should also be reserved to the managers of any 'voluntary' school in any case of complaint against the local authority. With this freer system of grants the 'special aid grant' should be merged in the other Government grants in aid and the voluntary associations for its administration should be abolished as unnecessary and inconsistent with County districts.

LONDON AND THE COUNTY BOROUGHS

We have reserved the case of London and the 62 County Boroughs, where the need for educational improvement is less crying than in the rural districts, and the problem of unification more difficult. The administrative unity of all grades of education is, however, no less desirable in London and the large towns than in the country, and the malign influence of sectarian quarrels at School Board elections is apt to be even more severely felt. On the other hand the School Boards in these large towns are usually at least as efficient as the municipal authorities; the work to be done is large—in London colossal; and there would be some danger that unification would lead not, as in the Counties, to an increased expenditure on education, but to some slackening in the present rate of increase, if not to a positive limit. The School Boards in London and the County Boroughs, should therefore for the most part be left untouched. The County Council in London and the Town Councils in the County Boroughs would become the authorities for all education outside the powers of the School Boards, with spending powers in this department of their work as unlimited as in drainage or water supply. They should, of course, retain all their existing powers, and they should, moreover, have the same enlarged powers of providing new schools as are given to the rural County Councils.

These considerations do not apply to such County Boroughs as Bury, Chester, Lincoln, Preston, St Helens and Stockport, which have no School Board. Nor need they apply to County Boroughs like Wigan, where the School Board has no school; or like Blackburn, Oxford or Worcester, where only five to ten per cent of the children are in Board Schools; or like Bath or Exeter, where the Board Schools contain fewer than 2,000 children. In all these cases the School Board should be abolished, and the Town Council at once made responsible for all grades of education. This would leave about 47 County Boroughs in which, as in London, the School Board system may be deemed to have so firmly established itself, as to be entitled to be untouched. But even in these cases it should be open to the School Board, if it should come to think it desirable, to terminate its own existence, and transfer its schools and powers to the municipality. Meanwhile the School Board should be strongly represented on the education committee of the municipal body; and the management of the proposed grant in aid of voluntary schools should be dealt with by a statutory sub-committee, of which the School Board members should form one half.

II THE CENTRAL AUTHORITY

THE PRESENT DRIFT

The Board of Education Act of 1899 has substituted the Board of Education for the Education Department, the Department of Science and Art, the Charity Commissioners and the Board of Agriculture, but no provision has so far been made for the rearrangement of their over-lapping powers or for the internal organization of the new Department. The powers of the Treasury over university colleges, of the Local Government Board over poor law schools, of the Home Office over industrial schools and reformatories, and through the Prisons Com-missioners, over prison schools, of the India Office over the Engineering College at Cooper's Hill, of the Board of Agriculture over the agri-cultural colleges, and of the War Office and Admiralty over their own primary schools in garrison towns, and over military and naval schools, are still continued to these departments. A consultative committee has been created, but without specific powers beyond the framing of a register of teachers. So far as can be seen, the present intention is to organize the Board of Education solely into primary and secondary divisions, the latter being illogically sub-divided into 'technical education' and 'secondary schools'. Such a plan may easily reduce the whole 'reform' to a merely mechanical concentration of existing departments under a single roof. This is of no use if no real unity and no organic relation between the various kinds and grades of education is created. Failure to secure this would be particularly bad for elementary education, which it is the fashion to regard as mechanical and suitable for assignment to lower-grade minds. The education of the great mass of the people must not be isolated from the general intellectual movement either locally or at the centre.

OUR PLAN

The Board of Education should have, subject to the authority of Parliament, powers of inspection, criticism, and audit of all education of every kind and grade, which is maintained or aided out of monies provided by Parliament, or from endowments or trust funds derived from persons deceased; and the Board should therefore take cognizance, not only of such primary and secondary education as it controls, but also of universities and university colleges, non-local schools, and other endowed educational institutions, army and navy schools, training colleges, poor law schools, and industrial and reformatory schools and school-ships.

The official staff should be unified and divided primarily into departments on a geographical basis, so that the section of the office dealing with each area should take within its purview all the grades of education whether elementary, secondary or university, and all subjects of study, whether literary, scientific, technological or commercial, carried on in the day or in the evening, under public authorities or bodies of managers or trustees. Only in this way can we ensure a complete view of all the needs of the district, the organic unity of education within that district, and a differentiation of the requirements of different districts. This fundamental organization of the central department should be into ten or twelve 'provinces', each including all public education within a well-defined geographical area, such as London, Lancashire and Cheshire, Devon and Cornwall, the South-Eastern Counties and so on.

Each of these ten or twelve geographical sections should be under an official of high standing and varied experience, who might be called Provincial Superintendent. Through his hands should pass all the reports and other papers relating to any part of the education of his district, which should have its own staff of inspectors for different kinds of schools and different subjects of study. Each province would have its own special needs, and special difficulties, which should be treated without any striving after rigid uniformity.

But in order to secure the highest specialist efficiency, no less than national unity, all important proposals should pass from the heads of the geographical departments to one of three or four staff officers, of the rank of Assistant Under-Secretary of State, who should devote themselves each to one kind of education, and should deal with that kind of education all over the country. From him the papers would go through the permanent Under Secretary of State to the Board, that is the Minister for Education, for final decision.

The Board of Education should require (a) the provision of at least a prescribed minimum supply of all grades of education by each local authority separately or in conjunction with other local authorities; and (b) the provision of an adequate educational and administrative staff.

The Board of Education should make the following grants: (a) a fixed grant based upon a calculation of two-thirds of the necessary minimum expenditure on each grade; and (b) a variable grant based upon one-half of the additional expenditure on any grade up to a fixed maximum. In this way efficiency and enterprise would be promoted, and at the same time extravagance checked. If any educational authority expended less than the minimum in order to save the rates, that is, raised by rate less than one-third of the minimum expenditure, the Board should have power, in the first instance, to fine the locality by reducing or withholding all or part of its grant, *and of supplying the deficiency thus caused by ordering a special local rate to be levied*. If this failed to ensure the provision of the 'National Minimum' of education in the particular locality, the Board should have power, in the last resort, to remove the defaulting local authority from office, and appoint, for a short term of years, Government Commissioners in its stead, with power to rate. But such a drastic course would never be necessary. Meanwhile the Board's inspector should have the right to attend at all full meetings of the authority.

CONCLUSION

The democratic ideal in education is not merely that a ladder should be provided, whereby a few students may climb unimpeded from the elementary school to the university; though even this ideal has little chance of realization so long as some rungs of the ladder are under no one's care, and competing guardians squabble for the right to look after others. What the national well-being demands, and what we must insist upon, is that every child, dull or clever, rich or poor, should receive all the education requisite for the full development of its faculties. For every child, in every part of the country, at least a 'national minimum' of education must be compulsorily provided. Above and beyond that minimum we must see that ample provision is made for varying faculties and divergent tastes. Our plan is to extend popular control and popular assistance to every branch of education; to combine all the scattered and overlapping authorities; and to link together the municipal life of our local authorities with the intellectual life of the schools by the concentration of all local services under one local body. This plan, it is true, requires the surrender of some cherished illusions, and involves some delicate adjustments to suit transitory forms of organization, but if these difficulties are faced and met on the lines sketched out in this Tract, we shall bring the schools into intimate connection with the everyday life of the country and secure so far as official machinery is concerned a sound and efficient educational system.

The still more important and more difficult problems of what to teach and how to educate, remain for separate consideration.

III London Education

So great was the hostility of the non-conformists to the legislation of 1902 and 1903 that by the time the London Education Bill had appeared on the statute book the Webbs were in a state of acute anxiety. What they found infinitely depressing was the thought that the educational reforms for which they had laboured so long might be blocked by 'the lion in the path'—in other words by the threat of administrative perversion. As always London was the focus of their concern and the Progressives their *bête noire*. Beatrice was prepared to admit that there were Progressives who claimed that they favoured education 'with a big E', but when their aims were analysed it was only primary education of a mechanical and uniform type that was desired. Behind this group there lurked, in her view, the sinister forces of the 'Labour men' who opposed the public support of secondary and university education, and also the N.U.T. who wanted all appointments to fall into the hands of the elementary school teachers. So great was the concern of the Webbs that Beatrice was torn between a wish that the Progressives might be defeated in the next round of local elections and a pipe-dream that a new party grouping might emerge in London, held together through a broad and imaginative educational policy.[121]

It was thus in a mood of genuine perturbation that Sidney wrote 'London Education' for *The Nineteenth Century* in October 1903. His aim is to take stock of the present position in the nation's capital and to indicate the scope of work for the new education authority. He seeks to allay the fears of those who, following the example of 'the non-conformist revolt' elsewhere in the country, might wish to block the workings of the London Education Act by one means or another. Running through the entire article is a burning concern for his native city and a compassion for those we would call today the under-privileged. For all these reasons the article is reproduced in full.

The transformation effected in the course of three-quarters of a century in the manners and morals of the London manual working class is one of the most remarkable chapters of social history. Nothing but the unimpassioned revelations of the Blue-books, or the incidental references of contemporary newspapers to what they took as a matter of course, can give an adequate vision of the abominations that, within the memories of men still living, prevailed in all the working-class quarters —two-thirds of the whole child population growing up not only practically without schooling or religious influences of any kind, but also indescribably brutal and immoral; living amid the unthinkable filth of vilely overcrowded courts unprovided either with water supply or sanitary conveniences, existing always at the lowest level of physical health, and constantly decimated by disease; incessantly under temptation by the flaring gin-palaces which alone relieved the monotony of the mean streets and dark alleys to which they were doomed; graduating almost inevitably into vice and crime amid the now incredible street life of an unpoliced metropolis. It was with this problem, only partly alleviated in its gravity, that the educational reformers of 1860 and 1870 had to grapple. It is, in the main, out of this material that the present working-class population of London—taken, as a whole, perhaps the least turbulent, the least criminal, and the most assiduous in its industry of any of the world's great capitals—has been fashioned.

In this arrest of a nation's suicide, what influences have been most potent? We do not need to dwell upon the organisation of a preventive police, the elaboration of the sanitary code, and the ever-increasing regulation of the conditions of factory employment. But, potent as these remedial agencies have been, it is not by inhibition alone that men and women are rescued from deterioration. Hence the heroic efforts to establish church schools and chapel schools, night schools and ragged schools; and the gradual development of these by Government grants until more than a hundred and fifty thousand children were under their influence. Like all voluntary effort, this work was patchy, unorganised, and of very varying quality. It left, even at the period of its greatest development, two-thirds of the boys and girls outside its scope. Not until the establishment, under the Education Act, 1870, of the London School Board, was there any systematic attempt to rescue the whole of the children of London. Thus it is that to the School Board for London has fallen by far the largest share in the beneficent transformation. By the persistent efforts of its army of attendance officers it has, at last, got London's 800,000 children to school. The voluntary schools stand, numerically, almost precisely where they did in 1870. It is the School Board which has provided the buildings for the half a million additional scholars brought under the wonderful discipline of the public elementary school. These five hundred new public buildings, occupying 600 acres of valuable land, existing now in every one of London's fifty-eight electoral divisions, four to the square mile of the whole of London's surface, erected at a cost of fourteen millions sterling, constitute by far the greatest of our municipal assets. And improvement in quality has kept pace with increase in quantity. It is, in the main, to the School Board that London owes the transformation which has, in these thirty-three years, come over its elementary schools—the change from frowsy, dark, and insanitary rooms, practically destitute of apparatus or play-grounds, in which teachers, themselves mostly untrained, mechanically ground a minimum of the three R's required by the wooden old code into the heads of their scanty pupils, to the well-lighted and admirably decorated school buildings of the present day, with ample educational equipment, with pianos, school libraries, extensive playgrounds, etc., served by a staff of trained professional teachers, encouraged to develop the growing intelligence of their scholars in whatever subjects and by whatever educational methods they find best.

Yet great as was the stride taken by the establishment of the London School Board, the dominant idea was still merely the education of the poor; really, the rescue of children from the abyss. In the Government Code of 1860 the object was expressly limited to 'the education of children belonging to the classes who support themselves by manual labour', and as late as 1868 minute regulations were framed to admit the sons of policemen and porters, but to exclude from the public schools those of excisemen, clerks, and the humblest shopkeepers. The proceedings of 1870 were full of the same idea. It is refreshing to study the plucky audacity and persistence by which the London School Board, largely through the imperturbable zeal and ingenuity of Mr.

Lyulph (now Lord) Stanley,[122] has forged its way through Government red tape and the grumbling of Philistine ratepayers across all these social barriers to higher grade schools and advanced evening classes. For some years this audacity seemed to receive the sanction of the Education Department. Then came friction, resistance, and estrangement. In the end the courts were driven to decide that the legislators of 1870 had not authorised more than the elementary education of mere children. The limitation thus practically reimposed by the judges in 1900–1 was, as we now see, not due to any special perversity, but to the historical fact that English public education, unlike that of Scotland or Switzerland, had its origin in what I have termed rescue work.

Meanwhile the community had been approaching the problem from another standpoint. England experienced successive waves of uneasiness about the supposed lack of craftsmanship in the British workman, and the deficiency in technical knowledge of the foreman and superintendent. First, as usual, came voluntary effort—the early mechanics' classes, the technical colleges of the City Companies, Quintin Hogg and the polytechnics; presently to be magnified by the dramatic 'rolling up' of the City parochial charities under Mr. Bryce's Act. Then, at last, the London County Council, reluctantly taking up the duty put upon it by the Technical Instruction Acts, began to spend its 'whisky money'. Beginning where the legal powers of the School Board ended, the Council, through its Technical Education Board, has, during the last ten years, laid down the lines of a highly complex system of specialised education, partly in the dozen great polytechnics, partly in its own technical institutes and art schools, and culminating in the technical faculties of the reorganised University of London.

But, with all this, London was still without an authority competent to deal with education as a whole. Fifty years ago, Matthew Arnold, crying in the wilderness, pointed out the absurdity of confining collective action to this or that particular grade of education, or to any one section of the community. Imperceptibly public opinion gained a new point of view. The leaders of all the political parties unconsciously absorbed the idea that national efficiency depended on our making the most of the capacities of the whole population, which form, after all, as truly part of the national resources as our iron and coal. Indeed, as we now see with painful clearness, we have, in the long run, for the maintenance of our pre-eminent industrial position in the world, nothing to depend on except the brains of our people. Public education has, therefore, insensibly come to be regarded, not as a matter of philanthropy undertaken for the sake of the individual children benefited, but as a matter of national concern undertaken in the interest of the community as a whole. It is this notion which has, almost without the notice of the controversialists, been embodied in the Education Acts 1902–3. We no longer prescribe, as the sphere of the local education authority, 'elementary education', or 'technical education', or any other kind or grade of education. Thus the task of the new Education Authority for London is very different from that hitherto undertaken either by the School Board or the Technical Education Board. It is called upon to endow London with a complete educational system. To give to each of London's 800,000 children during the years of compulsory school attendance the most effective physical, moral, and intellectual training; to develop in them the utmost mental acquisitiveness; to arouse in as many as possible of them the indefinable quality that we call resourcefulness, initiative, inventiveness or the capacity for meeting new conditions by new devices; to provide for the whole of them the widest possible opportunities for continuing their studies after leaving the day school; to carry on, by a 'capacity-catching' scholarship system, all whose brains make it profitable for the community to equip them with more advanced instruction; to organise, as well for these scholarship-holders as for all others able to benefit by it, an efficient and duly varied system of secondary and university education, whether predominantly literary, scientific, artistic, commercial, technological, or professional in type; to provide the best possible training for teachers of every kind and grade; and so to organise the whole machine as, while increasing knowledge and efficiency, to promote everywhere the development of character and culture, and ultimately to encourage the highest scholarship and the most advanced research—all this, and nothing less than this, is the duty which Parliament has committed to the London County Council.

How much is yet accomplished towards that great task? To 'take stock' of London educationally seems to be the first need of the new Education Authority. It was the comprehensive survey of London's technical education, made for the County Council by Mr. Llewellyn Smith in 1892, which made possible the successful ten years' work of its Technical Education Board. A similarly comprehensive survey of London education as a whole, as it stands in 1903, would be of inestimable value to the new Education Committee. It is an inevitable characteristic of educational administration in so vast an area that those who are interested in it have seldom had personal experience of, or come closely into contact with, more than a small portion of the field. One member knows about elementary schools, another almost exclusively about secondary; one is interested in the teaching of science, and is quite unaware of the progress made in drawing or modern languages; others, again, have governed boys' schools, but have hardly an idea of what is required for infants or for girls, and may be only dimly aware of the technical college or the university. No complete or systematic description of the educational institutions of London at present exists.

To begin with the broad base of the public elementary school, such a survey would, I think, show that the great task committed to the School Board in 1870 has been at last accomplished; that, of the child population living in houses under £40 rental, practically all are now either on the rolls of schools recognised as 'efficient' or otherwise accounted for; and that, roughly speaking, there is a school place for every child. This does not mean that there need be no more building of schools, even if London's child population continues stationary, but that such buildings may, broadly speaking, henceforth be confined to coping with the shifting of the people from the centre to the suburbs, and to the necessary substitution, as time goes on, of new schools for old ones. At least a quarter of the present public elementary school buildings of London are old and insanitary, and will have to be rebuilt, if not by the foundation managers out of private subscriptions, then as 'provided schools' at the public expense.

Passing from the buildings to their inmates, it will be found that the children are, taken as a whole, more regular in their attendance than they have ever previously been, the average in 1902-3 being 85.6 per cent. This, however, is not satisfactory. If several dozen schools in London, some in poor districts, can maintain an average attendance of between 90 and 95 per cent; if all Leicester can achieve 88.7 per cent, and the whole of sparsely peopled Westmorland 89.3 per cent, London cannot remain content with only 85.6, which means that there are at all times over 120,000 children away from school. What is even more unsatisfactory is that a great part of the absences are made by the same 6 or 8 per cent of 'regular irregulars'—a body of perhaps 50,000 children who, by habitually missing half the possible attendances, escape most of the educational discipline of the school. Much has been done by the School Board of late years, largely at the instigation of Dr. Macnamara,[123] to look after these children, and various improvements are already in progress. More can be accomplished when the visitors are more closely associated with the teachers, with a view to promptly visiting every absentee, and when the voluntary schools, where the attendance is much below that of the board schools, are brought under the same central control.

Having got our children to school, the supremely important question remains: What is the quality of the education there given to them? On this point no materials exist for any confident answer. Since the abolition of the individual examination of the Government inspectors, no common measure has been applied to all the schools, and there is no statistical evidence to appeal to.[124] If, indeed, we confine our attention to the best hundred of the board schools, with their splendid new buildings, their unstinted equipment, their specialised departments, their completely trained staffs, and their energetic headmasters or headmistresses of the modern type, some complacency can be excused, for it may be doubted whether there is anything in the world equal to them.

Even if we survey the whole of the board schools, educating five-sevenths of the children, these may, with their high average of excellence of buildings and equipment, and their superiority in proportion of fully-trained teachers, safely challenge comparison, taken as a whole, with the schools of any other English town. But the difference in real educational quality between the best and worst London board school is pretty considerable, and it may be doubted whether anybody but the School Board's own inspectors knows how unsatisfactory the worst schools are, or what proportion the bad ones bear to the whole. Still greater divergencies exist among the 500 voluntary schools, which educate two-sevenths of the children. It would seem as if, speaking generally, the few Jewish schools, nearly all the Wesleyan and British schools, and the best score or so of the Church schools are of good average efficiency. But there is no resisting the inference that nearly all the hundred Roman Catholic schools, and probably 300 of the 331 Church schools—having, in the aggregate, more than 150,000 children —are, so far as secular education is concerned, calamitously behindhand. It is not merely that their buildings are inferior and antiquated, their equipment and furniture insufficient, and their teaching staffs inadequate and in too many cases inefficient. What is more serious is the extent to which these schools have fallen behind in educational ideas and methods; their inability to provide adequate instruction in the upper standards; and their comparative failure in such subjects as elementary science and drawing. No child in these 400 schools has any practical chance of winning a scholarship under any system of open competition, and is thus inevitably debarred, however gifted it may be, from access to higher education. Putting together what little is really known of all the thousand public elementary schools of London, including both board and voluntary, there are competent observers who declare that nearly half of them, containing about a quarter of all the children, would probably be condemned as inefficient, either in respect of buildings or sanitation, of staffing or equipment, of curriculum or real success in child-training, by a Swiss, a Danish, a Saxon, a Prussian, or a Massachusetts school inspector.

So grave a condemnation of the schools in which 200,000 London children are being educated—a greater number than the whole child-population of Manchester and Birmingham together—will come to most people, as it did to the present writer, with the shock of surprise. We must with all speed find out whether it is borne out by the facts. We simply cannot afford to leave 200,000 London children to this fate. At the same time we must take care to maintain, and even to multiply and improve, the excellent higher grade, higher elementary, and other superior schools which set the pace to the rest.

Any general levelling up of the London elementary schools will bring the County Council face to face with the most pressing of educational problems, the supply and training of teachers. The present practice of the School Board of appointing to its permanent service none but fully trained teachers will, of course, be adopted by the County Council for all the schools. But this will be to raise the number required by nearly one half, and to demand, for London alone, more than 40 per cent of the entire annual output of all the training colleges in England and Wales put together, and more than twice that of those situated in the London area. With the growing demand of the other counties and county boroughs, it is clear that London cannot possibly continue to get even as many as heretofore, let alone half as many again. There is already something approaching to a teacher famine. More than a hundred vacancies in the School Board's own staff remain month after month unfilled. It is only by each county training as many teachers as it needs (not in the least implying that each county should employ only those whom it has trained) that the total supply can be kept up. London, in fact, must somehow get established, primarily for its own supply, additional training college accommodation equal to an annual output of 500 teachers, chiefly women.

So far, no controversy arises among those acquainted with the needs; and we may confidently expect the London County Council to provide what is required. But there is as yet no agreement whether we should add to the number of residential training colleges, in which the future teachers are boarded, lodged, and instructed in a sort of 'seminary' fashion, or whether we should simply enlarge six- or eight-fold the existing 'Day Training College' established in connection with London University, in which the students live at home or in lodgings, and, whilst provided with special pedagogic training, obtain their academic instruction as ordinary students in the various university colleges. Strong arguments are urged in favour of both systems. The residential training college, when at its best, offers many advantages to the London boy or girl of eighteen, coming from an artisan or lower middle class home. The removal from the crowded household in a monotonous street, from the often narrow outlook of the family life, with somewhat restricted diet and scanty exercise, to an institution in the fresh air and generous space of the country, with a common table, and a collegiate life, with all its training in manners and discipline, under a regimen specially devised for healthy development of body and mind, inspired, we may add, by corporate traditions, and by the personal influence of a highly selected staff—all these circumstances have, in the past, made the two or three years at such colleges as that of the old 'Borough Road', at Isleworth, or for women at Stockwell, a veritable stride forward in health, conduct, and culture to the young men and women who were fortunate enough to gain admission to them. But there are drawbacks. The establishment of a dozen new Stockwells or Isleworths would mean a capital expenditure of half a million. Moreover, the segregation, for two or three years, of young men or young women, all of nearly the same social class and the same antecedent education, all bent on passing the same examinations and intending to follow the same occupation, all taught the same subjects by the same teachers—is not calculated to give either breadth of culture or knowledge of life. The alternative of a Day Training College, attached to a university, offers, it is said, at any rate to the abler and better educated of the pupil-teachers, a far more valuable training. The pupil-teachers entering, in London, University College or King's College, Bedford College or the School of Economics, as ordinary undergraduates, working for a degree in one of the faculties of the university, attending the lectures of men of distinction, and mixing, so far as university students in London mix at all one with another, with undergraduates of other antecedents, other faculties and other vocations in life, cannot fail to get a broader and more humane education than is possible at even the best seminary. The balance of advantage seems on the side of the university Day Training College. Its drawbacks are that only the ablest of our future teachers in elementary schools are at present sufficiently well educated to profit by the university curriculum; and that the pedagogic work which they necessarily have to add to that of the ordinary undergraduate makes it a severe strain upon them. And there is the practical difficulty of absorbing, in the existing university colleges of the metropolis, anything like so large a number as 1500 additional teacher-undergraduates. The inference seems to be that we must, in London, adopt both plans, making the best of each of them—on the one hand, enlarge as rapidly as possible the present excellent nucleus of a Day Training College, admitting both secondary and elementary school teachers, securing, in some way or another, the necessary corresponding enlargement or multiplication of the existing university colleges (especially getting one established in South London), and providing residential hostels for such students as need them; on the other hand, grasp eagerly at any opportunity of establishing in the country round London two or three new 'Stockwells' for those London girls who find themselves excluded from existing residential colleges because they are not members of the Anglican or Roman Catholic Church, and whose needs and circumstances make the university Day Training College unsuitable.

The provision of training colleges is, however, only half the problem. Between fourteen, the age of leaving the elementary school, and eighteen or nineteen, that of entering the training college, the future teachers have to be caught, broken in to teaching work, and given some sort of secondary education. Hitherto we have relied for this on the pupil-teacher system. This system, as it was, and as in many country districts it still continues to be, may fairly be denounced as a combination of child-labour and soul-destroying intellectual drudgery unworthy of a civilised nation. The boy or girl of thirteen, who a few weeks previously had been in the sixth standard, was often put straightway in charge of fifty or sixty younger urchins, whom he or she sometimes learnt to control and discipline, if not to teach, in a marvellous manner. At fourteen he or she would be regularly apprenticed to the teaching trade, receiving a few shillings a week, and being supposed to be instructed by the head-teacher. For the next four or five years the pupil-teachers would be slaving all day in the exhausting task of school-teaching, struggling with the large classes in the lower standards; and cramming up in the evening the woodenest of text-books with the scantiest of tutorial assistance, in order to pass the Government examinations on which depended their whole professional careers. It is difficult to imagine a more cruel and less enlightened way of preparing those who are to become the intellectual guides and inspirers of the masses. Fortunately, the whole system is in course of transformation, and the London School Board has long treated its pupil-teachers very differently. Yet notwithstanding all that is done for them, even in London the recruits fall short of the numbers required. To fill the annual vacancies among its assistant teachers, London needs, probably, 2000 new pupil-teachers a year, one-third boys and two-thirds girls, allowing for the percentage which drops out by the way. The School Board gets only about eight hundred and fifty and the voluntary schools perhaps half that number. With both the deficiency is greatest on the male side. The London boy has, in fact, nearly ceased to enter the teaching profession. In all London last year, with close upon five millions of people, the number of boys who became pupil-teachers in any kind of school did not reach two hundred.[125]

Instead of remedying this dearth of pupil-teachers, the Board of Education has just issued new regulations, which revolutionise the whole system. The pupil-teacher of fourteen or fifteen, as he exists to-day, is peremptorily abolished. The future teachers are henceforth to devote themselves exclusively to secondary education up to the age of, at least, sixteen; and their period of actual apprenticeship is limited to two years, which may begin as late as nearly eighteen years of age. The whole of the regulations point to an intention on the part of the Board of Education to make it impossible for the pupil-teacher of the future to be taken straight from the elementary school. However much we may welcome the spirit of this revolutionary change, it involves, even in London, and much more so elsewhere, some difficult readjustments. The present scarcity of pupil-teachers shows that the payment made to them between fourteen and eighteen cannot be reduced, and ought rather to be increased, especially for boys. The new Education Authority will therefore not only have to see that a sufficient number of efficient secondary schools are available for the appropriate instruction up to sixteen of all its future pupil-teachers. It will also have to pay them, in a new form, at least the equivalent of the wages which they have hitherto received up to that age, nominally in return for their services in the school. It looks as if the London County Council, merely in order to keep up the necessary supply of pupil-teachers, would find itself compelled to increase its junior county scholarships to 2000 a year, and to give two-thirds of the total number to girls, perhaps confining the last thousand to candidates who undertake to complete their pupil-teacher apprenticeship, and possibly modifying for such candidates its financial regulations.

The scholarship system which the Board of Education's new pupil-teacher regulations will thus revolutionise is one of the most successful developments of the past decade. Every year about eight hundred of the ablest boys and girls in the public elementary or lower secondary schools, between eleven and thirteen years of age, are picked by competitive examination for two to five years' higher education. These 2000 scholarships provide for the cleverest children of the London wage-earners a more genuinely accessible ladder than is open to the corresponding class in any American, French, or German city. In addition to these maintenance scholarships there are free places at most of the London secondary schools, from St Paul's downwards, which are utilised, as is found to be the case with all provision of merely gratuitous secondary education, by the 'lower-middle' and professional classes. Above these opportunities stand the intermediate and senior county scholarships, and others provided by various trust funds, probably altogether about six hundred in all, for candidates between fifteen and nineteen years of age. These serve partly to carry on the best of the junior scholars; partly to admit to the superior secondary schools the ablest children of parents ineligible for the lowest rung of the ladder; and partly to take the very pick of London's young people to the technical college and the university.

This scholarship scheme has now necessarily to be revised, to bring it into accord with the changes lately made in the school-leaving age and the pupil-teacher system. Practically all children now stay at school until fourteen, and it is no longer necessary for any substantial payment towards the maintenance of the poor scholar to begin before that age. On the other hand, there is a consensus of opinion that, when a child passes from an elementary to a secondary school, it should do so before the age of twelve, and should remain for not less than four years. It looks as if the limit of age for the normal junior scholarship should be reduced from thirteen to twelve, and its duration extended from two to four years, whilst the annual maintenance allowance up to the age of fourteen might be reduced to £5, rising to £10 and £15 in the last two years. And if the need for pupil-teachers causes the number of scholarships to rise to 2000 a year, it would perhaps be possible to effect the further desirable reform of beginning the selecting process by a preliminary examination, conducted by the head-teachers themselves, in their own schools, of all the children who had attained the fifth standard before the age of twelve; and of undertaking to award the scholarships, not to any fixed number of winners, but to all who, in the subsequent centralised competitive examination, reached a certain percentage of marks. Such a reform would organically connect the scholarship system with all the public elementary schools, instead of, as at present, only about a third of them; and would bring London's 'capacity-catching machine' to bear on every promising child.

There must, however, be an adequate supply of efficient secondary schools for these picked scholars to attend, not to mention the needs of those who can afford to keep their boys and girls at school until seventeen or nineteen. There is a common impression that the public secondary schools of London are few and inefficient. Yet, including only foundations of which the management is essentially public in character, London has to-day certainly not less than 25,000 boys and girls between seven and nineteen in its secondary schools, actually a larger number than either Paris or Berlin. In the background, and not included in this calculation, stand, in varying quality, the private 'commercial academies' and 'colleges for young ladies' of the genteel suburbs. To these is left the opportunity of justifying their existence by catering for special needs, and supplying a desirable elasticity to the necessary rigidity of any public system. The publicly managed schools number no fewer than eighty-five, well dispersed over the whole county, ranging from those like Parmiter's School (Bethnal Green) and Addey's School (Deptford), where the age at leaving is never more than seventeen, through the dozen admirable institutions of the essentially public Girls' Public Day School Company, up to such thoroughly efficient 'first-grade' schools as the North London Collegiate, for girls (St Pancras), and Dulwich College (Camberwell) and St Paul's (Hammersmith) for boys, which take rank among the very best that England contains. Yet so dense is London that, with one or two exceptions, the very existence of these schools is forgotten by the ordinary citizen, and is often ignored by the legislator or administrator. Many a middle-class family which could well afford to send its boys and girls to secondary schools is unfamiliar with those which exist within a mile of its home. Even to the best-informed educational administrators the real state and quality of the London secondary schools, taken as a whole, are far less accurately known than those of the elementary. All the information points to the conclusion that the efficiency varies immensely from school to school; that nearly all of them have good buildings, mostly well provided with science laboratories and suitable equipment; and that, where any school falls below the mark, the weak point is the staffing. In at least a third of the London secondary schools the income from fees and endowment is insufficient to provide more than one good salary, which goes to the head-teacher, whilst the assistants, who ought to be university gradu-ates, are paid, for the most part, less than is earned by an ordinary certificated teacher in a board school. Yet, even recognising all the shortcomings of these schools, the department of secondary education is not one which will give the London County Council any serious trouble. About half of the publicly managed schools are sufficiently well off to be independent of its aid, and these, nearly always charging high fees, and providing an education of high grade, may be left to themselves. The other half, including practically all those in need of help, have already shown by their cordial co-operation with the Technical Education Board their willingness to fall into line. It would, of course, be un-necessary to disturb the present governing bodies, on which the local authorities are already well represented, and it would be unwise for the Council to interfere in the details of administration. In no department is it so important to maintain variety and independent experiment as in the secondary schools. The policy should be one of very strenuous organising, supervising, criticising, subsidising, and advertising. What needs to be insisted on is that every secondary school should attain a high level of efficiency in its own particular line; that the quality of the work should be systematically tested by thorough public inspection, if not also by the new 'school-leaving' form of the London matriculation; that any short-comings in buildings, equipment, and curriculum should be promptly made good, and that, in particular, the science, drawing, and modern languages should be specially attended to; that accommo-dation be found, either by enlargements or by the establishment of new schools, for the necessary addition to the number of scholarship holders;

and, it may be hoped, also for the growing number of ordinary pupils; and above all that an adequate scale of qualifications and progressive salaries be adopted for the teaching staff, so that all future vacancies may be filled by the appointment of men or women of education and professional training, whose remuneration and prospects will be such as to secure stability and continuity of work.

But construct what scholarship ladder we will, the secondary schools can be used only by a small fraction of the population. For the secondary education of the masses there has been organised, by the School Board on the one hand, and the London County Council on the other, an extensive assortment of evening classes; providing instruction in every imaginable subject of literature, science, art, and technology. The classes of the School Board, which enrol over 130,000 students for the winter session and have an average attendance of half that number, are conducted in 400 of its day-school buildings, mainly by the younger and more energetic of its staff of day teachers. The work of the Technical Education Board, dealing usually with a more advanced stage and older scholars, is concentrated in the fifty polytechnics, art schools, and technical institutes under its management or control, which have in the aggregate about 50,000 students. Here the lecturers and teachers are specialists in their respective subjects, teaching in institutions specially equipped for their work. At six of the polytechnics, the highest classes have been included in the faculties of the reorganised London University, and duly matriculated evening students obtain first-class university instruction in their own neighbourhood, and are enrolled as 'internal students' of the university itself. These two schemes of evening instruction have now to be co-ordinated, differentiated, and developed. There can be no question of stopping either one or the other; on the contrary, both sides of the work will have to be increased. It ought not to be too much to ask that every boy or girl who leaves school at fourteen or fifteen should, up to twenty-one, be at any rate enrolled at some evening-class institution, even if attendance is confined to an hour a week. Yet there are in London over 600,000 young people between fourteen and twenty-one, and not a third of these are at present members of any sort of institution, recreational or educational. Out of 84,000 boys and girls between fifteen and sixteen, only 21,000 are on the rolls. What is happening to the others? We cannot, as yet, compel them to come in, as the Bishop of Hereford proposes, though this is done in various parts of Germany and Switzerland. But we might try the experiment of using the school attendance officers to look after those who have not joined an evening school, using the method of persuasion, just as they look after the younger defaulters from the day school. This, of course, means a large addition to the present staff. Meanwhile we could bring the whole of the evening instruction in each borough into a single harmonious organisation; we could allocate the work in such a way as to provide appropriately for each age and each grade, and avoid overlapping; we could take care that each subject is taught under the most effective conditions, and properly co-ordinated with more advanced instruction elsewhere; and we could arrange for the progression of the students from stage to stage, until they reach the highest classes of the nearest polytechnic, or the technical college itself.

Finally, we reach, as the crown of the whole educational system, the newly reorganised University of London, with its 600 professors in eight different faculties, its twenty-five constituent colleges, and its score or more of other affiliated institutions, several of which are more important than some of the colleges, its 3000 'internal'undergraduates, and its still larger army of unmatriculated students attending university courses, constituting already the nucleus—especially in medicine, science, technology, and economics—of a centre of academic teaching and research not unworthy of the great city that it serves. What is important in the present survey is the closeness with which the university has already connected itself with all the other branches of educational work. By its inspection of schools and its new 'school-leaving' matriculation examination, it stretches down its roots to the secondary schools, from which it is attracting a steadily increasing number of undergraduates. By the bold opening of many of the ordinary courses to the evening student, it has—though at the sacrifice of the professors' dining engagements!—put itself in touch with a new crowd of able and eager students. By its inclusion of the ablest professors and the highest classes of the several polytechnics, it has begun that de-centralisation of undergraduate teaching and that local provision of university instruction which so huge a province as London requires. Alike in respect of the training of teachers and the adequate development of the scholarship system, it has made itself indispensable to the elementary schools. It is a tribute to the far-sighted statesmanship of those who drafted the scheme of reorganisation, and also to the prudent catholicity which has marked its present administration, that the University of London, only five years ago an isolated examining board without professors, students, colleges, or local connections of any kind, forms to-day an integral part of the London educational system. This connection is evidently destined to continue, and to become even more intimate. The urgent need for an extensive enlargement of the Day Training College, and the improvement in the education of pupil-teachers, will bring to the doors of the existing university colleges hundreds of additional young men and women, for whose academic training between eighteen and twenty-one the local education authority will have to provide. The development of the scholarship system will add another contingent, whom it will not be profitable to have to send to Germany, to seek the instruction in chemical technology or specialised engineering which is lacking in London. The need for considerable developments in the provision of more specialised science and technology, to say nothing of modern languages and economics, is, indeed, too patent to require argument. The grant of £10,000 a year made by the London County Council towards such part of the university work as falls within the statutory definition of technical education, and the recent conditional undertaking of the Council to contribute £20,000 a year to the projected new College of Technology, warrant us in assuming that, with the wider powers conferred by the Act of 1903, the municipal authorities of London, like those of Liverpool and Manchester, Birmingham and Glasgow, will not be unappreciative either of the requirements of their local university or of its place in the systematic organisation of London's education.

This rapid sketch of the most prominent facts and problems of London education will have seemed to some to omit the most pressing and the most important of them all. Some such readers may have looked for a discussion of the relative merits of a controlling body elected *ad hoc*, and the common municipal authority of the county, whilst to others the all-engrossing issue will have been the relation between denominational teaching and the public purse. It is my personal opinion that the Acts of 1902–3 require amendment at many points. But it is the simple fact that none of these hotly debated political questions traverses the actual work of educational administration. Neither the political nor the religious difficulty is met with in the schools themselves. Thus, if people feel strongly on these issues, it is as legislators and electors, not as educational administrators, that they must decide them.

With regard to the first of these controversies, as to whether the London Education Authority should be the County Council or a body elected *ad hoc*, not much need be said. The attitude of the educationist will be that of real mother at the judgment of Solomon—so long as the babe remains whole it is of secondary importance which body takes charge of it. What is vital is that there should be no more delay. The interregnum is paralysing the daily administrative work. Now that Parliament has decided, the sooner the new Education Committee grapples with its great task, and makes the necessary reorganisation of the administrative machinery—a subject which would demand an article for itself—the better it will be for London's children. Whatever alteration is required in the constitution of the County Council itself can best be obtained when experience of the new work has been gained.

When we come to the religious question, the first impression of the practical administrator is that grave indeed is the responsibility of those who seek to disturb the *status quo*. From this standpoint it is a merit of the Acts of 1902–3 that, *so far as religious teaching is concerned*, they simply maintain the existing arrangements. They make no change whatever, and they require no change, in the religious instruction given in any London school. In the 498 board schools educating 71 per cent of all the children, there will go on the same 'undenominational Christianity', according to the widely accepted syllabus of the 'Compromise of 1871', which the County Council will certainly not dream of disturbing. In the 331 Anglican schools, with their 21 per cent of the children, the Church Catechism and the Book of Common Prayer will continue to be taught. The 100 Roman Catholic schools will go on providing their 4 per cent with the doctrines of their own Church. The 15 Wesleyan schools and the 7 schools of the British and Foreign School Society, with their 1 per cent of the scholars, will persist in giving exactly the religious instruction they prefer. The 9 large Jewish schools, with about the same proportion of the total, will inculcate their own faith and observe their own festivals. Exactly the same continuity is preserved to them all, and to any secularist or nondescript school. Whether this freedom in diversity represents an ideal arrangement or not, it has the great merit of existing; of having worked smoothly and well for a whole generation; and of exciting practically no objection among the children, the parents, the teachers, or, in fact, anyone actually connected with the working of the schools.

This diversity in schools involves, as every practical educationist knows, some segregation of teachers according to their views on the deepest problems of ethics and theology. It is easy for those who do not

face the problem to earn the cheap applause of the unthinking by de-
nouncing all religious tests. As a matter of fact, in the London board
school of to-day, the teachers are appointed to give religious instruction
on a syllabus involving the existence of a Personal Deity, the Divinity
of Christ, the Incarnation, the Resurrection, Heaven (if not also Hell),
and other highly controversial theological dogmas, in which many
persons in the teaching profession do not believe. Even the Bible cannot
be read as the Word of God without offending some consciences. In
one or two London board schools, by a convenient evasion to which no
one objects, the creed expounded is not that of Christianity at all; the
Gospels are implicitly put on a level with the Koran; and Jewish
teachers are deliberately selected in order that they may expound the
Jewish Bible to Jewish children, for whose convenience the whole
school is closed on the Jewish festivals. It is plain that in Roman Catholic, Anglican, and Wesleyan schools there is, for the most part, a similar
selection. This inevitable segregation of teachers, or, as some persons
choose to call it, this use of a religious test, is neither established nor
increased by the Acts of 1902–3. There ought to be no exclusions, either
by law or trust-deed. To put any such invidious distinctions on record
is inconsistent with the spirit of what is essentially a public service. But
as a mere matter of administrative practice, whenever we have Roman
Catholic or Protestant or Jewish children segregated in groups, it is
convenient to have each group taught, at any rate as far as some of the
staff of each school are concerned, by teachers of its own faith. It
cannot surely be suggested that men and women should be required,
or even encouraged, to give ethical or religious instruction in which they
disbelieve, that they should day after day stand before their pupils and
inculcate the supreme duty of veracity, with a more or less carefully
hidden lie on their lips. Nor is this position created by the existence of
schools connected with different ethical and religious systems. If we
made all schools 'undenominational', or even 'secular', and imposed one
particular form of moral instruction on all of them alike, we should
necessarily have to couch this in some phraseology of scientific, metaphysical, or theological exposition of the order of the universe; and by
any such uniformity, inevitably by implication either theistic or agnos-
tic, we should be erecting a far more restrictive test than is involved by
the present diversity. We should, in fact, in that case exclude, not from
this or that school only, but from the whole teaching profession, all
those who could not conscientiously swallow either the positive or the

negative implications of the one official formula for the time being. The diversity of creed of the parents and the children being accompanied by an equal diversity of creed among those who wish to be teachers, the actually existing diversity of schools involves, as a matter of fact, the minimum of exclusion on account of ethical views or religious beliefs, and thus makes the teaching profession compatible with the widest practicable variety of opinions.

What the Acts of 1902–3 do, as regards the voluntary schools, is neither to create nor to alter the existing diversity, nor yet to establish any new test, but, in consideration of the provision of the sites and buildings free of cost to the public, to make the salaries of the teachers and the current expenses of education independent of the charitable subscriber, and to charge these expenses to the public purse. Whether or not this is financially a good bargain for either party to it we need not now discuss. Educationally, as Dr Macnamara has consistently pointed out, it is pure gain. We cannot afford to go on trusting the educational efficiency of 218,000 London children to the whims and vagaries of individual charity. Nor need the ratepayer shrink from the burden. It so happens that the London County Council will make an actual profit by the transaction. The whole annual cost of the voluntary schools hitherto borne by subscriptions is only about £82,000 per annum, whereas the net increase in the total Government grant to London, which becomes payable only when they are taken over, is no less than £190,000 per annum. The financing of the voluntary schools and the substitution of the County Council for the School Board as the education authority, ought to mean therefore, not an increase, but a reduction of the rate by a halfpenny in the pound. It is true that to bring up to the same educational level as the best 100 board schools the 25 per cent of London's schooling which is now below the mark will require a gradual increase of expenditure during the next few years. It is, however, to be noted that the whole of this increase will be spent on the secular education, not on the religious instruction; that it will be required alike in the defective board schools and the defective voluntary schools; and that it will be spent in all cases directly by the London County Council, and as that body, not the managers, may choose.

There are those who advise the electors to refuse to the voluntary schools any support from the rates; and who are willing to see them close their doors if their present subscribers will not keep them efficient. Whether or not this would be fair, it would at any rate be ruinous to the

London ratepayer. The present 472 Anglican, Roman Catholic, Wesleyan, British, and Jewish schools stand on 150 acres of London land, nearly all freehold worth on the lowest computation, as land alone, something like £2,000,000. Their buildings, though often defective, are actually serving over 200,000 children, and they have to be rebuilt, whenever rebuilding is necessary, at the private subscribers' expense. We cannot arbitrarily take away from their present legal owners these sites and buildings, worth a rental of at least £150,000 a year, which the Act places gratuitously at our disposal. To discard them, relegating them to use as Sunday schools and Bible classes (which would in most cases satisfy their trust-deeds), and to build board schools for 200,000 more children, would cost the London ratepayers over £5,000,000.

There are some who imagine that the powers of control over the voluntary schools which the new Acts give to the London County Council are incomplete and inadequate. If this proves to be the case, they will very soon be strengthened. The managers will not find that they have much power. My own impression, based on some knowledge of the Council, is that this body knows how to make effective any control which is entrusted to it. What with its absolute authority over secular education, and its unique opportunities of training teachers and pupil-teachers; what with its fixing the qualifications and salaries of every grade of teachers in every school, and the annual increments of salary, which it can give or withold at its will; what with its carefully considered confirmation of every teacher's appointment, and its putting them all as its own officers on its own salary lists; what with the opportunities of evening employment which it has to offer to them, and the unparalleled field for promotion which it controls; what with its supply of approved books and apparatus from its own central store, and the teaching of special subjects by its own peripatetic instructors; what with its extensive staff of school inspectors, on whose reports the teachers' increments of salary will depend, and its no less influential staff of dilapidation surveyors, with whose requirements the foundation managers will have to comply, I shall be surprised if the London County Council finds any administrative difficulty in getting all the power it desires. Does anyone imagine that any of the Churches, however potent in its own sphere, is going to be able to 'draw out Leviathan with an hook' or 'bore his jaw through with a thorn'?

These objections to the Acts of 1902–3 are, as is now plain, not the serious point of the attack. In the end the person with whom we stand face to face is the conscientious objector. To propose to give under public auspices any sort of ethical or religious instruction which earnest men and women deem erroneous, is, in 1903, as in 1843 and 1870, to stir up a storm of passionate conviction. Against the full force of this conviction, electoral or financial considerations, the efficiency of the physical and mental training given to the children, or even the continuance of any publicly organised and subsidised education system at all, are as dust before the whirlwind. To the fervent Protestant it is an infamy that the Government should seem to support the teaching of Roman Catholicism. The earnest Free Church minister is wounded in his soul at any public countenancing of the errors of Anglicanism. To the conscientious Roman Catholic, mere participation in the indiscriminate reading and discussion of the Bible which goes on in all Protestant schools is to incur the damnable guilt of heresy, whilst the ordinary school history-book, with its Protestant version of the Reformation, is a blasphemy. To many a devout Anglican, incredible as it seems to his Nonconformist brethren, the 'undenominationalism' of the board schools is an evil monstrosity of the most pernicious tendency. The exclusion of every shred of religion, which the Comtist and the Secularist would prefer—the turning of God and the Bible out of all the public schools of the land—is vehemently objected to by everyone else. It is in vain that you point out that, as each denomination pays its own share of rates and taxes, each may be regarded as, in effect, paying only for the particular schools which do not offend its conscience. Those of us who have been brought up to regard all truth as relative to the person who believes it are apt altogether to underrate the horror and offence given to many an earnest soul by the very notion of deliberately 'subsidising error.'

To the problem thus raised I know of no solution. It is not enough to answer, as does the practical man, that the State, with all its thousand working compromises, must somehow go on. To all who feel deeply on such questions there comes a solemn parting of the ways—a point at which, at whatever hazard of personal or class or party interests, they resolutely refuse to participate in sin or to co-operate in bringing about a disastrous calamity to the community. The dilemma we are in is that the possession of conscientious feelings of this kind is no monopoly. It is not even confined to the conflicting bands of religionists. We must honour the motives of these idealists, and admit their several rights to struggle one against another in the Parliamentary arena for the triumph of what they respectively think of supreme importance. But they, in their turn, must recognise the existence of equally conscientious idealists, who will fight quite as hard for that on which, as it seems to them, the salvation of the nation depends. There are whole ranges of human thought and feeling, whole regions of our life in this world, indispensable to any education that is worthy of the name, which we cannot deal with in our schools without candidly accepting the principle that the State, if it is to educate at all, not only may, but frankly must, 'subsidise error'; that is to say, must accept as the basis and vehicle of its instruction that which some or other of its members deem to be error. Above all we must not allow these disputes to interfere with the current administration. There are fervent educationists to whom the point of conscience comes in the reflection that, whilst the various other conscientious objectors are disputing as to *how they would like to alter the existing status quo in the schools,* there are 800,000 London children waiting to be taught. To these particular conscientious objectors, who will make a stand for their faith, the supremely important thing is not whether this or that ethical or theological form shall be used as the medium of instruction, but that these 800,000 children shall not be denied the mental, moral, and physical training that we all agree must be given to them, up to whatever standard London can afford; that in all this great city, from this time forth, there shall grow up no human soul in the blindness of ignorance; that henceforth no spark of genius shall for lack of opportunity be lost to the world; and that, whatever fate may be in store for the British Empire, London, at any rate, in bringing its whole population up to the highest practicable efficiency, this day shall do its duty.

IV Secondary Education

Not until the period of self-criticism that followed its 1951 electoral defeat did the Labour Party officially adopt the implementation of comprehensive schooling as a major plank in its educational policy. Imprisoned within their historical context, students nowadays find it difficult to sympathise with those early twentieth-century socialists who were prepared to justify the rejection of the common school on the grounds that a variety of secondary school provision was more directly relevant to Britain's needs. Written in 1908 as a contribution to Henry Bryan Binns' *A Century of Education*, Sidney Webb's chapter on 'Secondary Education' is a supreme vindication of the good sense in developing different sorts of secondary schools to meet the demands of the day.

For Webb there is little merit in the American common school; on the contrary, the English system is the more justly 'democratic'. He is not ashamed to use the word in connection with such a differentiated system and goes so far as to regard the 'democratisation of the secondary school' as 'the essential function and social justification of that scholarship system'. There is no hint of apology here for the system being second-best. Webb's objections to a society divided on lines of class were not that it lacked cohesion, nor that it distributed its rewards unfairly, but quite simply because it was inefficient. A hierarchical system of selective secondary education would provide the best means to put things right.[126]

Sidney's position has been justified by some in view of the prevailing scarcity of resources. In 1902 secondary education had only just won its place in the national system. It would be a long time before there would be enough new schools on the ground. Until then, selection on the basis of merit would have to be the order of the day. It must also be said that Webb, cast as he was in a supremely English revolutionary mould, may in 1908 have visualised, with the growth of educational provision, the eventual passing away of this differentiated system. In 'Secondary Education' he does in fact refer to the disappearance of the Taunton third-grade schools as a result of the changing scope of elementary education. It is interesting to reflect whether he saw a similarly changing social situation causing a merging at some time in the future of the second- and first-grade schools. This however must remain a matter of pure speculation. What emerges unequivocally from this writing is a belief in the superiority of the system of secondary education prevailing at the time.

To the French Revolution, and to Condorcet in particular, England, amid much else, owes a certain equivocal terminology in educational organisation. In 1792 Condorcet was the reporter of a committee on public education, which sent up to the Convention a remarkable draft bill. Every village of 400 inhabitants was to have its 'école primaire', or elementary school, attendance at which was to be compulsory. At the other end of the scale there were to be, dispersed throughout the whole of France, nine university colleges and more than a hundred 'institutes'. Intermediate between these upper and lower grades, each Department was to provide one or more 'écoles secondaires', or secondary schools, this being the first occasion, so far as I am aware, on which that term was used. The particular bill thus influentially proposed never became law, though the Convention presently decreed the universal establishment (on paper) of primary schools and the compulsory attendance of children over eight. Condorcet's comprehensive plan for a graded educational hierarchy from the elementary school to the university, though destined almost immediately to influence educational organisation in France, and partly carried out by Bonaparte in 1802, apparently failed to inspire either Bentham or Whitbread, William Allen or Henry Brougham, so far as England was concerned. But what it eventually did for England was to give us a terminology of schools. This terminology dominated educational literature in France even during the Revolution; and, from about the middle of the nineteenth century, more and more submerging the ancient terminology of 'writing school' and 'Latin school' and 'grammar school', also that of our own country. We owe to Matthew Arnold, and to the Schools Inquiry Commission of 1864–68, the popularisation in England of the phrase Secondary Education, if not indeed, as an organised system, Secondary Education itself. But during the past generation the phrase has undergone a certain shifting of denotation. To Matthew Arnold, as to Condorcet, the secondary school included the school for children who intended to leave at fourteen, but did not include that of the youths who stayed until nineteen, who would be in the projected 'institutes' of 1792, and in the classical and commercial 'high' schools that Matthew Arnold desired. To-day we include in elementary education whatever can be provided for, and made accessible to, all the children of the population; whatever schooling can be effectually placed at the disposal of every boy or girl, irrespective of the affluence of the parent or of any exceptional talent or idiosyncrasy of the child. And the amount, the variety, and the duration of this elementary education is always rising. To-day the primary, or elementary, school has stretched its bounds from twelve or thirteen right up to fifteen and even, by statute, to the end of the school year in which the scholar reaches fifteen. Including as it may every subject of instruction that can possibly be dealt with in those years, it is in process of absorbing or superseding the province of what the Schools Inquiry Commission called the third or lowest grade of secondary school. On the other hand, the 'high school', classical or commercial, now definitely takes rank among secondary schools, of which it forms the first grade; and mechanical and even technological instruction is no longer excluded from its curriculum. By secondary education today we mean all the schooling, whether literary or scientific, artistic or technological, at whatever tender age it begins, which is arranged so as to continue up to a greater age than that of the elementary school; it is therefore a specially prolonged education organised for those boys and girls who are, on one ground or another, selected for this exceptional school training; it provides a richer and more elaborate cultivation of the faculties than the community can yet afford to extend to all its youth, or, indeed, yet knows how to adapt to all its intelligences, and one which accordingly comprises everything between the province of the elementary school and that of the university.

The most important item in any survey of secondary education in England and Wales in 1908 is not this or that arid parade of statistics, but the fact that secondary education has at last won its place in the national system. It is, so to speak, only the other day, and almost unawares, that we have come to admit that the secondary school has any necessary place in a national system of education. In spite of the really great achievements of the fourteenth and fifteenth centuries in providing grammar schools, all idea of secondary education, as anything but the luxury of the rich, seems to have been absent from the minds of the English reformers of the beginning of the nineteenth century. This slowness—and even a certain distinct reluctance—to accept the secondary school as a part of the national system is not altogether to be explained by the educational backwardness of England, or by the mountains of obstruction and difficulty which had to be got over by the nineteenth-century pioneers of national education. Unlike that of France or that of Scotland, the public educational system of England owes its real origin, not to any conscious appreciation of the function of the school among the institutions of the nation, but to what we may call philanthropic rescue work, in which the British and Foreign School Society has played so important a part. To William Allen and Joseph Lancaster, to Samuel Whitbread and Henry Brougham, what appeared so terrible was not the failure to utilise the most valuable of our national assets, the intellect of the race, but the fact that the children of the poor were growing up, by hundreds of thousands, untaught, undisciplined, and uncivilised, graduating, almost inevitably, in vice and crime. This led, not to national education in any real sense, but only to a movement for the universal provision of primary schools. Even so 'advanced' a thinker as Francis Place seems to have no other vision than an elementary school in every parish. To the 'Early Victorian' democratic reformers there came presently, from misapprehended descriptions of New England, the ideal of the 'common school', or school common to all social classes, in comparison with which the secondary school seemed merely a product of snobbishness and class distinctions. Right down to the end of the nineteenth century, we may detect, at the back of most of the educational demands of politicians of 'advanced' opinions, traces of the notion that what it behoved the public to provide, throughout the length and breadth of the land, was a sufficient number of schools of one and the same type, preferably the best possible type, freed from all fettering limitations of age, or curriculum, or expense; so that for every five or six hundred families there should be such a rate-supported educational institution, in which all the boys or girls of the locality—some said all the boys *and* girls—should sit side by side receiving the same education, whatever their particular needs, whatever their social position, whatever their religion, whatever the probable length of their school life, or whatever the occupation for which they were destined. Anything other than this glorified 'common school' was regarded merely as the private luxury of the rich. Upon this conception, which still crops out in the minutes of Treasury clerks, and even in the phrases of members of the late school boards, the ideal 'national system of education' consisted, as has been said, of nothing more than a sufficiently numerous supply of 'the best possible board schools—and Eton!'

What we have learnt, gradually and slowly, is that nothing worthy of the name of a national system of education can be built up out of schools of a single undifferentiated type, however numerous and however excellent they may be. The aspiration after 'common schools', in the sense of schools which should be effectually open to the poorest children, and should be used, without thought of class distinction, by children of different social positions, was and is an aspiration based on sound considerations, and one to be promoted in all possible ways. But 'common schools', in this sense, do not necessarily mean schools of a single, uniform, undifferentiated type—still less only elementary schools. In truth, the notion was part of the 'Early Victorian' habit, alluded to by Mr. H. G. Wells, of regarding as 'democratic' nothing which could not be provided for the entire community in a 'wholesale' way. But so infinitely varied is our individuality that, in matters of social provision as in tailoring, the wholesale supply, when we come more narrowly to scrutinise it, can be nothing better than a series of misfits. When a population is educationally as naked as was that of England half a century ago, it is socially so urgent to supply every one with some sort of outfit that accuracy of adjustment is of subordinate importance. The educational reformers of the middle of the nineteenth century were therefore right to insist on the provision of schools by wholesale. When, by the end of the nineteenth century, practically all our children were at school, the time was ripe for a further advance—for the provision of more accurately fitting educational garments. What was needed was, in all populous centres, the progressive differentiation of the publicly provided school—the 'common school' of our Radical grandfathers— into a number of specialised schools each more accurately fitting the needs of a particular section of children. 'The first requisite in organising education', reported the Schools Inquiry Commissioners as long ago as

1868, 'is to assign definite functions to the schools, so as to prevent all trying to answer every purpose, and thereby few succeeding in answering any'. Thus, a local education authority such as that of London is already providing, not only boys' schools, and girls' schools, and infants' schools, but, for each sex, three or four different kinds of higher elementary schools and schools for the feeble-minded; day schools and boarding schools; blind schools and deaf schools; schools for the crippled and 'open air' schools for the phthisical and anæmic; 'ringworm schools' and 'favus schools'; truant schools and industrial schools; domestic economy schools and a dozen varieties of 'trade school'; and, among all the other specialisations, not only one but three or four different types of secondary school. The duty of the nineteenth century in education was merely to supply enough schools for all the children, and to get the children into them. The twentieth century recognises that its task is the more complicated one of providing every part of the country with the highly differentiated educational organisation necessary to ensure to every child *the particular kind* of schooling that it needs. 'Without system, and concert, and thought', said Matthew Arnold, 'it cannot be attained.' This, at last, has now been recognised. And thus, by the Acts of 1902–3 and 1907—probably building better than we knew—we have not only placed every part of England and Wales in charge of a local education authority, but we have also made it the express duty of that authority to provide for all the people of its area, without limit of age or sex or class or fortune, without restriction in subject matter or cost, not elementary education alone, or technical education, but whatever kinds of education they may severally be deemed to require.

It is just because the task is not merely, or even mainly, to multiply schools, and roll up imposing statistical aggregates of children rescued from the streets, but the elaborate organisation, and the progressive specialisation, of a varied educational system for each locality, and the more and more precise adjustment of that system to the needs of the children of the particular locality, that the institution of a local education authority charged with the work is the paramount subject for congratulation. From the Act of 1802, for the protection of parish apprentices, to the Act of 1902, for the creation of an education authority in every part of England and Wales, what a stride! Those to whom nothing is significant but statistics may prefer to recite the new and additional secondary schools already provided since 1902 in nearly every county; or the really significant fact that, in spite of the continued isolation of the hundred or more so-called 'public schools', and of their 400 remarkable feeders, the private adventure preparatory schools of the wealthier boys,[127] there are in 1908 nearly 800 secondary schools actually at work under the Board of Education's regulations, inspection, and grants, with nearly 120,000 pupils, and a scholarship system in full working order which far exceeds in effectiveness and scope the corresponding provision of any other country. But in truth, though we have everywhere secondary schools and pupils in rapidly growing numbers, these schools are still so varied in form of organisation and many of them still so isolated in their independence that we have, as yet, no comprehensive statistics of secondary education as a whole. It is more instructive to notice the conception that our local education authorities are forming of the great task of educational adjustment that they have, notwithstanding the characteristic English disclaimers and complaints of the cost, really so eagerly and so cordially undertaken.

Confining ourselves to that part of the differentiation and specialisation of the 'common school' that concerns secondary education, we may note first the very general disappearance of the somewhat crude conception of a differentiation by the subjects taught. We realise now that there are no subjects which are 'elementary' and none which are 'secondary'. There is no subject from which an elementary school is debarred; none which in a secondary school must be tabooed. Nor is the distinction simply one of age. Our local education authorities know now that they cannot grade schools so that all the children under twelve or thirteen shall be found in the elementary schools; all those between twelve and fourteen in the higher grade schools; whilst the secondary schools would contain none but those between thirteen or fourteen and nineteen. In truth, there are no more any special entering ages for elementary and secondary schools respectively than there are special subjects. 'Too few pupils', deplores the Education Committee of the West Riding County Council, 'as yet enter the secondary school *at an early age.*' Up and down the country the local education authorities really seem at last to have incorporated what the Report of the Schools Inquiry Commission ought to have taught us forty years ago, namely, that the differential gradation of schools must depend, primarily, not on the entrance age of the pupil, but on the anticipated length of his school life.

Viewed in this light [said the Schools Inquiry Commissioners in 1868] education . . . can, at present, be classified as that which is to stop at about fourteen, that which is to stop at about sixteen, and that which is to continue till eighteen or nineteen; and for convenience we shall call these the third, the second, and the first grade of education respectively. The difference in the time assigned makes some difference in the very nature of the education itself; if a boy cannot remain at school beyond the age of fourteen, it is useless to begin teaching him such subjects as require a longer time for their proper study; if he can continue till eighteen or nineteen, it may be expedient to postpone some studies that would otherwise be commenced early. Both the substance and the arrangement of the instruction will thus greatly depend on the length of time that can be devoted to it.

Forty years' progress since the date of that report has, we may almost say, in London and other advanced educational centres, already eliminated the elementary school as it was understood in 1868. What the Schools Inquiry Commissioners had, perforce, to regard as a separate class, for whom nothing more elaborate could be provided than elementary education as then understood—namely, those who would leave school at twelve or thirteen—has practically ceased to exist in the Metropolis, and may, we hope, soon be everywhere ignored. Schooling up to fourteen at least we must now assume to provide for every child. Hence, instead of three grades of secondary schools, local education authorities find that they need to recognise to-day only two, namely, those in which a fair proportion of the pupils, however young may be their age at entrance, may be expected to remain until eighteen or nineteen (first grade secondary schools); and those in which the pupils, also whatever the entrance age, may be assumed to be intending to leave school at sixteen or seventeen (second grade secondary schools). 'It is obvious', said the Schools Inquiry Commissioners of 1868, 'that these distinctions correspond roughly, but by no means exactly, to the gradations of society. Those who can afford to pay more for their children's education will also, as a general rule, continue that education for a longer period.' It is a happiness to record the fact that this division by degrees of gentility no longer holds the field. Any such correspondence between first and second grade secondary schools, respectively, and what may be termed first and second grade social position is happily diminishing. What with scholarships and free places, what with the attendance of pupil-teachers at first grade secondary schools and the new grade of bursars, there is coming to be, in many districts of England, little difference in average social position between the pupils of a first grade and those of a second grade secondary school as such; although there are, of course, marked differences in this respect between school and school, irrespective of its educational grading. And though there are still essentially 'class' schools—not alone among the endowed boarding schools, and private adventure 'commercial academies' and preparatory schools, but even among those dependent mainly on public grants—the enormous multiplication of scholarships, the frequent reductions of fees, and the salutary requirements of county councils and the Board of Education, have already brought it about that the class distinction between elementary and secondary schools as such has everywhere been blurred, and sometimes practically obliterated. We may hope that this tendency will continue. Already we see the local education authorities, with the increasing co-operation of the Board of Education, progressing steadily towards a state of things in which, whilst the small minority of wealthy parents may, by heavy payments, still secure, even for their stupidest sons and daughters, the most pro-longed educational advantages, the great bulk of the population will, by free places and scholarships, by entrance examinations and judicious selection, have access to just the kind and grade of schooling that their attainments and idiosyncrasies require. This will mean that, whilst the first grade schools will always contain stupid sons and daughters of wealthy parents, the bulk of their accommodation will, so far at any rate as most of these schools are concerned, be occupied by pupils, whether from wealthy households or not, who have been deliberately assigned to these schools, because such first grade secondary schools are those in which the public interest requires them to be. And whilst the second grade secondary schools will equally always contain, as fee-paying pupils, even the stupidest of the sons and daughters of the middle class, the great bulk of the pupils attending these schools will be those who, whatever their social class, have been deliberately selected to have that advantage, instead of the equally efficient but less prolonged train-ing of the elementary school. This 'democratisation of the secondary school' is the essential function and the social justification of that scholar-ship system, which has, within the past decade, become so important a feature in English secondary education—a necessary feature of any really democratic educational system in which England is, without knowing it, now far in advance of France or Germany, Switzerland or the United States.[128]

If it be asked how far can England and Wales be said, in 1908, to have progressed in equipping itself with anything like a satisfactory apparatus of secondary education, the reply is difficult to give with any precision. It follows from the very nature of the task that the answer cannot take a statistical form. In the matter of primary education, it is easy at any rate to compare the total number of children of school age with the number actually at school. The more difficult business of specialising the common school to meet the needs of different sections of children does not admit of any such simple arithmetical measurement. Precisely how far we have adjusted secondary schooling to the requirements of our people, no blue book can inform us and no man can declare. What we can notice is the far-sighted energy with which the Education Committee of the West Riding, for instance, has divided its great area, which has nearly one and a half millions of inhabitants, into seven sections, each of which requires a first grade school for boys and another for girls; and the seven sections into forty-five sub-districts, for each of which its own accurately adjusted supply of second grade schools has to be provided. Only about half of these sub-districts have, as yet, any secondary schools actually within their respective areas; but no fewer than eighteen new secondary schools are already provided or in course of being provided in this county alone, whilst fifteen have been, or are being, enlarged, improved, or reorganised. Under an energetic and well-thought-out scheme, the number of pupils in public secondary schools aided or wholly provided by the local education authority has increased, within four years, from 4155 to no less than 7317.[129] Or we may turn to the county of Kent, with its population of nearly a million, principally agricultural in its occupations, to note a rate of progress at least as great as that of the West Riding. Kent, four years ago, had but a score of publicly managed secondary schools with under 2000 pupils. By 1908 its twenty-one districts have, nearly all of them, one or more secondary schools either within its area or conconveniently adjacent to it; the nineteen schools have increased to thirty-one, educating nearly 4000 pupils; and these do not include half a dozen first grade secondary schools which serve the county but do not receive aid from the local education authority.[130] The largest figures, though not the largest increases, are, of course, recorded by the Administrative County of London, with its four and a half millions of people, and no fewer than 106 secondary schools under essentially public management, of which at least a score are first grade. The past decade has seen, on an average, two new secondary schools opened each year, nearly all provided and maintained by the local education authority itself. How many pupils are now in attendance is not ascertained, as 40 per cent of the schools are neither maintained nor aided by the local education authority, though nearly all of them are attended by the scholars whom it chooses under the largest scholarship scheme in the world. The total number of boys and girls in secondary schools in London must now exceed 50,000. London, in fact, has now actually a larger number of publicly managed secondary schools and pupils than any other city in the world—more than either Berlin or Paris; though not yet, it must be admitted, a number proportionate to its vast population. And if we turn to the twelve Welsh counties, with their million of inhabitants, we find, under Government inspection and public control, nearly a hundred secondary schools—four-fifths of them the outcome of the last twenty years—with a total attendance of boys and girls which by 1908 must have reached 13,000.

A mere multiplication of secondary schools in every county—especially when, as is sometimes the case, these are provided in substitution for the old pupil-teacher centres—does not, in itself, guarantee any real progress of secondary education. But it is common knowledge that the numerical increase in schools and pupils has been accompanied by a most surprisingly rapid improvement in every other respect. In buildings and equipment, in curriculum and staffing—in short, in every tangible factor of educational efficiency—the progress has apparently been greater during the last five years than during the whole of the previous generation. And if one may judge by the relatively small sample of the whole that any one person can be acquainted with, the improvement in the spirit in which the schools are conducted has at least kept pace with the progress of the material elements and the teaching staff. He is a bold man who ventures to compare one nation with another. No man has in his head any accurate general survey of a whole country. But though the particular excellencies of a selected sample can seldom be equalled elsewhere, they may be more often paralleled than is commonly supposed. Balancing one consideration with another, the present writer assumes temerariously to doubt whether the provision in all its varied forms actually made for secondary education in England and Wales—only a generation ago a byword and a reproach, and still horribly short of what it might easily be—is, viewed as a whole, now inferior, either in quantity or in quality, to that actually enjoyed by the boys and girls of Scotland, of the United States, of Switzerland, of France, or even of Germany itself.

V London University: a Policy and a Forecast

A frequently recounted story in Webbian folklore concerns the time when Sidney was questioned about his conception of a university. Quite obviously he was puzzled. 'I haven't any idea of a university', he is alleged to have answered. 'Here are the facts.'

The story is retailed a good deal because it purports to give an insight into the workings of the Webb mind. As has so often been said, Sidney and Beatrice were not *a priori* thinkers. The case has earlier been made that theirs was for example a functional theory of education. But inevitably there came a stage at which it was necessary to take stock of a situation, tease out the underlying principles and make prescriptions for the future. This is the *raison d'être* of Sidney's 'London University: a Policy and a Forecast' which appeared in June 1902 in the *Nineteenth Century*, the journal which had emerged as the unofficial monthly of the efficiency movement. To Sidney this functional approach was the only one which could produce anything worth while. 'They are futile dreamers who seek to fit new circumstances to the old ideals', he declaims in his peroration. And he goes on: 'Rather must we strive, by developing to the utmost the opportunities that the present affords us, to create out of twentieth-century conditions new kinds of perfection.'

There is more than a hint here that all was not well with the new University that had come into existence with the sealing of the statutes in 1900. Or rather that Webb was not getting his own way as he had done for so many years as chairman of the T.E.B. Sidney, it will be remembered,[131] had been given a seat on the Senate as one of the two representatives of the L.C.C. whose grant in 1902 amounted to more than a quarter of the University's total income.

Moreover, it was believed for some time that Webb had a united L.C.C. behind him. In view of all this his place on the University's governing body should have conferred unique advantages.

But although Beatrice's diary entries seem on occasion to show her husband playing a disproportionately active part in the proceedings, the reality was often very different and not infrequently her pessimism breaks through:

Sidney has been absorbed in his administrative work. London University proves to be the most formidable addition to the L.C.C. and Technical Education Board. The Senate of fifty more or less distinguished folk, many unknown to each other, and drawn from all sections of society, without procedure and with extraordinarily incompetent officers inherited from the old 'examining board', is the most difficult body to get into working order. The Chancellor, Vice-Chancellor and Registrar are simple obstructionists, and represent apathy, stupidity and ill-will, each carried to its nth. All that is done has to be done in spite of them; and of course, as far as Lord Kimberley[132] and Sir H. Roscoe[133] are concerned, it is impossible to be otherwise than outwardly acquiescent and respectful. Sooner or later the running of the University will, I think fall largely to Sidney and Hewins and one or two others: at present it is chaos. Meanwhile, we have been spending our substance giving little dinners to diverse senators: trying to make them understand each other and accept Sidney's view of university organisation.[134]

What this view was Sidney revealed in two articles in *The Times* in June 1901, in the *Nineteenth Century* in June 1902, and in the *Cornhill Magazine* in April 1903.

For its comprehensive grasp and elegant exposition of a difficult subject, 'London University: a Policy and a Forecast' cannot be bettered. It provides moreover a splendid insight into Sidney's concern for his native city, whose higher educational needs are so very different from those being met by contemporary Oxford and Cambridge. To this end general culture is subordinated to the education of the specialist. While undergraduate education is to be dispersed, post-graduate work is to be centralised to meet the demands of the Baconian university. In the part it can begin to play as a university of world calibre it will be able to combine 'a

sane and patriotic Imperialism with the largest-minded Internationalism'. 'London University' ranks high as one of Sidney's most
incisive contributions to serious journalism.

After a whole generation of conflict and controversy, London has at last
got its teaching university. The heartbreaking pioneer work is done,
statutes and regulations are completed, and in the various centres of
undergraduate instruction some two thousand matriculated students are
already at work. Yet the plain man remains unaware that the teaching
university exists. Its separate fragments, constructed on inconsistent
bases, meet but do not cohere. Before the new senate can become an
effective body, co-ordinating and directing all the university teaching
in London, and generating, out of the scattered elements, a real intellectual force, two things are necessary—a definite university policy
and the driving force of money.

What kind of university is possible in London? Any practical policy
for a London University has, it is clear, to have regard to the limitations,
the needs and the opportunities of London life. It may at the outset be
admitted that, for any university of the Oxford or Cambridge type the
metropolis is perhaps more unfit than any other spot that could be
chosen. By no possible expenditure could we create at South Kensington, in the Strand or at Gower Street, the tradition, the atmosphere, the
charm, or the grace of collegiate life on the Isis or the Cam. Nor is it
possible to secure, amid the heterogeneous crowds of London and all its
distractions, either the class selection or the careful supervision required by the parents of boys fresh from Eton or Harrow, with two or
three hundred a year to spend in pocket-money. For good or for evil
we must accept the fact that nothing in the nature of collegiate life is
possible in London. Even the 'hostel' becomes merely a co-operative
lodging-house. The London University student must inevitably be free
to wander, indistinguishable in dress, to all parts of the great city; to
pry into all phases of its life, and to rub shoulders with fellow-students
of every age, of every rank and of every kind of home experience and
personal tastes. Now that Oxford and Cambridge are open to students
of all creeds and all races, no parent, living himself away from London,
and wishing to place a boy of eighteen amid safe and advantageous
social surroundings, would willingly send him to live as an undergraduate in London lodgings. With the exception of country students
coming to study medicine or engineering, the undergraduate class of

London University will, we may infer, be confined to London residents, and, among these, to students from the 99 per cent of London homes which are maintained on incomes under £1,500 a year.

This limitation must vitally affect the whole policy of London University. It governs the curriculum, the character of the teaching, and its geographical distribution. But it imposes practically no limit on its size; for the London over which the university senate is given jurisdiction comprises all the seven millions of inhabitants of the thirty miles radius, covering, therefore, no less than 2,830 square miles. It is not a city, but a province, even a whole nation in itself. Holland and Belgium, neither so rich nor called to such great responsbilities as the people of London, have each half a dozen universities for not dissimilar numbers, whilst Scotland maintains, for only two -thirds as many people, no fewer than four ancient and successful seats of learning. Among seven millions of people there are reared up thousands of doctors and lawyers, engineers and chemists, architects and surveyors, teachers and civil servants, clerks and business men, journalists and authors, who cannot go to Oxford or Cambridge, and whose education at present is often prematurely broken off, or lacks direction and stimulus—fails, above all, in subtle cultivation of the imagination and generosity of aim—because there is not in London, as there is in Paris and Berlin, a well-organised university in close contact with the life of the city. In this as in other particulars the very limitation of a London University becomes its opportunity. Being, *as regards its undergraduate class*, essentially a university for the sons and daughters of households of limited means and strenuous lives, it will not, like Oxford and Cambridge, set itself to skim from the surface of society the topmost layer of rich men's sons and scholarship winners. Wisely organised and adequately endowed, it must dive deep down through every stratum of its seven millions of constituents, selecting by the tests of personal ambition and endurance, of talent and 'grit', for all the brain-working professions and for scientific research, every capable recruit that London rears. Hence it must stand ready to enrol in its undergraduate ranks not hundreds a year but thousands. If we remember that Paris and Berlin, drawing from much smaller local populations, and exposed each to the competition of a score of other universities in their own countries, have each actually twelve thousand university students, we can see that any equally effective London University might easily number twenty thousand.

An undergraduate class of this nature involves a second limitation.

Practically all the undergraduate students of London University will intend to earn their livelihood in the competitive work of the world. Whatever may be the advantage of the 'Greats' school of Oxford or the Cambridge triposes, as a preparation in general culture for those who can postpone their professional training to later years, it must be accepted as axiomatic that no such leisurely curriculum meets the practical requirements of the young engineer or business man, the teacher or the solicitor, or even the future doctor and civil servant. Between the ages of eighteen and twenty-two the London student will necessarily have to get well forward with his specialised knowledge and professional training. This involves the revival of the older conception of a university course deliberately framed so as to prepare the undergraduate from the outset for the practical pursuit of his profession, but in such a way as to turn him out equipped, not only as a trained professional, but also as a cultivated citizen. The London University, like those of mediæval Europe and modern America, will therefore necessarily take on the character of a technical school for all the brain-working professions of its time—not alone law, medicine, and theology, but also every department of science and learning, from engineering and chemistry to pedagogy, banking and commerce and public administration. Some may regret this limitation, but the practical man will see in it a great opportunity. Exactly as the 'middle class' origin of the typical London undergraduate by opening up a clientèle of enormous extent, makes possible a large university, so his professional needs compel an intensive culture of each subject unknown at the older seats of learning. Young men eager to master a department of learning or science, in order to apply it to gain their livelihood, will require in their teachers a much higher standard of knowledge and suggestiveness than those following courses with a view to a cultivated understanding of the whole realm of knowledge. The very practical character of London University will inevitably force its teachers further and further away from the mere elements of their subjects, and compel them to be ever pushing out into the yet unknown—that is to say, into the region of original investigation and research.

And here we see opening out before us London's most pressing need and unique opportunity. The obvious and imperative duty of a rightly organised and adequate endowed London University is to become the foremost post-graduate centre of the intellectual world. For alongside the university democracy of the undergraduate class, brought about by the multiplication of brain-working occupations and widespread education, we see everywhere emerging, at the beginning of the twentieth century, a new aristocracy of advanced students, intent on pursuing their chosen subjects above and beyond the first, or 'bread and butter', degree. Every day it becomes more clear that, as an equipment for the highest grades of brain-workers, the three or four years' general course of the ordinary undergraduate is far from sufficient. In the United States we find a practically unanimous opinion that it is to the post-graduate courses started five-and-twenty years ago at the Johns Hopkins, and now general at all the great universities, that the advances in American technique and American scholarship are to be ascribed: an opinion explained by Lord Kelvin's recent statement that it takes now at least six years to make a competent scientist. The crowning years of this extended course, when the student is emancipated from schoolboy discipline and academic drill, are best spent under the added inspiration of a new tradition, novel methods and experiences and contact with the intellectual and moral distinction of a fresh environment. Thus mere change of university is, for the picked student, a valuable stimulus, an axiom which, during the last decades, has been winning acceptance throughout the educational world. The research scholarships given annually by the Commissioners of the 1851 Exhibition to the most brilliant scientific graduate in each university of the British Empire, are deliberately made tenable, not at his own, but at some other university. Every German and Austrian university encourages its students to spend part of their time at some other seat of learning, whilst the French and Belgian Governments are always paying the expenses at foreign universities of carefully selected graduates. At this moment private munificence and travelling scholarships are keeping several hundreds of American graduates at one or other of the universities of Europe. And, as if to set upon this movement the seal of modernity, our new and 'up to date' ally in the Far East has, within the last few months, decided to send, at government expense, two hundred picked graduates from the Japanese colleges to spend some years in post-graduate study in the capitals of Europe. Now, to all this large and growing class of well-equipped and highly selected students London offers extraordinary attractions. Here they can live according to their own standards of expenditure, obtain the food, keep the hours, and follow the religious observances befitting their temperament, class, or racial habits. The very distractions and sights, the contact with celebrities, even the dark

places and problems of the world's greatest city, are, to the adult student, an education in themselves. We need not, therefore, be surprised
that, even with the present meagre facilities for post-graduate study,
every year sees an increasing number of graduates from other universities, following in the hospital wards the celebrated operator or
physician, seeking admission to Professor Ramsay's[135] experimental
laboratory, or attending lectures at the Royal College of Science or the
London School of Economics. With a highly specialised staff of university professors in each faculty, the London University would attract,
not one or two here and there, but a continuous stream of the ablest
and most enterprising of young graduates from the colonies and the
United States, from every university of Europe and the Far East. In the
provision of facilities for this highest grade of students the senate of
the new London University has an opportunity of combining a sane and
patriotic Imperialism with the largest-minded Internationalism. Moreover, in the organisation of these post-graduate studies, the senate will
be but responding to a characteristic need of London's own population.
In the homes and offices of the metropolitan area there exists the raw
material for a most fertile post-graduate department of native birth.
Among the thousands of young men and women whom we may expect
to see graduating year by year, there will be, in each faculty, a chosen
few who, either from intellectual interest or professional ambition, will
desire to continue their studies, and work for the higher degrees. Here
London makes possible a post-graduate life unattainable in the more
leisurely cloistered homes of university culture. Exactly because the
London University is set down in the very midst of warehouses and
offices, monotonous squares and mean streets, the poor and talented
graduate, living inexpensively at his own home, or already gaining his
livelihood, can, as a day or evening student, pursue his little bit of
original research, and work at the thesis which will gain him the coveted
doctor's degree. The very combination of two such distinct classes of
post-graduate students—the one bringing the training and experience
of alien universities, the other contributing the intimate knowledge of
the actual processes of bank or factory, government department or
merchant's office—constitutes in itself an extraordinarily stimulating
intellectual atmosphere for the advanced student.

But a university is, or ought to be, much more than a mere place for
teaching. Its most important function in the State is the advancement of
every branch of learning. For this highest function of a university the

character, conditions and numbers of the undergraduate students are relatively unimportant. Here what is vital is the professoriate and its environment. There are some who say that London, though it may become an important teaching centre, can never provide the environment for a university in this highest sense. What such critics have in mind is the absence from London of the fascinating atmosphere of general learning produced by the intellectual intercourse of men of different subjects, in a place where there is no competing distraction. We shall do wisely to recognise the truth underlying this instinctive consciousness of the limitations of London life. The all-round cultivation of the individual mind, the continuous appreciation of the finest literature that has been written, the balanced judgment due to a scholarly criticism of the past achievements of mankind, the refinement of humour and the sense of perspective of a Mark Pattison or a Jowett —all this is not, and can never be, promoted by London conditions. The vast distances between home and home, the differences in family circumstances and social position, the very strenuousness and bustle of London life, incline the brainworker to limit his social intercourse to those with whom he has actually to co-operate. The mere size of the professoriate of a London University increases this tendency. If the advancement of learning depends on the subtle intellectual stimulus gained by the professor of history's casual argument with the professor of biology, by the interplay of the theologian's mind with that of the philologist, by the interchange of the lore of the scholar of Arabic with the facts of the student of chemistry, the metropolis of the Empire is not likely to make any great contribution.

But the advancement of learning does not depend entirely, or even mainly, on a knowledge, however scholarly, of the past and present achievements of mankind. This, indeed, is culture, not science. What Bacon meant by the advancement of learning was the discovery of facts and laws hitherto unknown, new conquests of man over his environment. For this slow, hard and perhaps unlovely task of clearing new ground, quite different are the requirements from those which make for the highest culture. First and foremost, the scientific investigator in any of these fields, as distinguished from the scholar, must be provided, not with books alone, but with a perfect wealth of tools and raw material, costly laboratories and experimental workshops in physics and chemistry, hospitals and asylums for medicine and surgery, schools for pedagogy, documents, and social institutions actually at work for economics and political science. Above all, he must live and work under the stimulating influence of intellectual contact with the master minds in his own subject, English and foreign, whether these be fellow-investigators or practical experts applying and developing in their daily work the fruits of invention and research. For the advancement of learning in this, the Baconian sense, the conditions of London life, far from being adverse, are, in reality, in the highest degree favourable. Even without the staff or equipment of a great university, London has always contributed much more than its quota to scientific discovery. It was by no mere accident that Davy and Faraday, Huxley and Tyndall, Sir Joseph Hooker and Mr. Herbert Spencer, all worked in London. London's unparalleled wealth in 'material' for observation and study necessarily makes it the principal centre for every branch of English science. The intellectual environment is no less favourable than the wealth of material. The fact that all the learned societies meet in London is significant. No place provides, in each subject of study, so highly specialised a society, in which the ablest thinkers and investigators in any department of learning can meet, in friendly converse, not only their foreign colleagues visiting the great city, but also those who are, in the practical business of life, both needing and using the newest discoveries. Add to these natural resources of metropolitan life a university of the type required by London's needs—a large, closely knit and highly specialised professoriate in each faculty directing the researches of assistants and post-graduate students in the different branches of each science—and we shall have created, in the very heart of the British Empire, an almost ideal centre from which future generations of investigators and inventors may explore new realms of fact, discover new laws, and conquer new applications of knowledge to life. In the whole range of the physical and biological sciences, in the newer fields of anthropology, archæology, philology, pedagogy and experimental psychology, in the wide vistas opening out for applied science and the highest technology, in the constantly changing spheres of industrial and commercial relations, administration and political organisation, we may predict with confidence that a rightly organised and adequately endowed London University will take a foremost part in the advancement of learning.

What, now, should be the policy of the new London University? First and foremost we must accept, as the basic principle of its structure, an organisation by faculties, not by colleges or other institutions. Only on this principle can we develop a university structure adapted to the needs and opportunities of the metropolitan area. London, it is clear, can have but one university. For the small German town or provincial English centre, the university may suitably be of simple and, so to speak, unicellular type. Oxford and Cambridge, with their close aggregation of separate colleges of identical pattern, present us with what may be called a multicellular development of the same elementary type. By no such simple repetition of parts could we create a university for the huge area and dissimilar conditions of the metropolitan districts. Its unique combination of a widely dispersed undergraduate population and centrally segregated materials for research, its union of the most democratic student life with the most perfectly selected intellectual aristocracy of science, necessarily calls for a more highly organised structure. This is found in the establishment, as the principal organs of the university, of separate faculties, each of them highly differentiated in structure, so as to fit it for dealing, in its particular department of learning, with all the teaching and all the research from one end of London to another, and capable of indefinite expansion, without inter-fering with any other faculty, to meet the requirements of every part of the area and every development of the subject-matter. So long as the several colleges or other teaching institutions regard themselves, and are regarded, as the units of university organisation, their instinctive megalomania is a disruptive force, creating internecine jealousy and competition for students, and impelling each particular institution, irrespective of its local conditions or special opportunities, to strive to swell itself into a complete university on a microscopic scale. Make the faculty the unit, and the same megalomania, impelling the professors to work for the utmost possible extension and improvement of the faculty as such, serves only to extend the influence and enhance the reputation of the university as a whole. This is not to say that there is no place in the London University for separately organised institutions and auto-nomous governing bodies. It is impracticable and undesirable for the university senate or the university faculties to undertake the vast busi-ness of managing all the colleges and other teaching institutions within the metropolitan area. Whether these institutions devote themselves to particular departments of research, to special grades of teaching, to distinct subjects of study, or to the local requirements of their districts, the university will with advantage leave to their governing bodies a large autonomy in business management and finance, and concern itself only with seeing that such portions of their teaching staff and students, their courses of instruction and equipment, as are recognised by the university, are properly organised and co-ordinated with the larger life of the whole. The lines along which this co-ordination must necessarily proceed are marked out by the subjects of teaching or research; that is to say, by faculties. At present there are eight such faculties—namely, arts, science, medicine, law, music, theology, engineering, and economics. But the number of separate faculties will gradually increase, either by simply additions, such as pedagogy and philosophy, or, with the advance of the subjects, by the further differentiation into separate organisations of such large and comprehensive divisions as 'science' or 'arts'.

The internal organisation of all the faculties should comprise the same elements. Each will have to provide undergraduate teaching, to afford facilities for post-graduate work, and to promote, through the researches of its professors and advanced students, the discovery of new truth in its own subject-matter. Let us begin, as regards each faculty, with the broad base of the university organisation, the crowds of matriculated students following courses of study for the ordinary degree. Here the policy must clearly be that of the Open Door. It is the duty, as it will be to the advantage, of the senate to see that every section of the vast population committed to its charge has easy access to university teaching of the kind best adapted to undergraduate needs. It is at once plain that, in order to accommodate the undergraduates furnished by seven millions of population, spread over 2,830 square miles, we must give up all idea of concentration at any one centre. It takes longer to journey from Stratford or Beckenham to South Kensington or Gower Street than it does to go from Edinburgh to Glasgow or from London to Oxford. The cost of a daily railway ticket between Plumstead or Croydon and a central London laboratory exceeds the entire fees charged by a German or Scotch university. Whether we consider expenditure of time or expenditure of money, the only way to make a university education possible for the bulk of London's matriculated students is to bring it close to their own doors, giving the lectures and opening the laboratories at the hours most convenient to the students themselves. Thus, instruction will have to be provided in the evening as well as in the day-time, and it should be carried on, with proper relays of teachers, practically continuously throughout the whole year. There is no harm, and indeed great advantage, in these university courses being attached to polytechnics or technical institutes whose other departments are of less than university rank. The university will, of course, take care to appoint or recognise none but thoroughly competent teachers; it will see that the courses of instruction are given the genuine university spirit; it will maintain a high standard in laboratory accommodation; and it will naturally admit, as university students, only those who satisfy its matriculation and other requirements. Subject to these conditions there can be nothing but advantage in an indefinite multiplication of opportunities for undergraduate study in the whole of the vast area extending from Maidenhead to Gravesend, from Guildford to Bishop's Stortford. In the popular faculties of science and engineering there will, not improbably, soon be an effective demand—measured by the presence of fifty or a hundred undergraduate students at each place—for complete degree courses at forty or fifty such centres. Even such a multiplication would give, for each centre, a population as great as that of Aberdeen or Plymouth. The teachers at these exclusively undergraduate centres, who will be chosen, it may be hoped, from the ablest post-graduates of London or other universities, must, of course, be members of the faculties and boards of studies in their respective subjects, and every possible opportunity should be given for them to meet, for the discussion of how best to advance their particular branch of learning, not only their contemporaries, but also their more distinguished colleagues, the chief university professors, whose pupils they will probably have been. Only by the frank acceptance of some such policy of extreme local dispersion of the mere undergraduate teaching, coupled with a highly organised intellectual intercourse between all the university teachers in each subject, can the London University rise to the height of its opportunity as the university for seven millions.

Those who shrink appalled from this vision of ten or twenty thousand undergraduates dispersed among forty or fifty teaching centres at such unacademic places as Tottenham and West Ham, may find comfort in the arrangements for the post-graduate students, whom we may expect to see numbered at least by hundreds. Here the policy must be one of extreme concentration. It should be the policy of the university to attract the post-graduate student to the one or two highest colleges without, however, limiting his freedom of choice; to extend to him there the warmest welcome, with the fewest formalities; and to regard the suggesting and criticising of his work as the principal teaching duty of the ablest and most distinguished of the university professors. The seminars and specialist lectures of the more central colleges of the university should, in fact, be organised with primary reference to the needs of the post-graduate or advanced student, and should cater for undergraduates, if at all, only as a secondary and entirely subordinate consideration. For it will be, in the main, by these specialist courses and highly selected seminars that the university will be judged by other universities; and it will be by the patient work of the post-graduate students, and in their friendly personal intercourse with the professor, that will be trained, not only the future teachers and professors for universities all the world over, but also those to whom we look for the advancement of science and learning.

We come now to the character of the professoriate in each faculty. Here the keynote should be multiplicity of grade and diversity of type. The old conception of distinct colleges, each covering the whole range of the university curriculum, and able therefore to afford and employ only a single professor for each of the numerous subjects dealt with, is as we have seen, for many reasons unsuited to London. The newer conception of university organisation, embodied in the creation of faculties each composed of coequal professors of identical type, teaching the same subject at different institutions, is only one step in the right direction. What London University requires in each of its faculties is not a mere conference, but, under the guise of an advisory committee of the senate and its three subordinate councils, a highly organised and differentiated organ of academic administration. By a natural division of labour within each faculty, the different professors will find themselves undertaking research and teaching, not in the whole, but in particular aspects or departments only of their science. But there will have to be a further differentiation. We must abandon the simple ideal of equality, identity, or uniformity among professors, whether of tenure or salary, attainments or duties, time-table or holidays. The principal professors, on whom mainly we must depend for research, should, of course, have life tenures, high salaries, and abundant leisure, whilst the bulk of the university teachers required by so extensive an undergraduate population as that of London will necessarily be engaged for short terms, earn only modest salaries, and work at times and seasons convenient to those whom they serve. All the members of the faculty will, we may hope, be inspired by one and the same enthusiasm for the advancement of their science, but this oneness of spirit will go with diversity of gifts. If we are really in earnest in wishing to provide the best and most varied instruction, in the best way, to London's crowds of undergraduates, we must impose no tests on candidates for these teacherships, other than knowledge and capacity to impart it. Among these junior teachers may be found some who will distinguish themselves by original research, and rise to the highest academic distinction. But we must eschew anything like promotion by seniority. For the highest posts, it is, indeed, vital to choose comparatively young men: what we have to do is deliberately to survey the universities of the world and attract to London, by good salaries and the provision of the greatest opportunities for research, the most fertile brains of Europe and America. And we cannot afford to waste the most distinguished scientific talent on the drudgery of lecturing day by day to the mere undergraduate. 'It is not my business to make chemists, but to make chemistry', rightly urged one highly placed professor. No university policy can be successful unless it keeps in mind constantly that the duty of the principal professors is not the mere teaching of what is known, but the discovery of new truth. Thus, instead of the teacher's life being subordinated to the needs of the student, as in undergraduate centres it must and should be, every other task imposed upon the professor should, in the post-graduate centres, give way to the professor's own researches.

For this supreme end of original investigation and research should be organised the costly and specialised laboratories and collections of the central colleges of the university. Hence, it is indispensable that these colleges should be entirely independent of ordinary undergraduate classes. For undergraduate classes their buildings and equipment ought, indeed, to be unsuited. Instead of the merely elementary science benches thronged by hundreds of freshmen, the central colleges will need the most perfectly provided experimental laboratories, equipped with every new instrument of investigation, and open only to a chosen few. Here will be the meeting-place for all the teachers in the faculty; here will be received the foreign specialist or the practical expert; here will meet the learned society or the professional association; here, in fact, will be the intellectual headquarters of the particular department of learning.

The faculties of London University will therefore inevitably become large and varied bodies exercising, in their advice to the senate, important functions of academic administration. It is an important detail in their organisation that they should each be provided, not only with a convenient headquarters and a specialist library, but also with an adequately paid business manager or secretary. This officer should neither teach or investigate, but attend to the multifarious business of the faculty and of the boards of studies connected with it, for which the professors themselves have neither time nor training. In constant consultation with the principal and the registrars, he would see that his faculty, and the boards of studies connected with it, attended properly to all the requirements of the senate and its councils. But much more should be required from him. It should be his business to find out from the professors what further materials or plant they required, and see to its being supplied; to receive and enrol the post-graduate students and advise them as to the subjects dealt with by the various professors in his faculty; to keep his eye on every district of the metropolitan area, with a view to seeing that its particular needs in the way of undergraduate teaching were, so far as his faculty was concerned, adequately provided for. He would in every way act, for all the concerns of his faculty, as the confidential lieutenant of the principal of the university, in consultation with whom he would be always on the look-out to get, from local authorities, from bodies of trustees, or from individual donors, additional resources for the work of the faculty, in its twofold aspect of teaching and research.

The pivot upon which will turn this organisation by faculties of London University is the reality of the power exercised by the senate. This depends, to put it bluntly, upon how much money the senate itself has the spending of, irrespective of the separate 'schools' or other institutions. The senate itself, not this or that particular institution must necessarily appoint and pay, at any rate, all the principal professors in each faculty, even if they are assigned for research or teaching to the laboratories and lecture-rooms of particular institutions. The senate itself, not one or other of the mutually competing colleges, must be in a position to find the money for the appointment of the additional teachers required in each faculty, in order to be free to place them where they will be most serviceable. The senate, moreover, must be in a position to develop the newer or the weaker, the less popular or the less obviously utilitarian faculties, or departments of faculties, and even to create new faculties, in the direction and to the extent that the interests and reputation of the university may require. Only by wielding the power of the purse can the senate make its supreme authority effective, and serve as the co-ordinating brain that gives unity to the whole organisation. For, potent as must necessarily be the influence of the faculties in advising upon the curriculum, the character of the teaching and the opportunities for research, it is of the utmost importance to the welfare of the university that the ultimate decision should not be in their hands or in the hands of their co-ordinating committee, the Academic Council, any more than in those of the separate colleges. We cannot afford to give any faculty complete autonomy, even within its own field of science or learning. The existing professors and teachers of whom the faculty will consist must not have either the temptation or the opportunity to fill vacancies exclusively from among their own pupils, their own assistants, or the adherents to their own views; to exclude or discourage particular classes of students, or particular methods of teaching or investigation, which may from time to time offend their professional prejudices or seem to encroach on their vested interests. Even in academic matters it is vital that the supreme power should rest with a strong representative body essentially lay in character, accessible to new suggestions and independent criticism from the outside world, able, unbiased by the separate interests of particular faculties, to decide how best to meet the constantly changing conditions of a progressive community.

So comprehensive a scheme and so far-reaching a policy may seem hopelessly out of the reach of the newly constituted university, of which Lord Rosebery has become the first elected chancellor. But neither scheme nor policy involves anything revolutionary. They amount, in fact, to no more than an explicit writing out of what is already contained in the actual legal constitution of the university. Parliament and the university commissioners definitely rejected the plan of making the colleges the units of university structure, and created eight faculties, co-ordinated by a joint committee of themselves, called the Academic Council, as the principal organs of the teaching university. Over these faculties there is placed a strong senate, in which not only the professoriate and the graduates, but also the Inns of Court, the City Companies, the City Corporation, and the London County Council, are represented. In this senate sit eminent doctors and lawyers, engineers and business men, as well as some of the leading professors. For its work it has secured the services of a most distinguished man of science and organiser, in the capacity of principal. Nor has the senate to build up from the ground either the teaching or the research which it is charged to promote. Between thirty and forty centres of undergraduate teaching, dispersed all over London, are already at work, attended by some thousands of students. It has a university professoriate already hundreds strong, including in each faculty men of eminent distinction in their subjects. The existing laboratories and libraries, lecture-theatres and class-rooms, though far from adequate, represent a capital value of not less than two millions sterling. Thus, all the framework and many of the materials of a great university are ready to hand. What we have to do is to put the new senate in a position to adjust all these materials into their proper places; transform them so as to fit them for their most effective uses; fill up the obvious gaps, and weld the whole into a smoothly working machine.

To lift the new London University out of its present *impasse*, we have, first and foremost, to provide for a great development of postgraduate work, specialist teaching and original research; along with this to free the principal professors and the older and more central colleges from their present dependence on undergraduate classes, upon which they are largely wasted; and finally to multiply the centres for undergraduate teaching in the localities requiring them.

Let us begin with the Faculty of Arts. Here the characteristic need and special opportunity of London is of a great school of languages, the establishment of which, by the senate, would serve to organise the whole faculty. The varied activities of London bring it into contact, somewhere or another, with practically every known tongue. No city in the world sends so large a contingent of its citizens to other lands, none has so great an opportunity for the advancement of learning in philology. Yet others—notably, Paris and Berlin, Vienna, and even Leyden—put London altogether to shame in the extent of their provision for teaching and studying foreign tongues. There seem to be at least fifty distinct languages, from Annamese to Zulu, from Basque to Malay, from Russian to Persian, now being scientifically studied and practically taught in other European universities, sometimes only for comparative philology, but often also for the benefit of officials and traders. In London, with a far larger population from which to draw students, and organise post-graduate work, the department of philology is of the scantiest, and half of the fifty tongues are not represented at all. In the London University school of languages Greek and Latin would form the base, and classical archæology an important feature, whilst not only the philology and literature, but also the vernacular, would be throughly dealt with, of every tongue with which the missionary, the trader, or the official can come in contact. To maintain even one professor and one assistant for any particular tongue demands at least £700 a year; to provide for the whole fifty languages requires a new income of thirty or forty thousand pounds.

In the Faculties of Science and Engineering, clearly destined to be London's strongest side, the systematic organisation of the faculties depends on an extensive provision for post-graduate work and original research on two distinct but closely connected lines. On the one hand, we need to free our leading professors of chemistry and physics, mathematics and mechanics, from their present daily grind of under-graduate teaching; to transform their laboratories from crowded theatres of comparatively elementary teaching into silent homes of experimental research; and to establish thus—presumably at University College—a great centre of original investigation in pure science. On the other hand, a no less obvious deficiency, pointed out in two articles in *The Times*, is the absence of anything in the nature of an institute of scientific technology adapted to post-graduate work and the experi-mental application of science to industrial processes.

The same national neglect which lost us the great industry of coal-tar colours—positively a British discovery that we failed to utilise and abandoned to Germany—now bids fair to lose us one branch of applied chemistry after another. At the present moment perhaps the most promising outlook in the scientific field is presented by electro-chemistry, including both electrolysis and the manifold applications of the electric furnace. This new science has already transformed the commercial production of copper and aluminium, and given us such new products as carbide of calcium (for the economical production of acetylene) and carborundum. It bids fair, moreover, to revolu-tionise the whole alkali industry. Yet, beyond certain small experiments, due to the personal initiative of two or three professors, London offers no means and no opportunities for instruction and research in the subject. If electro-chemistry is destined to transform the world's industry, it is to Germany and not to England that the advantage of the first start seems at present likely to accrue. . . The same deficiency is found in other branches. . . Practically nothing in the nature of a school of chemical technology exists in the metropolis. . . How much of the future of industry may not turn on the proper working out of the possibilities of high-tension transmission and poly-phase currents ? Where, too, is our school of electric traction, which will enable us to keep, at any rate, part of this rapidly growing industry in our own hands ?

What London University wants, on this side of the science faculty, is, to put it briefly, a British 'Charlottenburg'—an extensive and fully equipped institute of technology, with special departments for such branches as mining and metallurgy, naval architecture and marine engineering, railway engineering and hydraulics, electric traction and power-transmission, electro-chemistry, optics, the various branches of chemical technology, and all possible applications of biology. Such an institution, which could be begun on any scale on the land lying vacant at South Kensington, should admit only graduate students, or others adequately qualified, and should lay itself out from the first to be a place of research in which there would be no teaching, in the ordinary sense, but only opportunities for learning—for every sort of investigation, carried out by professors and advanced students, individually and in co-operation.

Paradoxically enough, in the Faculty of Medicine, the way to increase post-graduate work and original research of advanced character, and thus pull the whole faculty together, is to transform the present arrangements for elementary teaching. Its peculiar need relates to the first two years of the medical student's life, during which the future doctor does not 'walk the hospitals', but applies himself exclusively to chemistry, physics, anatomy and physiology. The four or five hundred students who annually enter upon their medical course in London are now dispersed among twelve different medical science schools, where twelve different sets of poorly paid science teachers preside over twelve imperfectly equipped laboratories. It has long been recommended, and is now on all hands agreed, even by the twelve medical schools themselves, that it would be far better to concentrate the preliminary scientific studies of all the medical students in one great science school, controlled by the university itself. Such a school—which might with advantage be in two departments, one in East London and the other in West London—should provide laboratory accommodation for at least a thousand students, and might cost a quarter of a million to build and equip. The result would undoubtedly be a vast improvement in the scientific education of our doctors. What is of even greater importance is that it would set free the existing accommodation at the twelve hospital schools, together with their funds, for the further study of disease. Notably in cancer and phthisis are we sadly in need of more systematically organised research—research not undertaken at present because the accommodation, funds and energies of our great hospitals are partly devoted to teaching raw students the elements of chemistry or the mysteries of 'bones'.

Nor must we overlook, in a university for the greatest commercial, financial, and administrative centre, the need for post-graduate work and further discovery in all that is comprised under higher commercial education, the faculty of 'Economics and political science (including commerce and industry)'. The university commissioners shrank from establishing a 'faculty of commerce', but rightly separated economics from arts, and started a new faculty for the whole range of subjects which appeal to the statesman and the financier no less than to the banker and business man. Besides University and King's Colleges, which continue their old-established courses in economics, the teaching in this faculty is mainly carried on by the London School of Economics and Political Science, as a school of the university, now housed in the new building at Clare Market which it owes to the munificence of Mr. Passmore Edwards[136] and Lord Rothschild. This gives us a nucleus of some five hundred students, drawn from banks and shipping firms, railway administrations and Government departments, with a considerable intermixture of post-graduate students from all over the world. In this faculty what is needed is not more buildings but more professorships. What with specialised instruction in currency and banking, international trade and foreign exchanges, economic or industrial geography and commercial history, the higher accountancy and the principles of actuarial science, the methods of statistics and the organisation of business—what with the necessity of providing separate courses of practical instruction for the young merchant and the banker, the civil servant and the railway administrator—not forgetting, meanwhile, the research student in all these branches and a school of history, the needs of this faculty in the way of endowment cannot be put, if we are to see London level with Paris, or even with New York, at less than a capital sum of a quarter of a million.

In the Faculty of Law, whilst such undergraduate teaching as exists remains, at present, outside the university, there is practically no provision in London for post-graduate study or advanced teaching. This is a faculty in which the initiative rests with, and the work must practically be undertaken by, the Inns of Court and the Incorporated Law Society. Besides the comparatively elementary instruction of the young solicitor and bar student, there is room for a considerable development of specialist and advanced lectures in legal history, scientific jurisprudence, comparative legislation, and international law, for which we may hope that the great and wealthy lawyers will one day provide, either individually or in their capacity as benchers of the Inns of Court, the necessary ten thousand a year.

Thus, London University wants, on what may be called its higher side of post-graduate work, specialised teaching and original research, something like £500,000 capital for building and equipping a 'Charlottenburg', £250,000 for building and equipping a school of preliminary medical studies, and £250,000 for the necessary extension and re-equipment of University College, and possibly one or two other central institutions, in order to transform their buildings and laboratories from the needs of undergraduate to those of post-graduate work and research. It requires, moreover, an income of, say, £30,000 a year, so as to enable the senate to take the principal professors in each faculty into its pay and set them free from dependence on undergraduate classes, £30,000 or £40,000 a year for a great school of languages, £20,000 a year for the upkeep of the institute of scientific technology, £10,000 a year for all the ramifications of the economic faculty and higher commercial education, and £10,000 a year for the law faculty.

With resources of this magnitude at its disposal, the senate would find little difficulty in transforming the central colleges into essentially post-graduate centres, including research departments under the principal professors, the faculty libraries and the faculty headquarters. University College seems marked out for science, the Central Technical College for engineering, and the London School of Economics for its own faculty, whilst King's College, besides serving as the headquarters for theology, might usefully be made that of the school of languages. This work of concentration of the higher teaching and original research could be carried out by degrees. Meanwhile the multiplication of the centres for undergraduate teaching would have to keep pace with the local demands. To the fifteen existing science and engineering centres would be gradually added at least half a dozen others, notably in the outlying districts, at a cost of several thousands a year each.

To sum up. What London University needs to make it equal to its great opportunity, in its triple division into undergraduate teaching, post-graduate study, and original research, is an expenditure of one million sterling in buildings, alterations, and equipment, together with the provision, by way of endowment, of a new income between £120,000 and £150,000 a year, equal to, say, four millions. For five millions sterling—only half what has been given by a single benefactor to a single university in the United States—London's University can be fairly launched. This sum could with advantage be drawn from distinct sources. The new buildings and equipment, together with the endowment of the principal professors in all faculties—say, two and a half millions in all—must come practically as capital and might be collected from individual donors. The other half of the total cost, including the annual maintenance of the school of languages and of the institute of technology, together with the whole provision of undergraduate teaching and of scholarships, would be within the compass of a halfpenny rate, which the local authorities concerned, if appealed to in a sufficiently striking way, might perhaps be persuaded to levy.

But whether or not the necessary sum is at once forthcoming, the authoritative formulation of a comprehensive scheme for the university as a whole is urgently required. Such a scheme, once adopted by the senate, could be taken up in such parts and at such times as commended themselves to private or public benefactors. Individual donors could transform University College into a post-graduate centre and headquarters of the science faculty, establish a central medical science school, build and equip a 'Charlottenburg', or endow the faculty of economics, without impairing the chance of subsequently dealing with equal completeness with other needs. The authoritative promulgation of such a comprehensive scheme would offer untold advantages over the present chaotic struggle of separate institutions to extend and supplement themselves in all the departments of learning, without regard to what is done elsewhere. Such a scheme, moreover, would immensely improve the chances of securing gifts both small and great. 'University education' is too vague a term to attract any large measure of support. We must present each part of the work to the class or section to whom it most appeals. It may be that we must forego in London University the culture born of classic scholarship and learned leisure. But if we can show that there is no incompatibility between the widespread instruction of an undergraduate democracy and the most effective provision for the discovery of new truth; between the most practical professional training and genuine cultivation of the mind; between the plain living of hard-working students of limited means and high intellectual achievements, we shall not, I venture to believe, appeal in vain. London University must take its own line. They are futile dreamers who seek to fit new circumstances to the old ideals; rather must we strive, by developing to the utmost the opportunities that the present affords us, to create out of twentieth-century conditions new kinds of perfection.

VI The Organisation of
Commercial Education

Two months after the appearance of his article in *The Nineteenth Century* in October 1903, *London Education* was published by Longmans. What emerges very strongly in this little book is Webb's concern for the creation of an educational system worthy of the capital of Empire, a system which is to be founded as always on the concepts of 'the national minimum' and 'national efficiency'. It is in fact Webb's specification of an educational minimum which forms the bulk of the writing.

Chapter III of that work is entitled 'The Organisation of Commercial Education' and it is reproduced here in its entirety. It is of particular interest in that it gives an insight into Sidney's views on what would be called today his 'theory of the curriculum'. It is at once obvious that that theory owes nothing to epistemological considerations, nor to any concern for psychologically geared concepts such as 'interest' or 'motivation'. In its broadest sense it is a sociologically determined curriculum: its function is to prepare people for their efficient functioning in the world of work. It is in essence a view of education which subordinates 'intrinsic' to 'extrinsic' ends.

This view demands some elaboration. Sidney is writing about the educational needs of London, a vast commercial entrepôt, whose business community is in touch with every corner of the world. Education for the world of work is therefore, at least in this context, a preparation for an effective contribution to this commercial enterprise. In the past the necessary skills and bodies of knowledge have been acquired on the job. But supply has not kept pace with demand, nor can the English clerk be relied upon to pursue his studies in his spare time. The result is that strange phenomenon: the import of large numbers of Germans to fill the vacancies in the City's commercial and business houses.

The new century is then an appropriate time to take stock. In the process, Webb is not so intolerant as to banish the liberal, classical curriculum completely. Such a prescription would have been out of character. Instead it is treated in a mildly contemptuous manner. One is led to believe that it may have a small part to play for the minority of rather perverse people intent on entry to places like Oxford or Cambridge.[137] For the rest, what is important is the development of expertise at all levels.

As far as interest and motivation are concerned, Webb seems to beg all manner of questions. The assumption is that a preparation for the world of work will automatically involve the interest of children and young adults. He may of course be right: certainly the first half of the present century saw all manner of vigorous developments in commercial and technical education. In later years, a philosopher like A. N. Whithead was prepared to see the possibilities of full intellectual growth resulting from such curricula and by 1938 the Spens Committee wrote into their *Report* proposals which favoured the extension of this approach to learning. It has been the post-Newsom period, from 1963 onwards, that has seen an attack developing on a front which is broad enough to encompass both left-wing egalitarians and philosophers of education. In the case of children up to sixteen a broad general education, now restored under new classifications of knowledge, seems to be putting paid, for the time being at any rate, to the sort of curriculum planning that Sidney Webb was describing in this chapter from *London Education*. What should be emphasised however is that Sidney's curriculum is never narrowly conceived. Subjects like shorthand and book-keeping for example have no part to play in any school. In conclusion, it is perhaps not too maudlin to say that those teachers who have experienced the distinct sense of satisfaction that comes from operating in the sort of educational milieu favoured by Webb may well feel that a very promising development has become prematurely and unnecessarily tarnished.[138]

It is now nearly twenty years since the London Chamber of Commerce, with an initiative which does it credit, convened a conference to consider how we could improve our commercial education in London. For nearly twenty years the subject has been debated and discussed by schoolmasters and merchants, administrators and educationists; but the time has not been wasted. We have, I believe, all learned a great deal about needs and possibilities. We have discovered that we have already at our disposal much more commercial education than we imagined. Much has been done, meanwhile, to increase and improve that provision. And we are, I think, able with some confidence, and wide general concurrence, to lay down the lines on which the commercial education of a great city such as London can be, and should be organised.

We know now, for instance, that by commercial education we must mean, not merely instruction in any one subject or set of subjects, judged superlatively useful—nor yet education of any one grade or kind, regarded as specially lacking—but simply the best possible education of the man (or woman) who expects to spend his working life in an 'office' or in 'business' of one sort or another. We no longer accuse each other of ignoring 'culture', or excluding what Dr. Arnold called the education of the citizen. Nor, on the other hand, do we denounce any subject not visibly subservient to office routine as 'mediæval pedantry'. We find that we all really want the same thing, namely, the particular sort of education, whatever it may prove to be, which will enable our 'business men' to fulfil most perfectly all their functions, however diverse, in the organised community of which they form part. We have, in a word, when training the future business or any other man, to see his life 'truly', and to see it 'whole'. The old-fashioned grammar-school master was too ignorant of the world and too prejudiced to see it 'truly', and Mr. Gradgrind was too uncultivated to see it 'whole'.

We realise, too, much more clearly, the immensity and diversity of the class of citizens about whose education we are concerned. London is, above all other cities, the city of offices. It has not only far more clerks, and more kinds of clerks, than any other city, but probably more also in proportion to its total population. And though London also carries on, in the aggregate, more manufacturing industry, and more kinds thereof, than even Glasgow or Birmingham, yet owing to the decay of apprenticeship and the refusal of many London manufacturers to cumber their highly-rented workshops with boys, a much larger proportion of London lads go into offices than is the case in other cities. London, too, is in nearly every business, the head office of the world. Great banks, insurance companies, railways, and international enterprises of every kind, with branches and works all over the United Kingdom or the world, have their principal centre of administration, or one of their principal centres, in the 'five million city'. Then there is the great and growing service of public administration. There are 20,000 civil service or municipal clerks and officers in London, without including as many more messengers and other subordinates. There are 30,000 merchants, brokers, factors, commercial travellers, etc. The bankers and their clerks number over 8000, whilst those engaged in the great business of insurance exceed 5000, and there are no fewer than 8000 clerical officers at work in London at the administration of the railways. These large numbers are irrespective of the great army of merely commercial or business clerks, not further defined, of whom there are in London over 100,000. We have thus a total of at least 200,000 persons at work in London offices, before we begin to count the dealers, manufacturers, and shopkeepers themselves. Commercial education in London means, therefore, the education of at least one-fifth of the whole population.

The man who realises these figures is driven to admit that the problem of providing commercial education is a bigger and more complicated one than he had supposed when he began to think about it. When, in 1893, the American Bankers' Association sent an able professor across the Atlantic to find out how other countries provided for the education of business men, that professor passed over the United Kingdom altogether, on the ground that there was no education of business men there! It would be sad, indeed, if one-fifth of the people of London, including a large proportion of those by whose activities it lives and thrives, were, as recently as 1893, getting no systematic education in preparation for their life-work. But Professor James was misled by the talk of the business men themselves. To this day the foreigner is amazed at the contrast between the skill and energy with which our leaders of commerce and finance manage their ever-increasing business, and their ingrained disbelief in there being any desirable 'commercial education' at all. The fact is that business men usually forget (or are, indeed, unaware of) how much they themselves owe to their schools and colleges. They think that what they know they have 'picked up' in the city. It does not seem to occur to them to inquire by what long process of mental training they came to be able to 'pick up'. Nor do they stop to think what they would do if they had not at their command clerks and subordinates able to do what they themselves cannot accomplish; skilled in languages, acquainted with the business organisation of other countries, versed in the intricacies of currencies and international exchanges, up in foreign tariffs and port dues, competent to form a judgment as to the effect of a new tax or a new law on the course of trade, able to calculate actuarial probabilities and insurance risks—above all, trained to apply a well-informed intellect to the minor problems on which the smooth and succesful working of any considerable business depends. This cannot be 'picked up' in the city. We need not dispute, as one eminent German said to me, that the English merchant or banker enjoys, in his daily converse with his equals, the best commercial education in the world. 'What he needs', continued my friend, 'is more instruction in commercial subjects.'

Let us see what we have got in London to supply this need, and where we still fall short, in quantity or quality. We must divide the provision into three grades. There is first the instruction and training of the youth before entering business life—the school, whether primary or secondary in grade. No less important are what may be called the continuation or supplementary provisions—the evening classes available for the young clerk, or the day commercial courses supplementing the secondary school. And thirdly, perhaps most important of all to the community in the long run, there is the provision of what we call higher commercial education, required by the subaltern officers of the commercial army, if not also by the gifted and possibly heaven-sent commercial field-marshals themselves, and therefore to be sought for by every able and ambitious subordinate.

We have therefore to consider—

I   The day school for the future business man, primary or secondary in grade.

II The continuation or supplementary classes, day or evening, for the youth who has left school.

III The commercial department or faculty of university rank.

I OUR COMMERCIAL DAY SCHOOLS

(A) PRIMARY

The great majority of the eight or ten thousand recruits who each year join our army of two hundred thousand clerks and business men come straight from the public elementary school. London has at last caught up its arrears in the way of primary school accommodation, and the thousand existing separate school buildings, scattered over 120 square miles, would contain all the child population, if only it would not shift steadily outwards, from the centre to the suburbs. These schools, partly under the School Board, partly under denominational management, have steadily improved in general efficiency. They set themselves, under the direction of the Board of Education, to give their boys and girls a thorough grounding in speaking, reading, and writing English, in arithmetic, in modern history and contemporary geography, in elementary science, with the addition, as regards many of the boys, of some elementary knowledge of French. It is from these schools that we must draw our office boys and, to a large extent, our junior clerks. We do not call them commercial schools—a term which, in England, is abandoned to the private venture school—but they are, and must necessarily be, the schools in which all the lower ranks of our commercial army are educated. How do they perform the work?

Now, it is common to hear employers declare that these schools, whatever they may do in other directions, are a failure as places of commercial education. 'What I want', said one of them, 'is a boy who can write plainly and quickly; who can spell and can be trusted to turn out a decent letter; who can add up with accuracy, and who has some "gumption" about his work. That is all I ask for, and that is what I cannot get.' That is all he asks for, in a boy of fourteen! I wonder how many of us at that age could have come up to such a standard. The fact is, that employers have an altogether exaggerated idea of what, under the conditions of the problem, is physically possible. They expect too much from boys on leaving school. To catch the entire child-population of a great city, to drive into school and keep it there, to train it to cleanliness, order, and disciplined obedience, to make it master the intricacies of the most difficult of all languages in spelling and pronunciation, and acquire the habit of quick and correct hand-writing, and a capacity for accurate arithmetic—all this constitutes a herculean task. One can only most devoutly thank the school authorities and teachers for succeeding as well as they do. The employer who wants what a century ago would have been considered an Admirable Crichton of a junior clerk must not try to get it at the age of fourteen or at ten shillings a week.

All that we want further for commercial education from our elementary schools is really only a levelling-up on quality. They teach the right subjects, and they aim at the very standard that our grumbling employer sets up. The trouble is that in only a certain proportion of instances is that standard attained. What we have to do is to strengthen the staff and screw up the efficiency of the Board Schools to the high level of, say, the Fleet Road School; and (what is still more needed) raise the denominational schools to the level of the Board Schools. The most serious evil is the fact that so small a proportion of the children stay on long enough, or attend regularly enough, to get through to the highest class. This defect is being somewhat remedied by the slowly increasing stringency with which regularity of attendance is enforced, by the progressive extension of effective school life to at least fourteen, and by the development of what are called higher elementary or higher grade schools. Ten years ago London had scarcely a dozen public elementary schools where adequate instruction could be given to clever children between thirteen and fifteen; now it has at least fifty. Ten years ago there were fewer than 18,300 boys and girls over thirteen in the public elementary schools; now there are over 48,000. Nevertheless, it is estimated that at least 68.5 per cent of the boys and girls who reach the fourth standard still leave school before reaching the seventh standard.

It is all-important that this 'upper standard' work should be strengthened and encouraged. Unhappily the School Board and the Board of Education have been on such bad terms with each other, and the law has hitherto been in such an unsatisfactory state, that discouragement has been the rule. The Board of Education offers large grants in aid of higher elementary schools, but insists in such schools on a larger proportion of physical science than the School Board for London has approved. The result is that we have in London only seven such schools, though we could quite well do with many more. The Technical Education Board of the London County Council has supported the request of the School Board for an alternative curriculum, allowing, at any rate in some schools, more time to languages and literary subjects; but the Board of Education—perhaps not altogether without reference to legal and financial difficulties—has not yet seen its way to make this concession to the 'city of clerks'. What will be the solution of this particular problem we cannot yet see. It may possibly be that the 'higher elementary' minute, adopted only to meet an emergency, may be quietly superseded or left on one side by a better arrangement. With the ever-increasing number of children over thirteen in the schools, and the steady rise in the efficiency of the higher standards; with the growth of sixth and seventh standards in schools where, quite lately, no such advanced work was possible; with the possible doubling of the numbers in these standards by the extension of the plan of 'senior mixed' departments; and with the inevitable strengthening of the teaching staff in these upper standards—there does not seem any insuperable obstacle in presently making every large elementary school in London into what, ten years ago, would have been considered a good higher grade school. The exceptional will have become normal, and the very success of the higher grade school may thus cause it, as a distinct kind, to cease to exist. And if the Board of Education, instead of or in addition to its present very high grants to 'higher elementary schools'—confined to those which adopt an excessively scientific curriculum of very doubtful value, and limited by many cramping regulations—would make a moderate addition to the present block grant for children over thirteen under efficient instruction in the seventh or ex-seventh standards, this beneficient transformation of every large school into a higher grade school would, to the special advantage of commercial education, be greatly accelerated.

(B) SECONDARY

The practical distinction between primary and secondary schools, as we now recognise, lies not in the subjects taught, but in the age at which the scholars intend to leave school. For the boy or girl expecting to leave school at fourteen or even fifteen, the best we can do in the educational way is to provide the most efficient higher grade or 'higher elementary' school. But some boys and girls will remain at school until sixteen, seventeen, or eighteen, either because their parents can afford it, or (as now in increasing numbers) because they have been picked out by maintenance scholarships. For them the curriculum needs to be dealt with in a different way. The work, spread over a longer time, can be taken with a wider outlook and with greater reference to cognate subjects. There is time for more attention to mental training and cultivation, as distinguished from mere instruction. The scholar's own reading, the scholar's writing of essays, even the scholar's powers of dialectic, become much more important allies of the class teacher than is possible with children of less cultivation or more tender years. The foreign language studied may itself be made an important instrument of cultivation, and a second—even a third—language can be added. Thus, the secondary school is, and must always remain, essentially different from the primary school, however we may widen the range and improve the quality of our elementary education. From the secondary schools come a large proportion of those who enter city offices as clerks; practically all the bank and insurance staff and the civil service, and nearly all the sons of business men who are destined to succeed to their fathers' positions. Here, accordingly, we need a 'commercial' education, even more than in the elementary and higher grade school.

So unaware are we Londoners of what London is, that few of us realise that the great city has now a more extensive series of secondary schools, under essentially public management, maintained out of public funds, and many of them giving a more characteristically 'commercial' education, than any other city in the world. Including the very efficient dozen London schools of the Girls' Public Day School Company and similar bodies (only in form joint-stock companies, and administered with entirely public objects), there are at the present moment no fewer than eighty-five publicly managed secondary schools within the administrative county, thirty-nine for boys, thirty-nine for girls, and seven for both boys and girls. These schools, distributed all over London, charge fees varying from the fifteen to thirty guineas a year of St Paul's School, University College School, Dulwich College, Merchant Taylors', Blackheath, Westminster, and other 'first grade' schools, down to the two or three pounds a year of most of the Polytechnic day schools, and such endowed 'second grade' schools as Raine's. Between these extremes lie the great mass of public 'intermediate' schools, such as Owen's, Alleyn's, Aske's, Central Foundation, Roan, Latimer, and others, distributed over all parts of London, charging four to eight pounds a year, and giving, for the most part, a very efficient education of an excellent modern type. In a few cases reduced fees are charged to pupils coming from elementary schools. Some of them have valuable entrance scholarships, and others 'free places'—which, strange to say, cannot always be filled. And recruiting them annually by some 600 of the cleverest boys and girls from the elementary schools, there is the effective 'scholarship ladder' maintained by the London County Council. Some of these schools are old, and some are new; but the old ones have nearly all been drastically reformed within the past twenty years. During the past ten years, in particular, during which forty-six of these schools have been under the supervision of the Technical Education Board of the London County Council, they have all been considerably improved. The teaching of science has been revolutionised, with a view of making it of practical use as an instrument of education. Dozens of school laboratories and manual workshops have been built and efficiently equipped. Drawing and modern languages are now being gradually brought up to the same level. But there has been no attempt to plane these schools into uniformity. Each of them has its own incorporated body of governors, usually including some representatives of the County Council, and sometimes, also, of the Borough Council. Each has its own distinctive character, its own characteristic tone and tradition, and its own peculiar curriculum. In no city in the world is there such a wide range of choice for the parent, or such excellent variety; and certainly in no English city is there, taken as a whole, a more efficient or more suitable provision of secondary education.

Judged merely as 'commercial' schools—that is, as schools adapted to give the wisest possible education to the youth who will enter a business office at sixteen or eighteen—these schools naturally vary in excellence. Nearly all of them make a strong point of English and arithmetic, and all of them teach French. Practically all of them give a second modern language, usually German, but at least in three cases Spanish. The 'first grade' schools are perhaps, from the special point of view that I am now occupying, more open to criticism. It is to my mind an unsatisfactory feature of these schools, viewed from the standpoint of the education of the business man, that they should remain so completely subservient to classical or mathematical requirements of Oxford and Cambridge—very largely the effect of the scholarship and school examinations conducted by those universities. In spite of all the improvement in English middle-class schools, since Matthew Arnold bewailed their inefficiency —an improvement which I believe to have been greater in London than anywhere else—most of them still seem to me to suffer from not being quite sure what they are aiming at. I do not pretend to know what school curriculum will fit boys most successfully to be clerks or merchants, civil engineers or bankers, actuaries or chemists. Such a curriculum would perhaps have no very obvious connection with their future work. But I cannot believe that the best curriculum in each of these separate cases is identical with the best curriculum for all the rest, and for a university career. The idea that a 'good general education' of a literary or classical type is an adequate, if not indeed the best, preparation for every kind of career, sounds like a survival from the Middle Ages.

This has, during the last few years, become increasingly recognised in some of these London schools. The headmaster will often admit that there should, at any rate, be a clear distinction between an educational course which ends at sixteen or eighteen and one which is intended to be continued up to twenty-two or twenty-three. Yet so strong in England is the tradition that education is one and indivisible, that most of the 'first grade' schools go on pretending that all their scholars are preparing for Oxford or Cambridge, habitually working up to the same system of examinations, and pursue accordingly much the same curriculum with merely minor variations as to the relative time allowed to the several subjects, though they know that the majority of them will go straight into the city. This muddling up together of 'gymnasium' and *realschule*, of *lycée* and *école commerciale*, cannot but be detrimental to both varieties. There must be room for some schools, which need not be called commercial schools or bear any other badge of supposed inferiority, but which should reject all connection with the classical or mathematical sides of the university, which should decline to follow its traditional curriculum, and which should arrange a course of studies deliberately based on the needs of boys who will become clerks in commercial offices at sixteen or eighteen. We want, in fact, at least three kinds of secondary schools—one aiming at university scholarships; another giving a carefully devised, predominantly scientific training, with languages and literature taking a second place; and yet a third, in which the languages, literature, and history of at least two modern countries besides our own will be made the basis of the intellectual training, with economics, geography, and physical science holding a subordinate position.

This, I know, will be misunderstood, as involving a too early 'specialisation', the loss of culture, and so forth. It is the crudest of misconceptions to suppose that such a curriculum would be made up of shorthand and book-keeping, or the playing at commercial transactions —once tried (and, I believe, abandoned) in some German 'commercial institutes'. The inimitable Stock Exchange school, described in R. L. Stevenson's novel *The Wreckers* is scarcely a wilder parody. What I am advocating involves no 'narrowing' of the curriculum. It implies, on the contrary, the inclusion of much more culture, the taking of a

wider view of existence, a great deal more of 'seeing life truly and seeing life whole', than the average secondary schoolmaster, experienced
only in one narrow line, is as yet either capable or conscious of. One
of the greatest difficulties in the way is, indeed, the lack of adequately
trained teachers. But it does mean the abandonment of scholastic
prejudice and tradition in favour of a purposeful adaptation of means to
ends. It means putting a great deal of deliberate contrivance into the
business of making the most of three or four years of a boy's life.

At any rate, the experiment is worth trying, and it is now being
tried, in one of London's most efficient 'first-grade' schools. In 1899
the Technical Education Board of the London County Council began
to send a few selected teachers to study at the best French, German,
Italian, Swiss, and Belgian institutions for high commercial education,
with a view to their learning the best methods at work. With the
experience thus gained, a special department was established at University College School for the purpose of providing the most carefully
planned and the very best commercial education, of first-grade secondary type, that money could buy. Here the commercial department
shares in all the tradition and corporate life of the school. It is recruited,
not from the dull boys, but from those of exceptional ability. Every care
is taken to make the three or four years' course thoroughly educational
in character, with full regard for culture and intellectual training, rather
than mere instruction. But the department prepares for no external
examination, and follows no traditional curriculum. Greek and Latin
find no place. Modern languages are taught in the most approved
practical way, with quite remarkable success. Every subject of study,
every method of teaching, the whole distribution of school-time has
been deliberately planned with the sole object of giving the best
possible education for the youth who is expected to enter an office at
eighteen, and eventually take a responsible position in the business
world. The department is still only in its fourth year, so that it is too
soon to ask for results. But the reports of those who have inspected the
work are full of encouragment. In 1903, for the first time, half a dozen
of the boys from this school presented themselves for the Intermediate
B.Sc. examination of the University of London, in the newly organised
faculty of economics and political science, which includes in its scope
commerce and industry. Their success, after three years of mere school
work, was such as to astonish the university examiners. Alike in modern
languages and in sound training in economics, alike in powers of

thought and literary expression and in the knowledge of the organisation and problems of modern commerce, these boys of eighteen demonstrated how fallacious is the assumption that the secondary school cannot, without sacrificing its highest qualities, give any useful training for the merchant's office. The experiment of this commercial department at University College School, which now includes sixty or eighty boys between fifteen and eighteen, deserves more attention from those interested in secondary education than it has yet received. It may go far to revolutionise the traditional curriculum.

II OUR CONTINUATION CLASSES IN COMMERCIAL SUBJECTS

But whether the youth leaves school at fourteen to fifteen or sixteen to eighteen, it is clear that his commercial education can be, at that age, by no means complete. Every youth in a business office ought to be attending evening classes in such subjects as shorthand and book-keeping, which are unfit for a school curriculum; and in French, German, and if possible, a third language. Ample provision for such commercial education is now made in London. There are, first, the 400 centres at which the School Board has conducted, either gratuitously or at a trifling fee, somewhat rough-and-ready evening classes in all these and many other subjects. About a dozen of these are designated 'commercial schools', in which special attention is given to the subjects favoured by the young clerk. Standing above these in pretension, and, I venture to think, also in quality, are the evening classes in commercial subjects at the Birkbeck College and other polytechnics, or similar establishments, supervised and aided by the London County Council. Here, at one or other of about twenty centres, the young business man can find practically every subject and every grade of instruction that he needs, at convenient hours and low fees—not only French and German, but also Italian, Spanish, Portuguese, and Russian; not book-keeping only, but also economics, industrial geography, and commercial law. During the last few years the London Chamber of Commerce has conducted evening classes which aim at being even more specially adapted to business men than those of the Birkbeck College; and these have, at any rate, supplied a third alternative method of enrolment. By admitting the clerks of all subscribing firms without fee, many clerks have been induced to attend, if only for a few evenings, who have not hitherto been attracted either by the School Board free classes, or the fees of the Birkbeck.

Classes in commercial subjects of this continuation or supplementary type are held also in the daytime at the Northern Polytechnic, the Goldsmiths' Institute, and various other polytechnics. At the South-Western Polytechnic they have developed into a regular day 'college', which now exceeds the evening classes in the magnitude of its work. Here we have systematic instruction for young men and young women, from the age of sixteen upwards, in all the subjects needed by the clerk, the private secretary, the commercial agent, or, in fact, any kind of office work. It is not exactly a school, and it can scarcely aspire to be a university college. But it is much more than a congeries of isolated classes, and the extent to which it is taken advantage of proves that it fills a useful place in London's commercial education. A similar development will shortly take place in the city itself, in the projected extension of the City of London College, for which the Mitchell Trustees have advanced £15,000, and the balance of £10,000 is being collected among the City Companies and other friends. The new building will be devoted to commercial subjects, and, as at Chelsea, the experiment will be tried of adding morning and afternoon to the evening classes, so that the boy fresh from a classical or mathematical school may be able to spend a few months, or even more, over his French and German, his arithmetic and handwriting, his geography and economics, before actually entering an office.

The greatest deficiency in all this range of work appears to be the inadequacy of the teaching of modern languages. Even the number taught at all is curiously small. One would have supposed that, in a city like London, coming into contact with every race on earth, and having at least a quarter of a million business men to draw from, there would have been a demand for teaching in every language under the sun. At Paris and Berlin between twenty and thirty modern languages are regularly taught, often gratuitously, to all comers. In London, where, so far as I can discover, only a dozen appear in the prospectuses, the clerk or business man who wanted to learn Malay, Maltese, Armenian, Japanese, Annamite, Tamil—to say nothing of the Scandinavian languages, or even Welsh or modern Greek—would find considerable difficulty in getting instruction at low fees and convenient hours. There ought to be provision—the most fitting place seems to be the City of London College—for instruction in every language under the sun with which the trader, the missionary, or the official ever comes in contact.

And though evening classes ought to be held, the provision should not be confined to these. It ought to be possible for a man who has received an appointment, or who sees a chance of one, or who expects to be going abroad in a few months, to put in continuous work, under an expert teacher, for hours and days and weeks at a time. This is how really determined men learn a language when they need it. They will often pay a substantial fee for the necessary tuition. At present no public institution in London can provide for this need.

On the whole, however, it must be said that the provision in London of commercial education of this 'continuation' or supplementary kind fully keeps pace with the demand for it. Except at such specially successful centres at the Birkbeck and the Regent Street Polytechnic, the existing class rooms are often far from full, and some advertised courses fall through from lack of students. The root of the evil is a certain lack of desire on the part of the young men themselves, and the failure of the employers to make their clerks aware that they ought to attend evening classes. The numbers on the rolls, great as they are, represent only a small proportion of the young men between sixteen and twenty-five, and I fear we must conclude that the majority do not trouble about anything but football or bicycling after their office-day. This is where the German clerk gets ahead of us. 'I much prefer English clerks,' said the head of one of the very largest firms in the city, 'but I find my office full of Germans. The English clerk takes no intellectual interest in his work, and seems to give his mind to sport.' But this, I venture to think, is largely the fault of employers. If they made a point of pressing their younger clerks to attend evening classes, and considered the fact in their promotions, the students would soon be multiplied three- or four-fold.

III OUR COMMERCIAL UNIVERSITY

Compared with Paris, the most conspicuous deficiency in London's commercial education has been, until lately, the absence of any provision for higher commercial studies.

When the Technical Education Board began its work [reported in 1899 its special committee on commercial education] the only provision of anything approaching to commercial education of this grade consisted in one or two courses in abstract economics, commercial law, etc., at University and King's Colleges, which did not succeed in attracting many persons designed for or engaged in commercial pursuits. It was seriously doubted whether any demand existed for more teaching of this grade.

Yet in Paris the visitor may see, in the very heart of the city, a splendid building which cost over £100,000—the École des Hautes Études Commercielles—exclusively devoted to the training of young men between nineteen and twenty-two in the special subjects needed by the merchant or banker. Here are studied economics, and especially the history and present organisation of the world commerce; industrial and commercial geography; the outlines of the commercial law of the principal trading nations; their customs, tariffs, and commercial systems; their factory laws and other regulations affecting industry; and the methods and routes of transport by sea and land. In another street the visitor will find the École Libre des Sciences Politiques, where the future diplomatist and consular officer, the future financial or customs administrator, goes through a similar training, specially adapted to his official duties. These are both institutions of university status—indeed, largely of post-graduate rank—very widely supported and disposing of ample means. They provide, in effect, a university curriculum as carefully adapted to the needs of the undergraduate who is going to be a leader in business or the official world, as the medical faculty does for the undergraduate who is going to be a doctor. We have long needed in London a high commercial and administrative College of this type, the absence of which was specially regretted in 1894 by Lord Cowper's Commission on the reorganisation of London University. Acting on this hint and the contemporaneous proposals of the London Chamber of Commerce, the London School of Economics and Political Science was established in 1895, to carry out the suggestion of the Cowper Commission, and care was taken that the more strictly commercial side of the work should not be neglected. It is, indeed, largely owing to this side that the school has been from the first a success, having now over a thousand students, from eighteen years of age upwards, mainly drawn from the ranks of those engaged, or about to be engaged, in banking, shipping, foreign trade, insurance, railway administration, and the national and municipal civil service. The aim of the governors is to provide, for the business or official administrator, an education which should be genuinely of university rank, such as has long been available at Paris and elsewhere. As expressed in the prospectus of the school, by 'Higher Commercial Education' is here meant 'a system of higher education which stands in the same relation to the life and calling of the manufacturer, the merchant, and other men of business, as the medical schools of the Universities to that of the doctor'. The curriculum of the London School of Economics includes, on its commercial side, economics and statistics, including particularly the concrete description of the organisation of the modern business world at home and abroad, the history and geography of the world-commerce, international trade, economic and industrial history, methods of transport, railway administration, accountancy, insurance, banking and currency, commercial and international law, finance, and taxation. But all these subjects are not taken by all the students. 'Experience shows', remarked the Special Report on Commercial Education from which I have already quoted, 'that commercial education of this high grade requires to be differentiated according to the occupations for which its students are preparing, or in which they are engaged.' In fact, if you offer the clerk or business man simply an undifferentiated something which you call commercial education, he will, quite rightly, pass by on the other side. It is useless to appeal to the business man as such. He disdains and despises—perhaps rightly—any academic instruction under such titles as 'Methods of Commerce' or 'Business Training'. The great army, which seems to the academic student to form a single class, must be broken up. The merchant, the shipowner or shipbroker, the corn-factor, the produce-broker, and their principal employés, form, perhaps, one complex group, which is between twenty and thirty thousand strong in London. The insurance clerks, actuaries, and public accountants,—numbering, perhaps, another ten thousand—have quite different requirements, and need themselves to be split up again into three or even four distinct groups. The great army of railway officials, from the assistant traffic managers down to the junior clerks in the secretary's office, need yet another kind of instruction. The eight or nine thousand clerks in banks and finance houses have specialised wants of their own. Finally, there are the twenty thousand clerks employed in public administration, national or municipal, for whom a distinct curriculum has to be provided. For each of these groups a distinct and highly specialised curriculum has to be prepared, of a character beyond the scope of the ordinary professor. Let us take as an example that great section of the business world engaged in the railway service. Various great railway companies now send each year to the London School of Economics a selected contingent of their clerks and assistant managers to go through carefully planned courses of instruction in railway law and railway accountancy, the application of economics to such specialist problems as railway rates and railway electrification, the organisation and formulation of railway statistics, together with railway history and railway geography, and the comparative study of the methods of administration, and relations to the state, of the railway systems of other countries. This curriculum has been worked out, in the eight years' experience of the school, by the help of frequent consultation with such practised railway administrators as the late Sir Joseph Wilkinson of the Great Western Railway, Mr. Inglis, his successor on that line, Mr. Gibb of the North-Eastern Railway, and Mr. Bury of the Great Northern Railway. Other sections of the business world, such as the bankers and dealers in the foreign exchanges, those engaged in general merchanting and the shipping trade, the various branches of insurance, the actuaries and accountants—to name only some of the different groups—are dealt with on similar lines. Such a differentiation of curriculum, coupled with the need for highly trained teachers, and the occasional services of expert business men themselves, makes commercial education of this high grade quite exceptionally costly. But there is no other way of providing anything that is not a useless sham, and if London is to have anything like the advantages of Paris, considerably increased funds must be devoted to this part of the work.

Something more than funds is, however, required. In 1893 Professor James noticed the absence of academic recognition of higher commercial education as the greatest obstacle to its progress.

What then [he said] is lacking in this economic (commercial) education to make it in demand? It lacks only the sanction which crowns university studies. It is not sufficient to open the doors of entrance into the schools of commerce, one must also open the doors of exit. Nothing further can be done until the legitimate demands in favour of economic instruction shall be met, and it shall be placed on a par with classical education.

This lack of academic recognition is now remedied. During the protracted negotiations which led, between 1894 and 1900, to the reorganisation of London University, the London County Council strongly urged the desirability of making distinct and separate provision for higher commercial education.

We regard it as important [said the Special Committee of 1899] that commercial education of this high grade should form an integral part of the reconstituted London University, and that it should be distinctly recognised, as constituting a separate faculty or department of a faculty. Such university recognition is essential in our view both to give *status* to the higher branches of commercial education and to increase their attractiveness to students of the highest mental capacity. But it is also of the utmost importance to commercial education itself, as tending to ensure a high intellectual standard, and to counteract a tendency to an unduly narrow utilitarianism.

The University Commissioners met this demand by the establishment of a separate 'Faculty of Economics and Political Science (including commerce and industry)', having its own curriculum in its own subjects, and leading to its own distinct degrees of B.Sc. and D.Sc. This faculty now comprises more than twenty professors, all at work in London, teaching one or other of the subjects that have already been described. The largest part of this instruction is centred at the London School of Economics, which has not only complete degree courses, both day and evening, but also makes a speciality of the original investigation and research on which the D.Sc. is awarded. University College, too, less favourably situated for business men or Government clerks, makes considerable provision for instruction in the subjects of this faculty, which is also represented at King's College. And besides these centres, the Birkbeck College has its steadily successful classes in economics under recognised teachers of the University.

The new 'commercial' faculty of the University of London thus fitly crowns the organisation of commercial education in London. The whole field is mapped out, and to some extent covered. What is wanted to make the whole organisation worthy of the greatest commercial city that the world has ever seen is, in the first place, more appreciation by the public of what exists, and more sympathetic attention by business men to what is actually being provided for them. This increase of knowledge and sympathetic attention by heads of business houses would soon lead to greater zeal for commercial education among their subordinates. And if to this greater publicity and greater zeal could be added the potent stimulus of an intelligent donor—a man who knew how to put down his money, whether it be one or one hundred thousand pounds, in the way to produce the greatest results—there could be added the almost indefinite extension produced by additional annual subsidies from national and municipal funds. What is most wanted at this moment in commercial as in other higher education in London, is the driving power of conditional private donations, large or small.

Envoi: The Webbs' Visit to the Soviet Union

When in 1932 the Webbs visited Russia they were leading figures in the British Labour Party. Not only had Sidney rewritten its constitution in 1918[139] but he had been a minister in the minority governments of 1924 and 1929–31.[140] World economic depression had shattered their faith in 'the inevitability of gradualness'. Their earlier attitude towards Marxist political organisations in Britain, had been, on the face of it, little short of contemptuous. Now, however, the durability and the outward idealism of the first Marxist republic had obviously won their respect, especially as Russia seemed impervious to the searing economic winds that were desolating western capitalistic society. By 1932 the Webbs were ready to be converted and the faith that they embraced on this visit to the Soviet Union was to sustain them for the rest of their lives.

What they saw on their travels deeply impressed them and this enthusiasm, shared, let it be said, by most visiting western intellectuals, resulted in the publication in 1935 of their massive *Soviet Communism: a New Civilisation?* By 1937, when the second edition was published, the question mark had disappeared. The conversion was complete.[141]

Soviet Communism, though it does on occasion reveal the merest hint of an ironic detachment, was undoubtedly a panegyric on the part of two people to whom the concept of 'national efficiency' was no less important in the context of the 1930s than it had been a generation earlier in Edwardian England. The nation state endowed with an organic unity possesses great advantages. The Soviet Union was fortunate in that Marxism as a creed provided not only that essential unity but also the dynamic for social change.

The Webbs admired too the élitist role of the Communist Party, noting for instance that it had something of the character of the 'Samurai', the self-recruiting aristocracy of service lauded by H. G. Wells in his writings.[142] The place of science—not simply in providing material benefits for the community, but also in creating new men and women through a transformation of the environment—they found vastly impressive. They also approved of the stern discipline, the predominantly puritan ethic and, not least, because in itself it was the very instrument to attain those self-same ends, the Soviet educational system. Contrasting with their earlier and more limited view of the purpose of the school, they could now see it as having a part to play in the creation of the future. It must be said that this is still an instrumental viewpoint but one directed to a situation far removed from the parameters of the present.

As the good Marxist fulfils himself primarily through work, education should therefore be geared to that end, though not in a narrow vocational sense. But even in the trying circumstances of the 1930s Soviet man does not fulfil himself entirely in this way: there is an honoured place for leisure in his life and here the word 'culture' acquires much prominence. Education is seen as much more than schooling and to this end the state ensures that young people are prepared for physical, political and artistic 'culture'. Museums, art galleries, the theatre, concerts, the vast output of books and pamphlets—all play their part in strengthening the values that the Soviet school seeks to engender. It is true that the Webbs are a little uneasy about the amount of political indoctrination in the schools, even if, as they say, it is no worse than the sort of indoctrination which is a characteristic of the British educational system. This is perhaps to take a liberty with language. But what cannot be doubted is that here in Britain today many teachers would find the powerful alliance between the schools and the mass media extraordinarily reassuring. Given such a combination, what cultural heights cannot be scaled?

In view of the curriculum ferment that is a characteristic of so many of our contemporary schools, the Webb summary of the rise and fall of progressivism in the Soviet school system of the 1920s is not without relevance. So too is what they have to say about 'learning by doing', a technique whose chief value is to be seen in its application to a world dominated by the concept of the nobility of labour, rather than because of its pedagogic efficiency, an area in which, in any case, the Webbs say they are not competent to pass judgment. Echoes of Sidney's earlier educational writings continue to reverberate. Education must possess utility. Anything which is conducive to leisurely day-dreaming is to be banished. Yet when all is said and done, this means in effect that only the classics are to go. One is left with the feeling that the stress placed upon the arts by a society which saw education as a preparation for total citizenship had to some extent tempered the basic philistinism of both members of the partnership.

In conclusion, what was the Webbs' attitude in the evening of their lives to the issue which dominates so much of our thinking to-day? More specifically, to what extent had they moved away from their earlier meritocratic assumptions towards the extreme egalitarian position? The answer is easy to determine: the great attraction of the Soviet Union to the Webbs lay in the fact that it was the meritocratic state *par excellence*. Given this context, it followed logically that a nation's educational system must act as the sifting agent in the deployment of talent and ability. To this extent their view of the role of the school had in no way changed since 1908. What had changed, however, was their thinking about the age at which the vital decisions concerning a child's future were to be taken. In his work on the Technical Education Board nothing had given Sidney more pleasure than the rapid expansion of London's scholarship ladder. In the 1930s this was no longer enough and he was now prepared to pour scorn on those 'advanced Liberals in contemporary England' who saw the ladder satisfying the demands of social justice. In the common school, where there was 'none of the segregation or grading of pupils according to parental rank or profession, wealth or income', Russia had found the answer. Selection can wait until sixteen or seventeen. Nearly thirty years before the British Labour Party decided that comprehensive schooling was to be one of its 'signposts for the 'sixties', Sidney and Beatrice Webb, while in no way abandoning a fundamentally meritocratic philosophy, had decided that the common school was the more effective instrument to that end.

Table of Dates

Select Bibliography

A. MANUSCRIPT SOURCES

Diary of Beatrice Webb (Passfield Papers).
Letters from Sidney to Beatrice (Passfield Papers).
Letters from Beatrice to Sidney (Passfield Papers).
Other letters between Beatrice and Sidney and their contemporaries (Passfield Papers).
Henry Hutchinson Trust Papers comprising correspondence, Webb's notes, circulars and reports.

B. PRIMARY PRINTED SOURCES

1. *Minutes*

Minutes of Evidence, Royal Commission on Secondary Education, 1895.
Minutes of the London County Council, 1892–1904.
Minutes of the London Technical Education Board, 1892–1904.
Minutes of the Higher Education Sub-committee of the T.E.B., 1893–1904.
Minutes of the London School Board, 1892–1904.
Minutes of the Senate of London University, 1900–3.
Minutes of the conference between the respresentatives of the Senate and the T.E.B. on the proposed Day Training College, January 1902.

2. *Reports*

Second Report of the Royal Commission on Technical Instruction (Samuelson), 1884.
Report of the Commissioners Appointed to Inquire into the Elementary Education Acts, England and Wales (Cross), 1888.
Report of the Royal Commission on Secondary Education (Bryce), 1895.
Report of the Selborne Commission, 1889.
Report of the Gresham Commission, 1894.
Education Department, *Special Reports on Educational Subjects*, vol. ii, 1898.
L.C.C., Technical Education Board, *Annual Reports*, 1894–1904.

Llewellyn Smith, H., *Report to the Special Committee on Technical Education*, 1892.

L.C.C., Technical Education Board, *Report of the Special Sub-committee on the Education Bill*, 1896.

L.C.C., Technical Education Board, *Report of the Special Sub-committee on the Building Trades*, 1899.

L.C.C., Technical Education Board, *Report of the Special Sub-committee on the Relation of Science to Industry*, 1899.

Fabian Society, *Annual Reports*.

British Association, *Report*, 1894.

Hewins, W. A. S., *Brief Report on the Work of the School since 1895*, 1899.

L.S.E., *Director's Report on the Work of the School*, 1924–5.

Report of the Hutchinson Trustees on the Termination of the Trust, July 1904.

3. Pamphlets

'One Who Knows', *Phillimore and Webb for Deptford—A Letter to the Ladies of Deptford*.

Webb, S., *Nine Years' Work on the L.C.C.: A Letter to the Electors of Deptford* (1901).

Phillimore, R. C. and Webb, S., *Fifteen Years' Work on the L.C.C.: A Letter to the Electors of Deptford* (1907).

McKinnon Wood, T., *The Progressive Policy—Past and Present* (1904).

Webb, S., *The Work of the London County Council* (London Reform Union 1895).

Technical Education (London Reform Union, Leaflet No. 38).

The Profession of Teaching and the New University of London (1899).

4. Fabian Tracts, etc.

Webb, S., *Facts for Londoners* (No. 8, 1889).

—, *Figures for Londoners* (No. 10, 1889).

—, *The Workers' Political Programme* (No. 11, 1890).

—, *Questions for Parliamentary Candidates* (No. 24, 1891).

—, *Questions for School Board Candidates* (No. 25, 1891).

—, *Questions for London County Councillors* (No. 26, 1891).

—, *London's Heritage in the City Guilds* (No. 31, 1891).

Shaw, G. B., *The Fabian Society: What it has done and how it has done it* (No. 41, 1892).

Martin, J. W., *State Education at Home and Abroad* (No. 52, 1894).

—, *The Workers' School Board Programme* (No. 55, 1894).

Oakeshott, J. F., *The London County Council: What it is and what it does* (No. 61, 1895).

Shaw, G. B. (ed), *Fabianism and the Empire*. A Manifesto by the Fabian Society (1900).

Webb, S., *The Education Muddle and the Way Out* (No. 106, 1901).
—, *Twentieth Century Politics: A Policy of National Efficiency* (No. 108, 1901).
—, *The Education Act, 1902: How to make the best of it* (No. 114, 1903).
—, *The London Education Act, 1903: How to make the best of it* (No. 117, 1904).
Bland, H., *After Bread, Education* (No. 120, 1905).
Webb, S., *The Teacher in Politics* (No. 187, 1918).
Davies, A. Emil, *The London County Council, 1889-1937: A Historical Sketch* (No. 243, 1937).
Cole, G. D. H., *The Fabian Society, Past and Present* (No. 258, 1952).
Cole, M. I., *Beatrice and Sidney Webb* (No. 297, 1955).

5. *Parliamentary Papers*

Technical Instruction Act, 1889
Technical Instruction Act, 1891
London University Act, 1898
Education Act, 1902
London Education Act, 1903
Hansard (1903)

6. *Newspapers and Periodicals*

British Journal of Educational Studies
British Journal of Sociology
Commerce
Contemporary Review
Cornhill Magazine
Daily Chronicle
Daily Mail
Economica
Economic Journal
Fabian News
Fortnightly Review
London: A Journal of Civic and Social Progress
London Technical Education Gazette
Manchester Guardian
Nature
Pall Mall Gazette
St. Martin's Review
South-Eastern Progressive and Labour News
The Educational Record
The New Age
The Nineteenth Century
The Observer
The Speaker
The Times
The Woman's Signal
Westminster Gazette

7. *Other Sources*

Science and Art Department, *Directory*, 1897.
Webb, S., *Draft to the Fabian Sub-Committee on Education*, December 1902.
L.S.E., *Prospectus*, 1895–6.
L.S.E., *Prospectus*, 1896–7.
L.S.E., *Calendar*, 1903–4.
L.S.E., *Handbook of the Students' Union*, 1925.
London University, *Calendar*, 1926–7.
London University, *Calendar*, 1956–7.

C. SECONDARY SOURCES

Acland, A. H. D. and Llewellyn Smith, H. (eds.), *Studies in Secondary Education* (Percival 1892).

Allen, B. M., *Sir Robert Morant: A Great Public Servant* (Macmillan 1934).

—, *William Garnett, A Memoir* (Heffer 1933).

Argles, M., *South Kensington to Robbins* (Longmans 1964).

Armytage, W. H. G., *Civic Universities: Aspects of a British Tradition* (Benn 1955).

—, *The German Influence on English Education* (Routledge 1969).

Banks, O., *Parity and Prestige in English Secondary Education: A Study in Educational Sociology* (Routledge 1955).

Barker, R., *Education and Politics, 1900–1951* (O.U.P. 1972).

Beveridge, J., *An Epic of Clare Market* (Bell 1960).

Binns, H. B., *A Century of Education, 1808–1908* (Dent 1908).

Caine, Sir Sydney, *The History of the Foundation of the London School of Economics and Political Science* (L.S.E. 1963).

Cole, G. D. H., *A Short History of the British Working-Class Movement, 1789–1947* (Allen and Unwin 1948).

—, *The Second International, 1889–1914* (Macmillan 1956).

Cole, M. I., *Beatrice Webb* (Longmans 1945).

— (ed.), *Beatrice Webb's Diaries, 1912–24* (Longmans 1952).

— (ed.), *Beatrice Webb's Diaries, 1924–32* (Longmans 1956).

—, *Servant of the County* (Dobson 1956).

— (ed.), *The Webbs and Their Work* (Muller 1949).

Creighton, M., *Life and Letters of Mandell Creighton*, vol. ii (Longmans 1904).

Dugdale, B. E. C., *Arthur James Balfour* (Hutchinson 1939).

Eaglesham, E., *From School Board to Local Authority* (Routledge 1956).

—, *Foundations of Twentieth-Century Education in England* (Routledge 1967).

Ervine, St. J., *Bernard Shaw: His Life, Work and Friends* (Constable 1956).

Fitzroy, Sir A., *Memoirs* (Hutchinson 1925).

Gautry, T., *School Board Memories* (Link House Pub. 1937).

Gibbon, Sir G. and Bell, R. W., *History of the London County Council 1889–1939* (Macmillan 1939).

Haldane, E., *From One Century to Another* (Maclehose 1937).

Haldane, R. B., *Richard Burdon Haldane: an Autobiography* (Hodder & Stoughton 1929).

Halévy, E., *Imperialism and the Rise of Labour* (Benn 1951).

Hamilton, M. A., *Sidney and Beatrice Webb* (Low 1933).

Hewins, W. A. S., *The Apologia of an Imperialist: Forty Years of Empire Policy*, vol. i (Constable 1929).

Hobhouse, S., *Margaret Hobhouse and her Family* (1934).

Hobsbawm, E. J., *Industry and Empire* (Weidenfeld and Nicolson 1968).

Hogg, E. M., *Quintin Hogg: a Biography* (1904).

McBriar, A. M., *Fabian Socialism and English Politics, 1884–1918* (C.U.P. 1962).

Magnus, Sir P., *Educational Aims and Efforts, 1880–1910* (Longmans 1910).

Martin, Kingsley, *Editor* (Penguin 1969).

Maurice, Sir F., *Haldane, 1895–1915: The Life of Viscount Haldane of Cloan* (Faber 1937).

Muggeridge, K. and Adam, R., *Beatrice Webb* (Secker and Warburg 1967).

Pease, E. R., *The History of the Fabian Society* (Fifield 1916).

Rhys, E., *Everyman Remembers* (Dent 1931).

Russell, B., *Portraits from Memory and Other Essays* (Allen and Unwin 1956).

Searle, G. R., *The Quest for National Efficiency* (Blackwell 1971).

Selleck, R. J. W., *The New Education* (Pitman 1968).

Semmel, B., *Imperialism and Social Reform* (Allen and Unwin 1960).

Shaw, G. B. (ed.), *Fabian Essays in Socialism* (Allen and Unwin 1889).

—, *Sixteen Self Sketches* (Constable 1949).

Simon, B., *Education and the Labour Movement, 1870–1920* (Lawrence and Wishart 1965).

Snell, H., *Men, Movements and Myself* (Dent 1936).

Webb, B., *My Apprenticeship* (Longmans 1929).

—, *Our Partnership* (Longmans 1948).

Webb, S., *London Education* (Longmans 1904).

—, *Socialism in England* (Sonnenschein 1890).

—, *The London Programme* (Sonnenschein 1891).

Webb, S. and B., *A Constitution for the Socialist Commonwealth of Great Britain* (Longmans 1920).

Webb, S. and B., *Soviet Communism: a New Civilisation?* (Longmans 1935).

Wells, H. G., *Experiment in Autobiography* (Gollancz 1934).

—, *The New Machiavelli* (Lane 1911).

Wood, E. M., *The Polytechnic and Its Founder, Quintin Hogg* (Nisbet 1932.)

Notes

A FUNCTIONAL THEORY OF EDUCATION

1. See, for example, Alan McBriar, *Fabian Socialism and English Politics 1884–1918* (1962), ch. VIII; G. R. Searle, *The Quest for National Efficiency* (1971), ch. VII; B. Simon, *Education and the Labour Movement* (1965), Part II; A. V. Judges, 'The Educational Influence of the Webbs', *British Journal of Educational Studies*, vol. X, no. 1 (November 1961). Also four articles by the present writer under the overall heading 'Sidney Webb and the London Technical Education Board', *The Vocational Aspect*, Autumn 1959–Spring 1962 and 'Educational Engineering with the Webbs', *History of Education*, vol. I, no. 2 (June 1972).

2. Following the London University Act of 1898.

3. Richard Burdon Haldane (1856–1928). Lawyer, philosopher, leader among Liberal 'collectivists' and Liberal Imperialists, and lifelong friend of the Webbs. Secretary of State for War and subsequently Lord Chancellor in the Liberal Governments of 1906 and 1910, Haldane became gradually converted to Labour and was Lord Chancellor in the first Labour Government of 1924.

4. A claim that Beatrice herself was apt to make retrospectively.

5. Henry Mayers Hyndman (1842–1921). War correspondent in 1866; associated with Mazzini and other Italian republican leaders. Converted to socialism through his reading of Marx whose political thought he expounded for English consumption in a number of works. In 1881 he joined with William Morris in founding the Social Democratic Federation which until 1914 was the most pronouncedly Marxist organisation in England. There is an element of mild disdain in most of Beatrice's diary references to Hyndman.

6. Rev. Stewart Duckworth Headlam (1847–1924). Christian Socialist, founder of the Guild of St Matthew, and a Fabian of many years standing. Member of the London School Board, 1886–1904, and a Progressive member of the L.C.C. from 1907 until his death.

7. The work which, according to G. D. H. Cole, was the most important single publication in the history of British socialism.

8. S. Webb, *Socialism in England* (1890), pp. 105–6.

9. In a letter to Graham Wallas, written in December, 1902, Sidney has this to say: 'I quite realise that the mass of children, having to go to work at 14 or 15 can get no other day-schooling than what is provided in the "primary" schools; and I want all these, whether denominational or not, to be made as perfect as possible. What the perfect curriculum for them is I don't assume to know—whatever it is decided to be by you and the other educationists, let us by all means

have it.' Quoted from R. J. W. Selleck, *The New Education, 1870–1914* (1968).

10. B. Webb, *My Apprenticeship* (1971), p. 61.

11. Ibid., p. 86.

12. In ch. 3 of *My Apprenticeship* Beatrice refers to visiting schools in Bacup.

13. Archibald Philip Primrose, Earl of Rosebery (1847–1929). Liberal Prime Minister 1894–5. First chairman of the London County Council in 1889.

14. Sir Robert Laurie Morant (1862–1920). Civil servant; architect of the 1902 Education Act. On returning to England from Siam in 1895, Morant entered the Office of Special Inquiries and Reports under Michael Sadler. In 1903 he became Permanent Secretary to the Board of Education where he had great influence. Differences with the elementary schoolteachers led him to resign in 1911 and to become Chairman of the National Health Insurance Commission. In 1919 he became Permanent Secretary to the new Ministry of Health.

15. Alfred Viscount Milner (1854–1925). After Gladstone's conversion to Home Rule, Milner became Private Secretary to Goschen, the Liberal Unionist. Under-Secretary for Finance in Egypt under Cromer, 1889–92, and then Chairman of the Board of Inland Revenue, 1892–7. British High Commissioner in South Africa, 1897–1905. In this capacity he was responsible for much of the policy which led to the South African War. Member of Lloyd George's War Cabinet from December, 1916. War Secretary, 1918–19; Colonial Secretary 1919–21.

16. In *The Quest for National Efficiency* (1971), G. R. Searle gives a masterly account of the growth and demise of this heterogeneous group. Although reading rather too much into the meetings of 'the co-efficients', B. Semmel's *Imperialism and Social Reform* (1960) is also a significant work, especially in the way the author traces the rise of 'social imperialism' as a historical concept.

17. This is very well brought out in two contributions to the *British Journal of Sociology* in June 1961, viz: M. I. Cole, 'The Webbs and Social Theory'; T. S. Simey, 'The Contribution of Sidney and Beatrice Webb to Sociology'.

18. The contempt of the Fabians for this sort of intellectual exercise is brought out admirably in a review in *Fabian News* of August 1900 of a work in which an attempt had been made to define the nature of 'justice':

> The author . . . sets himself to define justice as a prelude to forming a philosophy of Government. In our view he has undertaken a somewhat thankless task. We are content to leave that excellent word to the tender mercies of Parliamentary orators and newspaper leader-writers. It is a useful word, no doubt, in daily casual talk, but for serious thinking we prefer to leave it alone as an abstraction which belongs to what Comte would call the metaphysical stage of human evolution.

Quoted from McBriar, op. cit., p. 148.

SIDNEY WEBB, THE FABIAN SOCIETY AND MUNICIPAL SOCIALISM

19. It is true that some of the more prominent S.D.F. leaders were also 'middle-class intellectuals' but the group was essentially a proletarian organisation whose revolutionary zeal quickly gained it a dangerous reputation.

20. Formed by a breakaway movement from the S.D.F. led by William Morris.

21. The famous 'Fabian quartet' comprised Webb, Bernard Shaw, Graham Wallas and Sydney Olivier.

22. Stories purporting to illustrate the philistinism of the Webbs abound. Not surprisingly there is a marked apocryphal quality to many of them, not least in the one told by F. H. Spencer in *An Inspector's Testament*. When asked what he would do with a garden, Sidney is alleged to have replied that he would 'Pave, Light, Watch and Cleanse It'.

23. Edward R. Pease (1857–1955). One of the founders of the Fabian Society, which held its earliest meeting in his rooms. He was General Secretary of the Society between 1889 and 1914, and its Honorary Secretary both before and after those years, finally retiring in 1939.

24. Frank Podmore (1856–1910). Played an active part in establishing the Society but retired in 1888 from the Fabian Executive and devoted himself to literary work, producing penetrating studies of spiritualism and an excellent biography of Robert Owen.

25. E. R. Pease in 'Webb and the Fabian Society', *The Webbs and Their Work* (1949), ed. M. I. Cole, p. 17.

26. Webb wrote twenty-five of the first sixty *Fabian Tracts*. He dominated the Executive Committee 'not because he was in the least dictatorial, but because he was always wise and right'. Pease, *The Webbs and Their Work*, p. 22.

27. See p. 5.

28. By 1906 the policies advocated by radicals and socialists had brought about the 'New Liberalism' which was so strong a feature of the new administration. It is only fair to add, however, that its chief exponents would have been horrified at the notion that they were all budding socialists. Although the concept of 'the national minimum' had been widely accepted, there was still very much stress on the virtues of 'free enterprise'. Winston Churchill, one of the up-and-coming under-secretaries, summed up the prevailing philosophy in homespun prose: 'We want to have free competition upwards; we decline to allow free competition to run downwards.' Quoted in McBriar, op. cit., p. 257 f. The influence of the Webbs whom he had begun to cultivate in 1908 may be seen in a letter written to Asquith in that year: 'Thrust a big slice of Bismarckianism over the whole underside of our industrial system and await the consequences whatever they may be with a good conscience.' Quoted in Searle, op. cit., pp. 248–9. By 1918 the 'Universal Enforcement of the National Minimum' had become one of the four pillars of the new socialist civilisation that was the goal of a re-aligned Labour Party. Webb and Arthur Henderson were the constitution makers of the new Party.

29. Annie Besant (1847–1933). Left her clergyman husband upon becoming a convert to secularism and birth control, for which she and Charles Bradlaugh were the most popular and effective propagandists in the 'seventies. In the early 'eighties she became a socialist; she was an early member of the Fabian Executive, one of the seven contributors to *Fabian Essays*, and a brilliant speaker for the cause. In 1888 she led the successful strike of the matchgirls at Bryant and May's. In 1888 she suddenly abandoned socialism for theosophy and became a passionate advocate of Indian nationalism.

30. Headlam and Mrs Besant were elected to the London School Board in 1888; Graham Wallas was to become a member in 1894.

31. G. D. H. Cole, *The Second International* (1956), p. 121.

32. R. C. K. Ensor, *England 1870–1914* (1936), pp. 128–9.

33. October 1891.

34. McBriar, op. cit., p. 195.

35. It should be stressed that Webb, despite his belief in the hierarchical ordering of society, was far from being autocratic by temperament. In academic matters he was an early believer in 'participation'. In the Webbs' *Constitution for the Socialist Commonwealth of Great Britain* (1920), p. 307, he says that in the universities each subject should have its own board of studies, 'representative of teachers, researchers and writers of various grades, which should be enabled to have an effective participation in the administration', for it was vital that unorthodox views should not be excluded.

36. Under the Progressive banner were to be found not only trade unionists and Gladstonian Liberals, but Conservatives, Liberal Unionists and Roman Catholic and Church of England philanthropists.

37. McBriar, op. cit., p. 194.

38. E. J. Hobsbawm, *Industry and Empire* (1968), p. 110.

39. J. A. Froude, *Short Studies on Great Subjects*, vol. 11. Quoted in Searle, op. cit., p. 10.

40. In this report Arnold calculated that Britain had proportionally only one half of the number of people receiving higher education in France and Germany. For a fuller account of the growing power of Germany vis-à-vis Britain, see W. H. G. Armytage, *The German Influence on English Education* (1969).

41. A. H. D. Acland (1874–1939). Liberal politician and educationist, Vice-President of the Privy Council Committee on Education and Cabinet Minister, 1892–5. In this capacity he did much to promote higher education, effective inspection and better conditions in schools. After his retirement he devoted himself to the cause of co-operation and adult education.

42. Hubert Llewellyn Smith (1869–1945). Civil Servant. Historian of the 1889 London Dock Strike. Secretary, 1888–92, of the National Association for the Promotion of Technical Education, and member of the Royal Commission on Secondary Education. Permanent Secretary to the Board of Trade, 1907–19, and organiser of Labour Exchanges. One of the most valuable collaborators in the social policies of the Webbs.

THE LONDON TECHNICAL EDUCATION BOARD 1892–1904

43. 'In short, I grew up a patriotic Londoner, very early declaring that no place on earth . . . would content me for habitation other than the very middle of the London that I knew.' S. Webb, 'The London County Council', *St. Martin's Review*, December 1928.

44. Margaret Cole is of the opinion that 'during all his long career in public life, it is doubtful whether any work he did so deeply engaged his heart as his service

on the London County Council and his efforts for the higher education of Londoners.'

45. The words 'and Secondary' had been added in 1889.

46. Sir John Donnelly (1834–1902). Started his career as a soldier, served in the Crimean War and retired as a Major-General. After his retirement became Secretary to the Department of Science and Art, 1884–99.

47. Keir Hardie (1856–1915). The Scottish miners' leader who founded the I.L.P. and was the chief influence in the formation of the Labour Representation Committee which became the Labour Party. Hardie stands for the emotional appeal of socialism in the British working-class movement, his mind was out of tune with the Webbs and there was consequently a gulf between them.

48. Will Crooks (1852–1921). Trade unionist and socialist, member of the Coopers' Union, and an early Fabian. Mayor of Poplar, 1891, and Chairman of the Poplar Board of Guardians, 1898–1906. Labour M.P. for Poplar, 1903 till his death. A moving speaker on social conditions.

49. Webb seconding the vote of thanks to H.R.H. The Prince of Wales. *The London Technical Education Gazette*, vol. III, no. 28, February 1897.

50. B. Webb, *Our Partnership* (1947), p. 97.

51. *Fabian News*, January 1903. My italics.

52. B. M. Allen, *William Garnett: a Memoir* (1933), p. 61.

53. B. Webb, op. cit., p. 79.

54. See, for example, an election pamphlet of 1901 entitled *Nine Years' Work on the L.C.C.: a Letter to the Electors of Deptford*.

55. A. V. Judges, 'The Educational Influence of the Webbs', *British Journal of Educational Studies*, November 1961, p. 40.

56. The word used by Sir Sydney Caine in his *History of the Foundation of the London School of Economics and Political Science* (1963), p. 1.

57. W. A. S. Hewins (1865–1931). Resigned as Director of the L.S.E. in 1903 on his conversion to tariff reform and was for fourteen years secretary to Joseph Chamberlain's Tariff Reform Commission. Under-Secretary of State for the Colonies, 1917–19.

58. B. Webb, *Diaries*, 21 September 1894.

59. Ibid.

60. John W. Martin. An ex-school board teacher and the only other Fabian to write a tract on the subject of education up to 1905. His *State Education at Home and Abroad* (no. 52, 1894) and also *The Workers' School Board Programme* (no. 55, 1894) are extremely informative. Subsequently went to New York where he married the leading exponent of Fabianism in the U.S.A. and where he decided to remain.

61. Sir William Mitchell Acworth (1850–1925). Barrister and railway economist. Member of several commissions of enquiry into railway affairs.

62. Professor Bernard Bosanquet (1848–1923). Hegelian philosopher who also did much work in connection with University Extension and the Charity Organisation Society.

63. Enid Stacy, d. 1903. One of the most effective women speakers and lecturers in the 'nineties. A socialist from Bristol, she joined the Fabian Society in 1891, became lecturer to the Hutchinson Trust and a member of the Council of the I.L.P.

64. Herbert Somerton Foxwell (1849–1936). Professor of Political Economy, University College London, and owner of a unique library of books on political and social questions, which the Webbs tried in vain to acquire for the L.S.E. Foxwell's political views were strongly conservative.

65. Hubert Bland (1856–1914). Socialist, journalist and author. A founder member of the Fabian Society, whose treasurer he remained from 1884 to 1911. Married to Edith Nesbit, the writer of many children's books which to-day are enjoying an extraordinary popularity.

66. *Passfield Papers*, Shaw to B. Webb, 1 July 1895.

67. Sir Sidney Caine gives a very full treatment of the legal implications in chapter 2 of his book.

68. Fortunately for the student, Sidney and Beatrice wrote to each other nearly every day at a period which was crucial not only in the life of the London School of Economics but also in the wider parliamentary arena.

69. S. Webb to Rev. Archibald Robertson (Vice-Chancellor of London University), 3 January 1903.

70. In his autobiography, Haldane paid handsome tribute to the part played by Webb. R. B. Haldane, *An Autobiography* (1929), pp. 124–7.

71. Baron Davey of Fernhurst (1833–1907). Lawyer and Liberal politician, Solicitor-General, 1886; became Lord Justice of Appeal. Chairman of the Committee which drew up the constitution of the University of London and member of the Senate.

72. B. Webb, *Diary*, 28 February 1900.

73. S. Webb to Mrs G. B. Shaw, quoted in Caine, op. cit., p. 95.

74. Caine, op. cit., p. 95.

75. John Burns (1858–1943). The 'Man with the Red Flag', most prominent of the 'new' Trade Unionists and chief leader of the 1889 Dock Strike. Burns was elected to the L.C.C. in 1889 and to Parliament as a Socialist in 1892. At first the Webbs had high hopes of Burns, but his desire to play a lone hand grew on him more and more. He would not co-operate with Keir Hardie, and as President of the Local Government Board he proved to be a bitter enemy of the Webbs in the Poor Law agitation.

76. H. Llewellyn Smith, *Report to the Special Committee on Technical Education* (1892), p. 71.

77. S. Webb, 'The Organisation of University Education in the Metropolis', *The Times*, 4 and 8 June 1901.

78. S. Webb, 'London University: a Policy and a Forecast', *The Nineteenth Century*, June 1902. See pp. 184–201.

79. S. Webb, 'The Making of a University', *The Cornhill Magazine*, April 1903.

80. Nathan Mayer Rothschild, first Baron Rothschild (1840–1915). The millionaire banker who contributed so much to educational and other causes.

81. Sir Julius Wernher (1850–1922). South African millionaire, senior partner of Wernher, Beit and Co., art collector, philanthropist and much interested in technical education.

82. Alfred Beit (1853–1906). South African financier and diamond merchant. Partner in the firm of Wernher, Beit and Co. Life Governor of De Beers Consolidated Mines. Director of Rand Mines, Rhodesian Railways and other companies.

83. The I.L.P.'s largest political representation at this time was on the school boards.

84. B. Webb, *Diary*, 8 July 1903.

85. On occasion she goes into considerable detail.

86. B. Webb, *Diary*, 8 July 1903.

87. See p. 20.

88. M. I. Cole (ed.), *The Webbs and Their Work* (1949), pp. 81–2.

89. B. Webb, *Diary*, Whitsun 1896.

90. In London and forty-seven county boroughs.

91. S. Webb, *The Education Act, 1902: How to Make the Best of it* (no. 114, 1903); S. Webb, *The London Education Act, 1903: How to Make the Best of it* (no. 117, 1904).

92. *Passfield Papers*, Gorst to S. Webb, 25 June 1902.

93. Beatrice's words after Morant had been to dinner at their home, 41 Grosvenor Road, Westminster. B. Webb, *Diary*, December 1902.

94. *Passfield Papers*, Morant to S. Webb, 16 January 1903.

95. The Reverend J. R. Diggle was a London curate until 1879 when he was elected to the London School Board. He was Chairman of the Board from 1885 to 1894. 'Diggleism' was a blend of Church policy and the desire of the ratepayers, expressed through the Moderate Party, to cut back on educational expenditure.

THE TEXTS

96. B. Webb, *Diary*, 16 March 1900.

97. The changing pattern of the relationship between Rosebery and the Webbs is very well described in G. R. Searle, op. cit., pp. 122–41.

98. B. Webb, *Our Partnership*, p. 228.

99. Ed. Bernard Shaw, *Fabianism and the Empire: a Manifesto by the Fabian Society* (1900). In this tract socialists are adjured to support imperialism. In the face of a world dominated by empires, 'a Fabian is necessarily an Imperialist in theory'.

100. Bernard Shaw to S. Webb. Quoted in Janet Dunbar, *Mrs. G.B.S.: A Biographical Portrait of Charlotte Shaw* (1963), pp. 191–2.

101. Much of what is said in this article is also to be found in S. Webb, *Twentieth Century Politics: A Policy of National Efficiency* (Tract 108, 1901).

102. Sir Henry Campbell-Bannerman (1836–1908). The Liberal Prime Minister of 1906. Like many of their Liberal Imperialist friends, the Webbs constantly underrated him.

103. Campbell-Bannerman to Herbert Gladstone, 12 September 1901. Quoted in Searle, op. cit., p. 126.

104. *Passfield Papers*, Rosebery to B. Webb, 3 September 1901.

105. Searle, op. cit., p. 131.

106. Campbell-Bannerman to H. Gladstone, 18 December 1901. Quoted in Searle, op. cit., p. 132.

107. Sir William Harcourt (1827–1904). Liberal politician; imposer, as Chancellor of the Exchequer in the 1892 Government, of the first death duties. Leader of the Commons in Rosebery's Administration. The rivalry between him and Lord

Rosebery accounted for much of the weakness of Liberal leadership around the turn of the century.

108. John Morley (1838–1916). Lord Morley of Blackburn, biographer of Gladstone, Secretary of State for India during the Morley-Minto reforms, resigned from the Asquith Cabinet in 1914 on pacifist grounds.

109. Sir Henry Fowler, later Viscount Wolverhampton (1830–1911). Liberal politician and leading Wesleyan. President of the Local Government Board, 1892–4.

110. Michael Edward Hicks-Beach, later Earl St Aldwyn (1837–1916). Conservative politician, first held office in 1868. Secretary for Ireland, 1886–7; Chancellor of the Exchequer, 1885 and 1895–1902.

111. Henry Chaplin, Viscount Chaplin (1841–1923). Conservative politician, M.P. for many years and 'Father of the House'. President of the Local Government Board, 1895–1900.

112. Walter Hume Long, Viscount Long of Wraxall (1854–1924). Conservative politician, in the inner counsels of the leaders before and during the First World War. President of the Local Government Board, 1900–5, and no friend to municipal enterprise. The Metropolitan Water Board, in whose constitution he succeeded in defeating the advocates of direct election, was set up under an Act of 1902.

113. Henry Labouchere (1831–1912). 'Labby' of *Punch*. Liberal M.P. for Northampton, 1880–1906; proprietor and editor of *Truth* when *Truth* was a Radical journal.

114. Charles Thomson Ritchie, Baron Ritchie (1838–1906). Conservative politician, M.P. from 1874 onwards, held various Government posts, rising to Chancellor of the Exchequer, 1902–3. As President of the Local Government Board (1886–92) played a considerable part in the setting up of County Councils.

115. B. Webb, *Our Partnership*, p. 81.

116. *Fabian News*, February 1901.

117. *Footnote by S.W.* 'Even these subjects may legally be taught in Town or County Council schools, if a proportional part of the expense is covered, as it always may be, by sources of income (such as fees or emoluments) other than the Town or County Council grant.'

118. *Footnote by S.W.* 'In December 1900, this peril was made both imminent and apparent. The Court of Queen's Bench decided (in R. *v.* Cockerton) that the London School Board could not, out of the School Board rate, conduct classes for the examinations and grants of the old Science and Art Department, or go beyond the Code of the Education Department, or give instruction of any kind to adults, whether in day or evening schools. This decision may perhaps be appealed against, but it will certainly be accepted by the Government as definitely limiting the powers of the School Boards.'

119. *Footnote by S.W.* 'The six English Universities would remain, as at present, independent of the local authorities, except in so far as these might aid them by grants, in which event conditions would naturally be mutually agreed. But the universities, no less than other educational bodies, should be subject to inspection, criticism and public report by the Board of Education itself. Such endowed, "non-local" schools as Eton and Harrow, and the various unattached colleges and specialized educational institutions, would occupy a similar position.'

120. *Footnote by S.W.* 'The law should, of course, be changed, so as to make women eligible for election for both Town and County Councils. See Fabian Tract No. 93.'

121. 'The planks would be (1) fairness to the voluntary schools, complete freedom for them to teach their religious doctrine in their own way; (2) unsectarianism in the board schools—these latter constituting, broadly speaking, the supply for the Nonconformist and secular children—and, as regards all kinds of elementary teaching, thorough efficiency in staff and structure; (3) development of secondary and technical education on the present lines of independent governing bodies aided and inspected by the L.C.C. and kept up to the mark on their educational side; but completely free to be as denominational or anti-denominational as the governing body chose. And, last but not least, a great London University—independent of L.C.C. but subsidised and influenced by it—not only a leading university organised on a democratic basis, but a great centre of the highest and most useful science, scholarship and metaphysics'. B. Webb, *Diary*, 15 June 1903.

122. Edward Lyulph Stanley, Lord Stanley of Alderley, later Lord Sheffield (1839–1925). Educationist and authority on social questions. Member of London School Board, 1876–85 and 1886–96. M.P. for Oldham, 1880–5.

123. Thomas James Macnamara (1861–1931). Elementary schoolteacher who became a Liberal politician. Member of London School Board, 1896–1902, and M.P. for North Camberwell, 1900–18; Coalition Liberal in 1918 election and Minister of Labour, 1920–2. A strong non-conformist and editor of *The School-master* from 1892 to 1907.

124. *Footnote by S.W.* 'On the School Board itself there have been grave searchings of heart as to whether the greater freedom now allowed to the teachers, beneficial as the change has been on the whole, may not have resulted, in all but the best schools, in a serious falling off in the accuracy and thoroughness with which the elementary subjects are taught. See the significant report, and the still more significant evidence, of the Special Sub-Committee of the School Management Committee, 1902.'

125. *Footnote by S.W.* 'Apart from the objections to attracting any continuous stream of immigrants to the already overcrowded metropolis, the extent to which whole sections of London's services are habitually recruited from the provinces is disquieting in its restriction of the opportunities practically open to the London boy. There is reason to infer that less than a third of the vacancies for male assistant teachers in London are filled by London boys. The competitive examinations for entrance to the great services of the Customs and Excise show an overwhelming proportion of non-Londoners among the successful candidates. Few London boys enter for the national scholarships for science and art teachers. In other spheres it may be noted that both the porters and clerks of the wholesale drapery houses are largely drawn from the country; that the London police are largely recruited from the country; that the Metropolitan Fire Brigade is nearly wholly drawn from sailors, comparatively few of whom are London-born; and that such a typically London industry as the building trade takes, nowadays, hardly any boys, and is mainly recruited by young journeymen from elsewhere. It must be remembered that the London boy seldom starts as a teacher, clerk, policeman, fireman, porter, bricklayer, or carpenter in any other town. It will be

deplorable if we have to infer that, apart from the great army of junior clerks, it is the still greater host of dock and other unskilled labourers which is recruited in the largest proportion by Londoners. We should at any rate take care that the London boy has the first steps to the entrance of all skilled occupations and professions made genuinely accessible to him.'

126. See R. Barker, *Education and Politics, 1900–1951* (1972), p. 16.

127. *Footnote by S.W.* 'It is a peculiarity of England—and one which makes our provision of secondary education look misleadingly small—that nearly every writer (the present being no exception) omits from his survey, not only the unknown host of so-called secondary schools conducted for private profit, but also the hundred or more so-called "public schools", which form the apex of our system and now contain some 30,000 boys; and, with them, their peculiar "feeders", the preparatory schools for little boys containing 10,000 more.'

128. *Footnote by S.W.* 'It is usually forgotten by Americans as well as by English admirers of the United States, that the most generous provision of free secondary education, *without scholarships covering maintenance*, leaves (even in the most advanced States) 80 per cent of the children excluded, in practice, from anything beyond the elementary school. In Chicago the percentage so excluded is 97. It is very doubtful whether even in Massachusetts or Connecticut the proportion of children actually obtaining secondary education in 1908 is greater that in Surrey or Kent; whilst it is plain that the proportion in New York or Chicago falls below that of London or Birmingham. And this is apparently true for the United States as a whole compared with England and Wales as a whole (See 'A Comparison between the English and American Secondary Schools', by G. L. Fox, in Board of Education's Special Reports on Educational Subjects).'

129. *Footnote by S.W.* 'First, Second and Third Annual Reports of the Education Committee, County Council of the West Riding of Yorkshire, 1905, 1906, and 1907; Statement in support of application to the Local Government Board for alteration of limit of expenditure on Higher Education, 1907.'

130. *Footnote by S.W.* 'Special Report on Higher Education in the County of Kent, 1906. (Kent Education Committee); Fourth Annual Report (Higher Section) of the Kent Education Committee, 1906–7.'

131. See p. 42.

132. Lord Kimberley (1826–1902). Liberal politician. Leader of the Liberal Party in the House of Lords from 1897 to 1902 and in 1899 Chancellor of the University of London.

133. Sir Henry Enfield Roscoe (1833–1915). Professor of Chemistry at Owens College, Manchester, examiner in chemistry for London University, author of many text-books, member of several Royal Commissions. In 1885 he was Liberal M.P. for South Manchester.

134. B. Webb, *Diary*, December 1900.

135. Sir William Ramsay (1852–1916). Chemist, Professor of Chemistry at University College London, 1887–1912. In 1904 he received the Nobel Prize for chemistry.

136. John Passmore Edwards (1823–1911). Philanthropist, Radical and pacifist; in his early days a Chartist and editor of an Anti-Corn Law League journal, later edited the *Echo* (first halfpenny newspaper) from 1876 to 1896 and became

President of the London Reform Union. Founded free libraries, hospitals, convalescent homes and supported many Radical causes.

137. In *A Constitution for the Socialist Commonwealth of Great Britain* (1920), Sidney entrusts only foreign policy to the graduates of the two ancient universities. One parliament will have this responsibility. A second and much more important parliament will legislate in the area of social and economic policy. This body will be dominated by the products of university institutions like the L.S.E.

138. The current stress in the United States on 'career education' provides an interesting example of a reaction in that country away from an over-emphasis on 'general education'. See E. J. T. Brennan, 'The "Vo-Tech" in the Context of the 1970s', in D.E.S., *Trends in Education*, May 1974.

139. Along with Arthur Henderson.

140. Webb was President of the Board of Trade in the 1924 Labour government and Colonial Secretary from 1929–31.

141. 'Old people', said Beatrice upon one occasion, 'often fall in love in extraordinary and ridiculous ways—with their chauffeurs for example: we feel it more dignified to have fallen in love with Soviet Communism.' Quoted in M. Cole, *Beatrice Webb*, p. 173. Mrs Cole also concludes that the communist faith, as Beatrice saw it being practised in Russia, had filled the fifty-year-old gap which had troubled her since her rejection of Christianity; 'she needed no other religion'. Ibid., p. 177.

142. As for example in his *Modern Utopia* (1905).

Index